MEDITERRANEAN DIGITAL SOCIETIES

This open access book provides a Mediterranean perspective on digital societies, focusing on core issues such as cultural heritage, tourism, smart city development, migration, humanitarian action management, maritime security, health data sharing, and the Mediterranean data space.

The Mediterranean Sea is not just a geographical place; it is a crossroads of cultures, economies, and political trends, all of which are now intertwined with data-driven technologies. Neither a national nor an EU versus non-EU perspective can fully grasp the variety and complexity of the resulting space and legal issues.

This book takes a multidisciplinary approach to Mediterranean digital societies by analysing the legal, societal and technical dimensions of the Mediterranean digital environment, with contributions by scholars and experts in this area.

The book is a key resource for scholars seeking to gain a better understanding of these under-explored topics and to do so from a Mediterranean, rather than an EU-centric, perspective. It also supports policy makers designing their digital strategies – both sectoral and general – in the Mediterranean region, and considers the impact of data-driven technologies on society and their geo-political dimension.

Mediterranean Digital Societies

Law and Technology

Edited by
Alessandro Mantelero

•HART•
OXFORD • LONDON • NEW YORK • NEW DELHI • SYDNEY

HART PUBLISHING
Bloomsbury Publishing Plc
Kemp House, Chawley Park, Cumnor Hill, Oxford, OX2 9PH, UK
1385 Broadway, New York, NY 10018, USA
Bloomsbury Publishing Ireland Limited, 29 Earlsfort Terrace, Dublin 2, D02 AY28, Ireland

HART PUBLISHING, the Hart/Stag logo, BLOOMSBURY and the Diana logo are trademarks of Bloomsbury Publishing Plc

First published in Great Britain 2026

A catalogue record for this book is available from the British Library.

A catalogue record for this book is available from the Library of Congress.

Library of Congress Control Number: 2026015830

ISBN: HB: 978-1-50998-367-4
ePDF: 978-1-50998-369-8
ePub: 978-1-50998-368-1

Typeset by Compuscript Ltd, Shannon

ACKNOWLEDGEMENTS

This book was co-financed by the DIGIMED project, a research project co-funded by the European Union (Project: 101047818 – DIGIMED – ERASMUS-JMO-2021-CHAIR, Jean Monnet Chair in Mediterranean Digital Societies and Law – DIGIMED).

CONTENTS

PART III
THE CULTURAL COMPONENT OF THE MEDITERRANEAN DIGITAL SPACE

LIST OF CONTRIBUTORS

Maria Belén Andreu Martínez is a full Professor of Civil Law and Research Coordinator at the University Institute for Research in Bio-Law at the University of Murcia (Spain). She leads the research group on Bio-Law, Ethics, Health, and Technology at this university. Her work focuses mainly on digital law, the protection of vulnerable persons, and health law.

Ayça Atabey is a post-doctoral researcher at the University of Edinburgh. She received PhD Enrichment Award from the Alan Turing Institute, where she worked on Child-Centred AI. She is an affiliate at the Centre for Data, Culture & Society of the Edinburgh Futures Institute. She conducts interdisciplinary research at the intersection of Law and HCI, focusing on fairness in design and regulation. She also works at the Digital Futures for Children centre at LSE focusing on AI in EdTech design, regulation and child rights.

Joseph A Cannataci is head of the Department of Information Policy & Governance at the Faculty of Media & Knowledge Sciences of the University of Malta. He co-founded and continues as Co-director (on a part-time basis), of STeP, the Security, Technology & e-Privacy Research Group at the University of Groningen in the Netherlands, where he is also Full Professor, holding the Chair of European Information Policy & Technology Law. A Senior Fellow and Associate Researcher at the CNAM Security-Defense-Intelligence Department in Paris, he was decorated by the Republic of France as *Officier de l'Ordre de Palmes Academiques* (2002).

Maria Samantha Esposito is an Assistant Professor of Private Law at the Polytechnic University of Turin. She holds a PhD in Civil Law from the University of Bologna. She has participated in several research projects focusing on digital societies and has been a member of the EU Jean Monnet Chair on Mediterranean Digital Societies & Law team. Her publications focus on data protection and fundamental rights, technology-related liability, and contract law.

Chawki Gaddes was a distinguished Tunisian legal scholar and professor of constitutional law, administrative law and human rights at the Faculty of Legal, Political and Social Sciences in Tunis. He was secretary-general, then vice-president, of the Tunisian Association of Constitutional Law. He served as president of the Tunisian National Authority for the Protection of Personal Data (INPDP) and was elected vice-president, then president of the Association Francophone des Autorités de Protection des Données Personnelles in 2019, a position he held until his retirement in 2023. He was a staunch advocate for the protection of personal data and played a key role in enshrining citizens' fundamental rights.

Lina Jasmontaite is a researcher and project manager at Archimede Solutions SARL. A lawyer and researcher specialising in personal data protection and the regulation of new technologies, she holds a doctorate from Vrije Universiteit Brussel (Research Group on Law, Science, Technology & Society), where among others she contributed to initiatives on data protection in humanitarian action and remains an affiliated fellow.

Alessandro Mantelero is an Associate Professor of Law & Technology at the Polytechnic University of Turin. He is a member of the EDPB Support Pool of Experts, the OECD.AI Expert Group, and scientific legal expert on AI for INTERPOL and UNDP. He has held visiting and research positions at several universities, including the Berkman Klein Center for Internet & Society, the Oxford Internet Institute, the Universitat Oberta de Catalunya, the Ada Lovelace Institute, and the Universidad de Murcia.

Lilian Mitrou is Professor at the University of the Aegean – Greece and President of the Institute for Privacy Law, Data Protection and Technology(EPLO). She was Member of the Hellenic Data Protection Authority and the National Council for Radio and Television. She was/is member of many Committees in the fields of privacy and data protection, communications law, digital governance and artificial intelligence. Her professional experience includes senior consulting and researcher positions in private and public institutions and projects on national and international level.

Miquel Peguera Poch is Full Professor of Law at the Universitat Oberta de Catalunya (UOC) in Barcelona, Spain. He has been Co-editor of the Journal of Intellectual Property, Information Technology and E-Commerce Law since 2011. His research focuses on the legal aspects of the internet, particularly copyright, trademarks, privacy, intermediary liability, and artificial intelligence. He has published extensively in these fields from both EU and US perspectives. He is also a consultant with the Spanish law firm Cuatrecasas.

Julián Valero Torrijos is a Full Professor of Administrative Law at the University of Murcia, Spain. He coordinates the iDerTec Research Group (Innovation, Law & Technology) and holds the Integra Foundation Chair on Identity and Digital Rights. His research focuses on legal aspects of information and communication technologies in the public sector, particularly e-government, data governance, AI regulation, and digital rights.

1

Mediterranean Digital Societies: A Common Path?

ALESSANDRO MANTELERO

1.1. Does a Mediterranean Digital Society Exist?

Does a Mediterranean digital society exist? Are the Mediterranean region and its countries different from others in terms of the development of digital technologies? Is the legal framework in these areas different when it comes to dealing with digital technologies? These are some of the questions that a reader might ask themselves when considering the reasons behind the initiative of various academics from different Mediterranean countries to write this book.

However, writing a book on Mediterranean digital society from the legal perspective that focuses merely on differences would be reductive. This would fail to capture the broader picture that investigating digital society in the Mediterranean region can provide. In the same way that Fernand Braudel's pathbreaking book, *La Méditerranée*,[1] changed the way historians approached the region, looking at the Mediterranean region first is a novel way to frame the discourse on law and technology.

The vast majority of international literature on law and technology tends to focus on major geopolitical actors such as the US, the EU, China and countries in the Global South. Areas of interplay such as the Mediterranean are often overlooked. The Mediterranean shores are so close together that they create a common space that transcends the transient geopolitical divisions of the current historical period. On a historical scale, the EU/non-EU dichotomy is negligible compared with the Roman Empire, the Muslim domain, and the many other geopolitical, religious, and cultural waves that have shaped and reshaped the Mediterranean region over the centuries.

This peculiar perspective is precisely the first reason to investigate digital societies in the Mediterranean region. The teenagers in Place Oudaya who look out to sea from the old town of Rabat do not use social networks in a different way to

[1] F Braudel, *La Méditerranée: les hommes et l'héritage* (Paris, Flammarion, 1985).

those who walk along the seafront in Barcelona. It is clear that the globalisation and consolidation of digital services, dominated by a small number of major players, affects the Mediterranean region as much as any other region in the world. However, the lack of a common geopolitical framework here, unlike continental Europe with the EU, means new forms of collaboration must be invented to outline a common path that is consistent with the needs and ambitions of the Mediterranean digital society.

This is because the Mediterranean is not just a mere geographical and political space; it is also a network of human interactions, maritime activities, tourist flows, research collaborations, joint projects in private and public sectors, and shared heritage sites. The two shores of the Mediterranean Sea are connected not only by the good times in our lives, but also by tragedies and difficulties, from humanitarian emergencies to migration and wars. These different elements all call for a perspective that considers this area a shared space common to different cultures and countries.

Against this scenario, there is a need for the singularity of the Mediterranean experience to be given space in the academic debate on digital society, which is often culturally dominated by a few policy and research centres in continental Europe situated far from the Mediterranean area and largely focused on the geopolitics of another sea: the Atlantic. For too many years, the rich debate within academia on both shores of the Mediterranean has been fragmented, local, and disconnected. The few outstanding scholars from this region who have achieved international recognition have often focused their attention on topics and areas far from the Mediterranean.

This book and the EU-funded project[2] that paved the way for this scientific work are the first responses to the lack of attention given to the legal and cultural dimensions of this area in the international and EU debates.

1.2. A Living Laboratory

The second core element of this book is the nature of the Mediterranean region as a living laboratory for studying the regulation of digital societies. Of course, digital societies can be investigated from a legal perspective anywhere in the world. However, the richness of the Mediterranean area, the mentioned multiple connections between its various actors and, at the same time, their differences, make this a varied setting in which new forms of cooperation can be tested, outside the 'safety zone' of the main geopolitical blocs.

In this respect, writing a book on Mediterranean digital society does not mean claiming that this society is inherently different, but rather highlighting

[2] Digital Mare Nostrum – Jean Monnet Chair in Mediterranean Digital Societies and Law [DIGIMED], https://digimed.polito.it. The project was co-funded by the European Union, Project: 101047818 – DIGIMED – ERASMUS-JMO-2021-CHAIR.

the different dynamics and environments in which similar processes are developing. Dialogue and collaboration between Mediterranean countries and those on the northern and southern shores are not just a political exercise; they are necessary. Macro phenomena such as migrations and regional interests ranging from commerce to tourism require significant forms of cooperation, but these must be established outside of the facilitating institutional framework provided by the main geopolitical blocs. The tension between the importance of creating a shared digital space that satisfies shared needs and interests, and the fragmentation of the institutional and digital industry systems, makes the Mediterranean area a privileged living laboratory for studying and developing regulatory solutions for digital society.

The need to define new hybrid solutions through trans-cultural and trans-national dialogue in this region, while bearing in mind the common core of the Mediterranean culture and space, has no equal in terms of legal experimentation in other areas. Here, the Mediterranean Sea provides the geographical and cultural basis for creating shared data spaces, enabling the development of a cross-country Mediterranean digital society. Rather than relying on top-down solutions facilitated by regional institutions, as is the case in the EU, a different bottom-up approach becomes the cornerstone on which to build this digital space. This provides a model that offers a different perspective to the dominant narrative, which focuses on the main geopolitical blocs, and it is also suitable for implementation in other areas.

Returning to the initial questions, which the authors of this book also raised at the beginning of this cultural and scientific journey, perhaps there is no such thing as a Mediterranean singularity in terms of digital society and culture, at least from a legal perspective. The Mediterranean region does not use, and has not developed, digital technologies that are significantly different from those used elsewhere. However, the convergent variety of the Mediterranean countries, their ties and differences, their common issues and different approaches, make the Mediterranean digital society unique and worthy of study beyond the EU/non-EU dichotomy. This paves the way for new forms of cooperation and highlights the cultural specificity of this region, which cannot be see through the lens of the logics and cultures of other parts of the world. In this regard, the vibrant pages written by Joe Cannataci in the final chapter of this book are the appropriate conclusion to the reflections that begin in this chapter.

1.3. The Methodological Approach

The methodological contribution of this book concerns digital regulation, in a broader sense, and the challenges involved in creating operational legal solutions within multilayered legal frameworks (ie national, regional/EU, and international) and multicultural spaces, which impact on the notion of dignity and the ethical values underpinning legal principles, as found in the Mediterranean region.

This relatively small regional area is rich in historical and cultural ties,[3] interconnected through international and cross-national initiatives,[4] and facing common issues.[5] Its multilayered and multicultural nature requires a methodological approach that combines a theoretical view with an empirical understanding of the region's complexity.

In this regard, for example, chapter two examines the difference between 'public good' and fairness as guiding principles in data processing through the lens of the concrete experience of humanitarian organisations dealing with challenging situations in the Mediterranean area. It looks at the best legal framework to ensure that the needs and expectations of vulnerable individuals are at the centre of data management practices. Similarly, chapter five contextualises the notions of data sharing and data spaces by examining existing constraints in the Mediterranean region and proposing a decentralised architecture built on contractual solutions, data portability, citizen engagement, certifications, open-source solutions and interoperability.

Finally, the complex mosaic of the Mediterranean context requires a specific methodological approach to finding legal solutions to the challenges it faces, which are examined in this book. More specifically, the lack of a common regional legal framework, coupled with the cultural and political limitations of an EU-centric approach, suggests developing different bottom-up strategies that focus on key principles, soft law instruments, contracts, and shared standards.

For example, the fairness principle can play a central role in balancing power dynamics and respecting the expectations of data subjects in the context of humanitarian action, including taking a culturally sensitive approach.[6] The same applies to the agreements that govern the various actors involved in international cooperation actions, setting out policy and technical solutions that ensure an adequate protection of human rights.[7] A similar approach has been recommended for developing the first building block of a Mediterranean health data space by promoting tools, such as digital wallets that enable citizens to manage their health data and share it with third parties if they wish.[8]

These strategies can be complemented by specific state agreements at the bilateral or multilateral level. This depends not only on the willingness of state actors, but also on the sectoral or general maturity of the legislation in the different countries, and on how closely their respective provisions align.

[3] See chs 8 and 9.
[4] See chs 2 and 3.
[5] See chs 4, 5, 6 and 7.
[6] See ch 2.
[7] See ch 3.
[8] See ch 6.

1.4. Digital Technologies for Human Rights Protection and Security in the Mediterranean Area

The first area investigated in this book relates to the critical issues and tragedies that have occurred in the Mediterranean region in recent decades. Humanitarian crises, migration and war have affected both shores of the Mediterranean Sea. Tensions originating in one area have spread throughout the Mediterranean region like the waves of the sea under the wind. This has necessarily connected the different countries in the region, which are involved in facing these challenges in various ways.

Part one of this book (chapters two to four) addresses these issues from various legal angles. In chapter two, Lina Jasmontaite and Ayça Atabey focus on the key role played by data and data processing in humanitarian actions. As with many other areas of life, humanitarian action is also increasingly data-driven, but this raises several challenging issues in terms of data protection.

Many humanitarian organisations are active in the Mediterranean region, seeking to protect, assist and empower vulnerable people in contexts of armed conflict, crisis, violence, and natural disasters. The work of many of these organisations is mission-driven and does not necessarily fit into a 'typical' legal framework. This is because they perform specific tasks under international law, based on their privileges and immunities.

Against this complex background in which many stakeholders participate in and contribute to international development assistance and humanitarian aid programmes, the two authors question whether the 'public good' narrative could encourage the sharing of excessive amounts of data without adequate safeguards. They emphasise that this concept must be examined closely through the lens of the fairness principle. This principle ensures that data processing aligns with individuals' reasonable expectations, and helps to mitigate power imbalance between organisations and affected populations. In order to explore its research questions, the chapter draws on real-life scenarios and case studies set in a Mediterranean context. This approach complements theoretical analysis with empirical evidence, in line with the methodological approach described above.

An important role in addressing the challenges posed by the various crises and critical situations affecting Mediterranean areas is also played by international cooperation. While humanitarian aid is more focused on specific needs and emergencies, some of which have become structural issues in the region, international cooperation has a broader, long-term scope. This cooperation takes various forms and involves a variety of local entities.

In this scenario, chapter three will discuss contractual solutions for protecting human rights in critical areas of international cooperation. As with humanitarian action, international cooperation is based on the interaction between different actors, with a key distinction between funding or leading entities and local contractors. The broad scope of this cooperation and the variety of its impacts raise issues that go beyond the data protection issues considered in the previous chapter.

Furthermore, the progressive datafication of the physical and social environment in the context of cooperation project development has often resulted in risks associated with digital ecosystems characterised by knowledge and information asymmetries. Significant power therefore lies in the hands of local technological partners, in terms of access to data, the development of data processing tools, and the potential reuse and sharing of data.

Building on the role played by the EU in the Mediterranean area – based on a partnership with the eastern and southern shores of the Mediterranean established back in 1995 – this chapter considers the challenges of implementing cooperation strategies in contexts where the legal framework fails to provide an effective, comprehensive level of protection for personal data and human rights, in terms of existing legislation and its implementation. In order to address the fragmented scenario of Mediterranean cooperation, the chapter outlines various strategies for promoting the responsible use of digital technologies and AI throughout the projects' lifecycle. These strategies can be implemented regardless of the level of protection provided by the local context in which the funded projects are developed.

The current tensions in the Mediterranean area also have a tangible impact on the region: migrants, humanitarian aid, as well as armies, cross the sea on vessels and boats. Maritime security is therefore a crucial component of a social environment in which the sea is the main charactering element. In this context, chapter four, the final chapter of part one, sees Lilian Mitrou discuss maritime security and its various aspects.

The progressive digitalisation of the maritime sector has opened up new scenarios with regard to security, including cybersecurity. The digital environment, coupled with the increasing number of geopolitical conflicts and challenges in the Mediterranean region, has introduced new risks while providing new ways to address them. This chapter analyses these multidimensional threats and the impact of the 'digitisation of security' on fundamental rights and freedoms.

The author focuses on border control and migration, examining concrete projects developed in the region that use a data-driven approach to security, employing tools such as drones and AI-enabled surveillance and analysis technologies. The chapter also discusses, from a perspective of fundamental rights protection, the impact of digitalisation and pervasive control related to search and rescue operations, as well as disaster and accident management in the Mediterranean Sea.

1.5. Digital Services and Mediterranean Cross-Country Cooperation

Having addressed the critical issues affecting the Mediterranean region and the challenges of balancing urgent responses with the safeguarding of fundamental rights in adverse conditions in part one of this book, part two turns to positive scenarios of digital societies. Tourism, health services and smart cities present different positive horizons for Mediterranean societies, offering new opportunities, better economic and living conditions, and social growth through digital technologies.

In chapter five, Maria Samantha Esposito and I focus on one of the most lucrative industries in the Mediterranean region: tourism. With over 232 million international tourists per year, the Mediterranean is the planet's leading tourist destination. In order to manage such large numbers of tourists, data plays a crucial role in optimising flows and offers, and in boosting this economic sector. However, the geographical, political, and functional fragmentation of tourism policies, coupled with the variety of actors involved, hinders the achievement of these results.

It is therefore necessary to develop synergies based on improved interaction, shared objectives and data sharing. In this respect, data spaces will play a central role. This chapter makes a contribution to the design of such spaces and their regulatory framework by analysing tourism data ecosystems.

Another crucial area for the people living on the shores of the Mediterranean Sea is health. While the health industry is important in many regional economies, it is not the focus of this book. Rather, the focus is on the importance of having access to efficient, high-quality health services. As in previous chapters, data and ICTs play a crucial role here.

In chapter six, Belén Andreu Martínez and Chawki Gaddes* analyse how sharing health data can improve health services in the Mediterranean context, where this category of data plays a significant role in various scenarios relating to people and service flows within the region.

Migrants and tourists need healthcare for different reasons. Collaborations between hospitals and research centres require data exchange. This variety of scenarios is based on different legal frameworks for data exchange, with the EU moving towards a common health data space and harmonised rules, but with much greater variability among non-EU countries.

The authors address the challenging question of how legal solutions could facilitate data exchange in the light of the operational scenarios and the existing framework of international relations. They propose an approach that, in line with the methodology adopted in this book for dealing with the complexity of the Mediterranean context, combines the active involvement of state actors in regulatory interoperability with bottom-up initiatives based on contractual instruments under private law.

* Chawki Gaddes will never read this book. He passed away in July 2025. I would like to honour his memory and his active role in protecting personal data at a national level, as well as his work at the Council of Europe, where we met several times. I still have the leather folder he gave me years ago during one of those meetings. Its Arabic style reminds me of the importance of strengthening ties between countries around the Mediterranean Sea. He demonstrated this in his work and reiterated it in his final message to me, in which he referred to 'ce lac qui nous unit, qui est la Méditerranée' ('this lake that unites us, the Mediterranean'). Sit tibi terra levis, Chawki.

Chapter seven, the final chapter of part two, also focuses on an emerging general trend in this area concerning smart cities: the progressive datafication and digitalisation of urban spaces, which are transforming into socio-technical infrastructures. Julián Valero Torrijos considers smart cities in the context of modernising public administration functions, particularly at a municipal level. This is a common issue in many Mediterranean countries, where administrations are often underfunded and bureaucratic.

Moreover, the traditional approach to the relationship between public administration and citizens in this area has, to varying degrees, been characterised by limited transparency. The design and development of smart city projects can address this by improving access to public sector information, not only in the context of administrative procedures, but also from a broader perspective involving various actors interested in providing public services. This includes adopting open data standards for commercial reuse. While these changes affect cities and their administrative management from legal and data-driven perspectives, they also present an additional challenge in terms of protecting the personal data of service users. This chapter analyses the implications of such an approach, emphasising the importance of combining innovation with the effective respect for fundamental rights within the EU and the broader Mediterranean legal frameworks.

1.6. The Cultural Component of the Mediterranean Digital Space

Part three of the book examines the cultural aspects of the digital Mediterranean space, shifting the focus from legal analysis to a broader multidisciplinary approach. In chapter eight, Miquel Peguera Poch considers the relationships between cultural heritage and data, which is an under-explored topic in the legal debate, but of paramount importance in a region that is the custodian of an immense cultural heritage.

From a legal perspective, data management lies at the intersection of heritage, personal and non-personal data, and intellectual property protection. Therefore, as in other areas explored in this book, it is crucial to establish the basis for creating a shared data space for cultural heritage.

The book concludes with a culturally stimulating chapter by Joe Cannataci, which takes an interdisciplinary approach to studying privacy in the Mediterranean area. This approach fuses legal thinking with anthropological, archaeological and architectural perspectives on the origins and development of privacy.

Starting with the way Mediterranean peoples have built their houses to ensure privacy, from pre-Hellenic domestic architecture onwards, the author proposes a cohesive, holistic methodology for 'the archaeology of privacy', taking into account the history and evolution of domestic architecture in both private and public spaces. This analysis combines evidence from archaeology and architecture with the broader approach offered by anthropology, with the aim of improving our understanding of the various privacy-related aspects of the human experience. It also provides a conceptual framework for addressing the most recent issues as the Mediterranean transitions into the eras of the digital society and the knowledge economy.

1.7. Towards a Mediterranean Digital Society

The journey presented in this book is just one possible path for discussing and exploring the interplay between law and technology in Mediterranean societies. The lack of legal studies in this field means it is not possible to draw conclusions on the basis of the research conducted by the authors of this book. In fact, the book's purpose is to initiate a new line of research in this area.

Our work reveals that the Mediterranean region should be considered as a whole rather than as a space divided by geopolitics. Although there are certainly areas of influence belonging to regional powers, this does not preclude a multidimensional framework. In such a framework, the traditional EU/non-EU dichotomy would be an oversimplification, hiding the common issues and ties that connect the two shores of the Mediterranean Sea.

Nowadays, this regional dimension is largely determined by the challenges that the different Mediterranean countries face in terms of digital transformation when addressing critical situations and social core interests. However, based on these needs, new regulatory strategies are emerging in this area that take a different approach to that of EU neighbouring countries. These strategies focus on key principles, soft law instruments, contracts and shared standards.

With regard to the main drivers of the digital society – namely, datafication and data-centric technological solutions, Mediterranean societies demonstrate similarities with global trends. When using digital technology to address crises and challenging situations, the focus should be on protecting human and fundamental rights. When it comes to using these technologies to promote societal development, key elements are creating data spaces, ensuring data flows, and guaranteeing technical interoperability.

The following chapters demonstrate how the Mediterranean 'laboratory' is gradually adopting these frameworks, and explore which solutions are possible or have already been implemented. The unique socio-cultural dimension of this region is evident in the various areas examined in the book, and even more specifically in the final part. This dimension is not explicitly reflected in a common regulatory approach, but facilitates the bottom-up approach mentioned above and makes it possible to use it to overcome political, institutional and legal fragmentation.

The brushstrokes on the cover of this book reflect the various perspectives of Mediterranean digital societies. Each tone and nuance is different, yet they are all connected by a common background.

PART I

Digital Technologies for Human Rights Protection and Security in the Mediterranean Area

2

Downstreaming Data Protection in Humanitarian Work: Why Revive Fairness Over Public Good for Individual Benefit?

AYÇA ATABEY AND LINA JASMONTAITE

2.1. Introduction

The idea of using technology and encouraging or facilitating data sharing among different types of humanitarian aid organisations seems to perfectly align with the default modes that underpin today's societies and policy making no matter the sector: datafication and data solutionism.[1]

Datafication consists of two connected aspects: the generation of a recorded trace that is shared as data beyond its original time and location; and the subsequent utilisation of that trace as a significant component in other processes.[2] In contrast, data solutionism legitimises digitalisation. As put forward by Morozov, this term represents the tendency to change 'all complex social situations either as neatly defined problems with definite, computable solutions or as transparent and self-evident processes that can be easily optimised', against the backdrop of 'unexpected consequences that could eventually cause more damage than the problems they seek to address'.[3]

These tendencies of the non-emergency world are visible in the humanitarian sector. That 'the importance of digital technology in the development agenda has been identified and recognised since the early 2000s' was noted by the Working

[1] See, Recital 2 of the Data Governance Act ('data-driven innovation will bring enormous benefits to both Union citizens and the economy, for example by improving and personalising medicine, providing new mobility').

[2] See A Beaulieu and S Leonelli (eds), *Data and Society: A Critical Introduction* (London, Sage, 2021) 4.

[3] E Morozov, *To Save Everything, Click Here: Technology, Solutionism and the Urge to Fix Problems That Don't Exist* (London, Penguin Books, 2014) 5.

Group on the Role of Personal Data Protection in International Development Aid (WG Aid),[4] which was launched in the aftermath of the 2015 Resolution on Privacy and International Humanitarian Action. WG Aid also highlighted that the main purpose of the use of technology in the humanitarian environment has been to realise and facilitate projects within the framework of international development aid and humanitarian assistance, in other words, enhance living conditions for affected individuals. At the same time, as explained by the Global Privacy Assembly, 'The increasing use of technology allows for a broader use of different categories of data processed and an increase in the amount and sharing of data'.[5]

More specifically, in the humanitarian sector personal data is mostly collected and processed in the following main lines of action: providing and securing shelter, habitat, and access to food and health and hygiene care; assisting in cases of forced displacements of population, restoring family links, providing victim support (sexual abuses, tortures etc); as well as providing education.[6] To this end, 'humanitarian organisations process the personal data of different categories of individuals in humanitarian emergencies, such as data of beneficiaries and contacts involved in their activities, as well as data of staff and goods/service providers, or even data of donors'.[7]

The term 'humanitarian organisations' can be defined as 'an organisation that provides aid to alleviate human suffering, and/or protects life and health, and upholds human dignity during Humanitarian Emergencies in accordance with its mandate and/or mission'.[8] Within the scope of this chapter we use this term as well as 'international aid organisations' to include humanitarian organisations such as the International Committee of the Red Cross (ICRC), United Nations High Commissioner for Refugees (UNHCR), International Organization for Migration (IOM), United Nations Children's Fund (UNICEF), United Nations Office for the Coordination of Humanitarian Affairs (OCHA), World Food Programme (WFP) and World Health Organization (WHO). It must be, however, recognised that community-based and local organisations also play an important role in providing humanitarian assistance. Consequently, not only are numerous organisations involved in providing international development aid, but mapping

[4] Federal Data Protection and Information Commissioner (FDPIC), Switzerland and Supervisory Commission for Personal Information (CCIN) Monaco, 'Report – Working Group on the Role of Personal Data Protection in International Development Aid, International Humanitarian Aid and Crisis Management' (2023) 22, https://globalprivacyassembly.org/wp-content/uploads/2022/11/2.2.h.-The-Role-of-Personal-Data-Protection-in-International-Development-Aid-International-Humanitarian-Aid-and-Crisis-Managment-Working-Group-English.pdf.

[5] Global Privacy Assembly, 'GPA Resolution on the Role of Personal Data Protection in International Development Aid, International Humanitarian Aid and Crisis Management' (2020), https://globalprivacyassembly.org/wp-content/uploads/2020/10/FINAL-GPA-Resolution-International-Aid-EN.pdf.

[6] See ibid 22.

[7] C Kuner and M Marelli (eds), *Handbook on Data Protection in Humanitarian Action* (Geneva, ICRC, 2020).

[8] See ibid.

the humanitarian sector is complicated. Despite the intrinsic complexity of the humanitarian sector, it is recommended that:

> Donors, competent organisations and agencies … mainstream data protection and privacy by design in a systematic manner in their international development aid, international humanitarian aid and crisis management programmes, in order to guarantee the rights and freedoms of the beneficiaries of these programmes.[9]

Against this backdrop, in this chapter we seek to further the debate on how the mainstreaming of data protection and privacy by design in a systematic manner in the context of international development aid could be done. Notably, the EU General Data Protection Regulation (GDPR) undeniably sets the gold standard for data protection laws across the globe, and many humanitarian organisations and international aid organisations have taken steps to implement data privacy and data protection guidelines and internal policies. At the same time, it is important to recognise that the legal set-up of international aid organisations presents unique legal challenges from the affected individual's perspective, given that these organisations work under privileges and immunities, which are necessary to perform their work independently.[10]

2.2. Unavoidable Data Collection and Sharing

As observed and noted by many, most international organisations collect data, including personal data, within the scope of various operations.[11] While recognising that data collected by humanitarians can be used – aid provided by local communities and by national governments is less likely to be reported than aid provided by international organisations – it is highly valuable as it can be used: 1) for analysis of humanitarian crises and assistance; 2) in order to support humanitarian policy decisions; and 3) to provide context for operational decisions (programme development).[12]

Data collection takes place within the operational data management. More specifically, operational data management, as explained by the Data Responsibility Working Group,[13]

[9] Global Privacy Assembly (n 5), 3.

[10] We use the term 'affected individuals' to refer to individuals who are affected by natural or man-made disasters (eg displacement due to a conflict) and whose personal data are processed in order to receive humanitarian aid or assistance.

[11] See T Gazi, 'Data to the rescue: how humanitarian aid NGOs should collect information based on the GDPR' (2020) 5 *Journal of International Humanitarian Action* 9.

[12] See United Nations, 'World Humanitarian Data and Trends 2017' (2018), doi.org/10.18356/b7f20438-en.

[13] The Data Responsibility Working Group is a global coordination body that works to promote data responsibility throughout the humanitarian system. It originated as an Inter-Agency Standing Committee (IASC) subgroup. The Inter-Agency Standing Committee (IASC) is a high-level

> occurs as part of humanitarian action throughout the planning and response cycle across clusters/sectors and includes activities such as situational analysis, needs assessments, population data management, registration and enrolment, case management, communicating with affected populations, protection monitoring, and response monitoring and evaluation.[14]

Such data management should ensure data responsibility in humanitarian action and the latter is understood as 'the safe, ethical and effective management of personal and non-personal data for operational response, in accordance with established frameworks for personal data protection'.[15]

It has been argued that apart from operational value, collected personal data 'may provide unique humanitarian aid actors with insight into the context, beneficiaries' needs, and the type of assistance required'.[16] For the collection, and therefore, the processing of personal data of affected individuals by an international aid organisation to be fair and lawful, it must be based on a legal ground.[17] It is at most important for any organisation processing personal data, including those involved in the provision of aid and other humanitarian assistance, to identify the legal ground correctly. That is the determining factor when evaluating the lawfulness of the processing. For this reason Bieker argues that 'The principle of lawfulness is central for data protection law'.[18]

Article 6 of the GDPR outlines the requirements for lawful processing,[19] many of which are also found in the data processing policies of international organisations. While these legal grounds seem to provide a range of situations that can be applicable to different contexts of processing, for organisations involved in the provision of humanitarian aid the selection of a legal ground may seem to be difficult. For example, Kuner and Marelli explain that 'In their humanitarian work, humanitarian organisations may rely on' the existing legal bases. However, they recognise that:

> In the emergency situations in which humanitarian organisations usually operate it can be difficult to fulfil the basic conditions of valid consent, in particular that it is

humanitarian coordination forum within the United Nations system. It brings together the executive heads of 19 organisations and consortia to formulate policy, set strategic priorities and mobilise resources in response to humanitarian crises.

[14] Inter-Agency Standing Committee, 'Inter-Agency Standing Committee, Operational Guidance, Data Responsibility in Humanitarian Action by Data Responsibility Working Group' (2023) 10, https://interagencystandingcommittee.org/operational-response/iasc-operational-guidance-data-responsibility-humanitarian-action.

[15] ibid 10.

[16] Gazi (n 11).

[17] See also Art 5 of the GDPR, which states that 'Personal data shall be: (a) processed lawfully, fairly and in a transparent manner in relation to the data subject ("lawfulness, fairness and transparency")'. This principle is also listed in other core data protection documents, such as the Council of Europe, Modernised Convention for the Protection of Individuals with Regard to the Processing of Personal Data.

[18] F Bieker, *The Right to Data Protection: Individual and Structural Dimensions of Data Protection in EU Law* (Den Haag, Asser Press, 2022).

[19] The requirement of lawfulness was also found in the Data Protection Directive (Directive 95/46/EC). It can be also traced to the Fair Information Practice Principles (FIPPs) as well as the OECD Guidelines, which requires among its eight principles: (1) collection limitation – data should be collected lawfully with the individual's consent; and Convention no 108 of the Council of Europe.

> informed and freely given. For example, this can be the case where consenting to the processing of personal data is a precondition to receive assistance. It could also apply to human resources, for example, if consenting to the processing is a condition for recruitment.

The two authors suggest that 'Processing by humanitarian organisations may often be based on vital interest or on important grounds of public interest, for example in the performance of a mandate established under national or international law'.[20]

At the same time, in cases of vital interest, it should be considered that there must be 'sufficient elements to consider that in the absence of processing the individual could be at risk of physical or moral harm' and, in cases involving important grounds of public interest, it must be clear that

> the specific processing operation is within a mandate established for the humanitarian organisation under national, regional or international law, or that the humanitarian organisation is otherwise performing a specific task or function that is in the public interest and is laid down by law.[21]

While international organisations providing humanitarian assistance endorse principles and various GDPR requirements listed in their privacy policies,[22] they are not bound by the GDPR. As Marelli argued, the international organisations 'have immunity from jurisdiction' and are considered to be third countries within the meaning of GDPR. For example, they can be recipients of data transfers, provided additional safeguards are put in place.[23] While it is important for international organisations to have access to privileges and immunities – as set out in the 1946 Convention on the Privileges and Immunities of the United Nations and the 1947 Convention on the Privileges and Immunities of the Specialized Agencies – as this ensures their independence, this can make their commitment to data protection principles practically unenforceable.

Finally, it is worth noting that considerable efforts have been made to standardise data protection practices among international organisations. For instance, the Data Protection and Privacy Policy for the Secretariat of the United Nations (ST/SGB/2024/1) was adopted on 13 March 2024. This policy aims to harmonise data protection and privacy policies across United Nations system organisations and ensure they align with best practices, providing more tailored and specific legal grounds to meet the demands of international organisations.[24]

[20] Kuner and Marelli (n 7) 60.

[21] ibid.

[22] See, eg, IFRC, 'Policy on the Protection of Personal Data | IFRC' (2020), www.ifrc.org/document/IFRC-Data-Protection-Policy.

[23] M Marelli, 'Transferring Personal Data to International organisations under the GDPR: An Analysis of the Transfer Mechanisms' (2024) 14 *International Data Privacy Law* 19.

[24] See United Nations, 'Data Protection and Privacy Policy for the Secretariat of the United Nations ST/SGB/2024/3' (2024), https://documents.un.org/doc/undoc/gen/n24/069/80/pdf/n2406980.pdf.

2.3. Unavoidable Data Sharing in Crisis Management

As rightly noted by the Data Responsibility Working Group,[25] 'the humanitarian sector is inherently interconnected' with many actors involved in the provision of aid at global and local level. Consequently, apart from collecting data, including personal data, international organisations share that data with others. The WG AID report found that the majority of aid organisations collect and share personal data with third parties and subcontractors for the purposes such as provision of: 1) humanitarian assistance; 2) cooperation with donors, partners and service providers; 3) litigation management; 4) internal and external audits; and 5) research.[26] These third parties include other humanitarian actors (eg agencies), national governments of the jurisdiction where aid is provided, donors and national governments where the entity providing aid is based.

In fact, it is desirable for international aid organisations to share personal data with other parties involved in the humanitarian intervention for two reasons.[27] First, data sharing prevents affected individuals from being subjected to multiple data collection initiatives. Second, it improves efficiency by reducing potential overlap in the services and assistance provided.

However, not all data sharing activities are equal. We posit that differentiation should be made between two situations based on their impact on the data rights of affected individuals: (i) personal data sharing with third parties based on data sharing agreements as a legal basis; and (ii) data sharing with third parties, in aggregated or in a disaggregated form.

In the first situation, the already collected personal data of affected individuals is shared with other organisations based on the agreement between organisations. The agreement serves as a legal basis legitimising the processing of personal data, which may, for example, include access and retrieval of such data. Within the scope of such agreements, at least theoretically, individuals can enforce their data subjects' rights (eg right to access or rectification).

In general, international aid organisations collecting personal data can enter into such agreements, as long as such data sharing is compatible with the purpose for which personal data was collected initially and affected individuals can enforce their rights not only with the initial data controller. It should be added that international organisations either enter into high-level interinstitutional data sharing agreements or use ad hoc templates for data sharing.[28] There is a great difference in terms of details and scrutiny that shared personal data is subjected to between

[25] Inter-Agency Standing Committee (n 14) 13.

[26] See FDPIC and CCIN (n 4) 35.

[27] Gazi (n 11).

[28] See UNHCR 'Trilateral Data-Sharing Agreement for Cash Assistance (UNHCR, WFP, UNICEF)' (2020), www.unhcr.org/media/trilateral-data-sharing-agreement-cash-assistance-unhcr-wfp-unicef; UNHCR, 'World Bank-UNHCR Data Sharing Agreement to Improve Assistance to the Forcibly Displaced' (2023), www.unhcr.org/uk/news/press-releases/world-bank-unhcr-data-sharing-agreement-improve-assistance-forcibly-displaced.

the two types of agreements. Interinstitutional agreements are typically followed by annexes specifying data protection obligations.

For example, the Trilateral Data-Sharing Agreement between UNHCR, WFP and UNICEF focuses on a specific type of aid: cash assistance, also sometimes referred to as cash transfers. One of the clauses in the agreement notes that 'UNICEF's agreement to share data with UNHCR and WFP will be in both refugee and non-refugee contexts' and it refers to an annex that includes the 2018 Data Sharing Addendum signed by UNHCR and WFP.[29] The addendum should form the basis on which agencies develop specific data-sharing clauses, taking UNICEF's mandate into account. In contrast, the IOM and third parties have adopted a template agreement on the transfer of personal data, which set outs a number of very specific obligations.[30]

In this regard, it could be added that data protection policies can be of great importance as they can provide for the general approach to address data sharing between organisations. For example, the aforementioned Data Protection and Privacy Policy for the Secretariat of the United Nations notes that in case of data sharing outside the United Nations, 'the data steward must make reasonable efforts to ensure that the receiving party affords appropriate protection for such data in a manner at least equivalent to the [UN] principles'.

The second situation includes data sharing with third parties, in aggregated as well as disaggregated forms. An illustrative example in this regard could be the tendency of donors (eg governments and private companies) to request to share disaggregated data with them, such as the gender, age, and disability markers.[31] Donors play a key role within the humanitarian sector as they enable funding for humanitarian programmes, and therefore, their need to collect data is justified by the purposes of accountability for funds spent, compliance, and efficiency and effectiveness of programme design. The Humanitarian Data and Trust Initiative that plays a critical role in this landscape raised the alarm that 'donors have begun to increasingly request various forms of disaggregated data, such as household-level survey results and data about the delivery of assistance disaggregated by demographics, geographical location and/or group dimensions (e.g. ethnicity, protection status, etc.)'.[32]

[29] ibid.

[30] These obligations include the following: adherence to the IOM's Data Protection Principles; strict confidentiality standards and appropriate access control measures for third parties, as well as encryption of all transmissions of the selected personal data; use of personal data only for the specified purpose, without further processing, disclosing or sharing without the IOM's consent; adoption of security measures by third parties to protect data integrity and limit access on a need-to-know basis; immediate reporting to the IOM of any data breaches or requests from data subjects or third parties regarding the data; and immediate updating, rectifying and/or erasing of the selected personal data upon instruction from the IOM.

[31] See L Fast, 'Data Sharing between Humanitarian Organisations and Donors' (NCHS Paper, 2020) 21, www.humanitarianstudies.no/wp-content/uploads/NCHS-paper-06-April-2022-Data-sharing-between-humanitarian-organisations-and-donors.pdf.

[32] Humanitarian Data and Trust Initiative, 'A Principled Framework for Responsible Data Sharing Between Humanitarian organisations and Donors – The Centre for Humanitarian Data' (2023), https://centre.humdata.org/a-principled-framework-for-responsible-data-sharing-between-humanitarian-organisations-and-donors.

Data sharing requests form part of the formal and informal frameworks that govern the collection and sharing of data between humanitarian aid organisations and donors. Data sharing agreements typically forms part of framework agreements. It appears that 'The amount of data increases and the risks become more complex with additional implementing partners',[33] where government donors contract humanitarian actors who, in turn, subcontract to other entities, often national or local NGOs. The latter – outsourcing aid delivery to the local level – is a standard practice, which in essence means that minimising data collection of affected individuals and its sharing is quite unlikely. Furthermore, trust and power dynamics (ie, the power asymmetry) between humanitarian organisations and donors may incentivise data sharing in expectation to receive further funding, whereas often such data is not used for analysis purposes by donors (eg because of lack of interoperability).[34]

Consequently, donors both encourage and incentivise data collection and analysis, and in some cases are direct users of data collected.[35] However, the increasing data thirst by donors is problematic because 'sharing seemingly innocuous data such as aggregated survey results can place already vulnerable people and communities at greater risk' of re-identification of individuals, communities and demographic groups, and as a result of this, affected individuals that received aid can be subjected to various human rights violations, including violence and other forms of harm.[36]

As a rule of a thumb, the processing of personal data for purposes other than those for which the personal data were initially collected should be allowed only where the processing is compatible with the purposes for which the personal data were initially collected. Humanitarian aid organisations can build on good data practices that have already been identified.

For example, there are numerous initiatives that advocate for the responsible management of data, such as the Inter-Agency Standing Committee (IASC) Operational Guidance on Data Responsibility in Humanitarian Action, the ICRC Handbook on Data Protection in Humanitarian Action, and A Principled Framework for Responsible Data Sharing Between Humanitarian organisations and Donors. Raising awareness of the sensitivity of data seems valuable. This could provide the missing piece of this puzzle – the lack of the voices of individuals whose data is processed – by placing their rights and needs at the centre of the two data-sharing scenarios discussed. In our opinion, this shift in mindset is desirable, as otherwise humanitarian organisations cannot be held accountable by the individuals whose data they collect.

[33] See Fast (n 31) 21.
[34] ibid.
[35] Humanitarian Data and Trust Initiative (n 32).
[36] Centre for Humanitarian Data, 'Responsible Data Sharing with Donors – The Centre for Humanitarian Data' (2020), https://centre.humdata.org/guidance-note-responsible-data-sharing-with-donors.

2.4. Data Sharing for Public Good: A Viable Solution in the Humanitarian Context?

The idea of sharing data, including personal data, for public good is closely connected with the Open Data movement, which has grown out of the initiatives in various research areas (eg meteorology and astronomy). The underlying premise of this movement is that data is a non-excludable resource. Sharing research data demonstrated that there are many opportunities, once data is pooled from different resources, such as to accelerate research; to avoid useless duplication of efforts and investment; and to increase the transparency and accountability of research by widening the peer group available to scrutinise results, to address mistakes and prevent fraud. Building on this positive experience, the Open Data movement has expanded and currently includes government and social services (through the idea of 'Open Government') 'as well as private industry and particularly large corporations'.[37]

The Open Data movement functions on the premise that data, including personal data, is a public good and can be reusable and, in this way, it goes beyond the right to know. The Open Data movement deems that data should not be commodified. More specifically, data are expected to be freely and widely available to anybody who wishes to use them. In support of this view, legal frameworks have been developed to facilitate data journeys while imposing the least possible constraints on who uses the data, why and how. For example, in the EU, the urge and need for access to more data and its reuse has been cemented by the Data Governance Act (DGA) and the Data Act.[38] The two acts include legislative measures on data governance, access and reuse of data, including personal data. The DGA, in general, requires anonymising (personal) data in order to ensure that neither identification of individuals nor disclosure of data containing commercially confidential information is possible.

Apart from resulting in the legal frameworks enabling data sharing, it must be pointed out that technological developments also shaped the Open Data movement. For example, it can be suggested that the smart city narrative encouraged a deep faith in the usefulness of data collected by public authorities to guide city

[37] See Beaulieu and Leonelli (n 2) 123.

[38] The Data Act, Art 2(16), introduces the concept of 'data altruism', which to some extent resembles the public good narrative. Data altruism is understood as 'the voluntary sharing of data on the basis of the consent of data subjects to process personal data pertaining to them, or permissions of data holders to allow the use of their non-personal data without seeking or receiving a reward that goes beyond compensation related to the costs that they incur where they make their data available for objectives of general interest as provided for in national law, where applicable, such as healthcare, combating climate change, improving mobility, facilitating the development, production and dissemination of official statistics, improving the provision of public services, public policy making or scientific research purposes in the general interest'.

leadership via Internet of Things (IoT) devices.[39] Then, big data initiatives, which were based on data collected from a variety of different sources, carried the promise of generating new knowledge by unlocking patterns, which had not previously been identified.[40] More recently, the economic and policy push to develop large language models has brought the debate over access to publicly available data to the forefront. For example, the European Commission concluded that in the EU 'there is not enough data available for innovative re-use, including for the development of artificial intelligence' and consequently there is a pressing need to open up data from public and private entities.[41]

There are also good intentions to allow and incentivise data collection and sharing in the humanitarian context. OCHA emphasised the need to access available data in 2013. Its 2013 report noted that the main value of collecting data is to identify humanitarian needs and

> to establish a common baseline of data that can be used to make comparisons across time. The information can be used for analysis of humanitarian crises and assistance, to support humanitarian policy decisions and to provide context for operational decisions.[42]

It has been suggested that the phrase 'data for public good' could be understood in two ways in a humanitarian context. First, 'data should be made available to help international organisations promote social good in the public sphere, i.e. that data should be more public to create more good impacts from it'; and second, 'data should be formally defined as a public good, because its potential power to fight poverty and disease and to inform emergency response is such that international institutions should have access to it'.[43]

In order to advance debates on access and reuse of available data, the UN Secretary-General created Global Pulse, an innovation initiative charged with accelerating discovery, development, and adoption of big data analytics as a public good. In one of its first reports, Global Pulse posited that

> current frameworks for data and privacy protection have not kept pace with advances in technology, and often do not account for big data. Big data collected by the private sector as part of their commercial services makes compliance in the context of repurposing those data sources for development and humanitarian action unclear.[44]

[39] See JI Lane (ed), *Privacy, Big Data, and the Public Good: Frameworks for Engagement* (New York, Cambridge University Press, 2014). See also ch 7.

[40] See Beaulieu and Leonelli (n 2).

[41] See European Commission, Communication to the European Parliament and the Council the European Economic and Social Committee and the Committee of the Regions, 'A European Strategy for Data' COM(2020) 66 final, https://eur-lex.europa.eu/legal-content/EN/TXT/?uri=celex%3A52020DC0066.

[42] A Thow et al, 'World Humanitarian Data and Trends' (OCHA, 2013).

[43] See L Taylor, 'The Ethics of Big Data as a Public Good: Which Public? Whose Good?' (2016) 374 *Philosophical Transactions of the Royal Society A: Mathematical, Physical and Engineering Sciences* 20160126, doi.org/10.1098/rsta.2016.0126.

[44] M Romanoff and S O'Shea, 'Big Data for Development and Humanitarian Action: Towards Responsible Governance' (Relief Web, 2015) 5, https://reliefweb.int/report/world/big-data-development-and-humanitarian-action-towards-responsible-governance-global.

More specific criticism of Global Pulse has concerned the fragmentation of the regulatory landscape, potential harms of data collection and use, assessment of justified purpose for data projects, and effectiveness of and the need for consent, as well as issues related to data security, accountability, and project transparency.

A decade has passed since these observations, and it is quite remarkable that despite many positive developments, such as the launch of data sharing initiatives (eg, the United Nations Big Data Platform, CGIAR platform for Big Data in Agriculture, and Mastercard's SpendingPulse), insight-generating platforms and governance tools, the adoption of the Resolution on Data Protection and International Organisations and many guidance documents, such as the ICRC Handbook on Humanitarian Data, many issues persist.[45] First of all, the term 'data' is generally used without a clear or consistent definition or specification of the type of data. Further, the challenges of data sharing are made more complex by intricate regulations, varying expectations from donors (both within and between donor governments at different levels), and diverse experiences with data sharing. Additionally, limited data literacy and differing perceptions of the risks involved in managing operational data lead to inconsistent practices in data sharing.

In other words, the tension between the two different objectives – mainstream data protection standards and sharing data for operational and other purposes – remains. The COVID-19 pandemic further heightened the need for providing easier ways to share data among private organisations and institutions, such as research labs and healthcare providers. Research studies in the aftermath of the global health crisis demonstrated that phone data can help to predict the spread of disease and even improve targeting of humanitarian aid.[46]

Against this background, the adoption of the Global Privacy Assembly Resolution on Data Sharing for Public Good followed in 2021.[47] The resolution established a working group that sought to

> focus on identifying practical and pragmatic approaches on how personal data can be shared and used to enable innovation and growth while protecting individual rights and promoting public trust and provide principles and best practices on key components of data sharing for public good.[48]

[45] See Fast (n 31).

[46] See A Aiken, 'Zooming in on Privacy Concerns: Video App Zoom Is Surging in Popularity. In Our Rush to Stay Connected, We Need to Make Security Checks and Not Reveal More than We Think' (2020) 49 *Index on Censorship* 24.

[47] The Global Privacy Assembly, formerly known as the International Conference of Data Protection and Privacy Commissioners, was established in 1979. It provides a platform for exchanges and collaborations for the world's data protection and privacy authorities.

[48] Global Privacy Assembly, 'Resolution on Data Sharing for Public Good' (2021) 3, https://globalprivacyassembly.org/document-archive/adopted-resolutions.

However, this resolution received little support from humanitarian actors actively involved in a parallel initiative, the Aid WG, at the Global Privacy Assembly. Furthermore, it seems that the term 'public good', which has been criticised, has recently been replaced by others. For instance, Global Pulse explained that it has rebranded the multi-partner Global Data Access Initiative (GDAI), which sought to harness big data for public good, as Data Insights for Social and Humanitarian Action (DISHA), as this better aligns with data usage goals on the ground. Provided that high-quality relevant data can be accessed and used effectively and sustainably, DISHA should help to unlock the potential of AI and big data to advance development and humanitarian efforts.[49]

In the following section, we examine the fundamental challenges associated with the term 'public good' from a data protection standpoint.

2.4.1. 'Public Good' as an Umbrella Term

One of the key challenges posed by the term 'public good' is that for many it is associated with the legal ground for processing personal data 'for the performance of a task carried out in the public interest or in the exercise of official authority vested in the controller'. However, it appears that the way it is used in policy debates is different. It is used as an end goal for which data, including personal data, are processed in the humanitarian context. From the data protection perspective, such a purpose is problematic as it would oppose one of the key data protection principles, such as the purpose limitation principle.

On the conceptual level, 'The principle of purpose limitation is designed to establish the boundaries within which personal data collected for a given purpose may be processed and may be put to further use'.[50] It is a safeguard that seeks to protect individuals whose data are processed by limiting how data controllers are able to use their data while also offering some degree of flexibility for data controllers. The principle of purpose limitation reinforces the fairness of the processing by preventing the use of individuals' personal data in ways (or for additional purposes) that they may consider unexpected, inappropriate, or objectionable.

The first building block of this concept is that personal data must be collected for 'specified, explicit and legitimate purposes' (purpose specification) and the second building block is for it not to be 'further processed in a manner that is incompatible with those purposes" (compatible use)'.[51] The EU data protection

[49] See United Nations, 'UN Global Pulse 2023 Annual Report: Inspiring Hope through Innovation' (2024) 14, www.unglobalpulse.org/inspiring-hope-through-innovation-un-global-pulse-2023-annual-report.

[50] Article 29 Data Protection Working Party, 'Opinion 03/2013 on Purpose Limitation' (WP 203) (2013) 38, https://ec.europa.eu/justice/article-29/documentation/opinion-recommendation/files/2013/wp203_en.pdf.

[51] Article 5(1)(b) of the GDPR.

regulators have argued that 'specification of the purpose [for which personal data are processed] is a prerequisite for applying other data quality requirements, including the adequacy, relevance, proportionality and accuracy of the data collected and the requirements regarding the period of data retention'.[52] In other words, organisations handling personal data are likely to fall short on the data governance side if they have not determined the specific purpose for which the processing operations are initiated. This is because they are more likely to fail to implement the core requirements stemming from the data protection frameworks.

Contrary to the purpose specification principle, the term 'public good' is a high-level concept which is invoked in policy and legal contexts. While an additional explanation sometimes follows its use, its meaning is often implied. For instance, the European Data Protection Supervisor suggested that 'As AI technologies advance rapidly, European Union Institutions must consider carefully when and how to use generative AI responsibly and beneficially for public good'.[53] Recital 75 of the Data Act refers to 'a significant public good' and explains that it could include responding to public emergencies.[54]

It can be suggested that there are several similarities between the terms of public interest and public good. First of all, the two terms are invoked in numerous contexts as justifications for action, as is the case with the legal framework enabling Open Data initiatives. Second, both concepts focus on the well-being and benefit of the general public, society at large or groups to whom measures are addressed, rather than prioritising individual or private interests.

Against this background, it should be added that the term 'public good' should be invoked with caution within the scope of data sharing agreements between international organisations providing aid as otherwise this could permit humanitarian exceptionalism: organisations providing aid would not be bound by the purpose specification principle.

The deviation from this principle could easily result in situations where data sharing and further processing would go beyond what people's expectations at the time of data collection. This could have a negative impact on vulnerable and affected individuals as information about them would be disclosed, and as this disclosure may 'deepen socio-economic divides through the categorisation and segmentation of individuals into larger groups, often reflecting existing inequalities'.[55]

[52] ibid.

[53] European Data Protection Supervisor/EDPS, 'Generative AI and the EUDPR. First EDPS Orientations for ensuring data protection compliance when using Generative AI systems' (2024) 6, www.edps.europa.eu/system/files/2024-05/24-05-29_genai_orientations_en_0.pdf.

[54] More specifically the recital says: 'When the safeguarding of a significant public good is at stake, such as responding to public emergencies, the public sector body, the Commission, the European Central Bank or the Union body concerned should not be expected to compensate enterprises for the data obtained. Public emergencies are rare events and not all such emergencies require the use of data held by enterprises.'

[55] United Nations (n 49).

The increasing reliance on datafication and data solutionism in the humanitarian sector, while aligning with broader societal trends, poses significant ethical challenges. Datafication – the practice of turning human experiences into quantifiable data – and data solutionism – the belief that complex social issues can be solved through technology – risk oversimplifying the needs of vulnerable populations. While these approaches can enhance operational efficiency, fairness requires that data collection and data sharing prioritise the rights and dignity of individuals. This is particularly relevant in humanitarian contexts where individuals may not have full control over their personal data or may not be able to give fully informed consent.

Moreover, we argue that the concept of the 'public good' as a justification for data sharing must be carefully scrutinised through the lens of fairness. While sharing data for the public good can improve transparency and decision-making, it can also conflict with the principle of purpose limitation and lead to the overuse or misuse of personal data. Fairness demands that data be used only for the purposes for which it was originally collected, respecting individuals' rights and vulnerabilities.

In a humanitarian context, where power imbalances are significant, fairness plays a crucial role in preventing the exploitation of vulnerable individuals. This principle ensures that data processing serves the best interests of the affected individuals,[56] rather than merely fulfilling organisational or public objectives, thereby respecting human dignity and rights throughout the data processing lifecycle and stages in humanitarian action settings.

2.4.2. From Public Good to Realising Fairness in Practice

The concept of the 'public good' in data protection law raises critical questions about whose interests are truly being served. While data protection is meant to safeguard the rights and dignity of individuals, particularly vulnerable groups, the notion of the public good often reflects the perspectives of legal scholars and decision-makers, rather than the expectations of data subjects themselves. Data protection law discourse concerning vulnerable groups focuses particularly on the added value of the core data protection principles, including fairness when addressing the need to mitigate power imbalances between controllers and data subjects.[57] This raises value-sensitive questions: whose public good are we talking about, and who determines what constitutes the public good? This is where the principle of fairness becomes crucial.

[56] See A Atabey and R Scarff, 'The Fairness Principle: A Tool to Protect Children's Rights in Their Interaction with Emotional AI in Educational Settings' (2023) 4 *Global Privacy Law Review* 5.

[57] See G Malgieri, 'The Concept of Fairness in the GDPR: A Linguistic and Contextual Interpretation' in Proceedings of the 2020 Conference on Fairness, A ccountability, and Transparency (Barcelona, ACM, 2020), 154–66, doi.org/10.1145/3351095.3372868.

The concept of fairness in data protection law is broad and context-dependent.[58] It involves balancing fundamental rights and freedoms while addressing power imbalances. Fairness therefore assumes several connotations: procedural fairness; fair balancing; preventing adverse effects (eg discrimination); and good faith (bona fide).[59] These four nuances have the common aim of addressing the power imbalances experienced by data subjects and vulnerable groups,[60] and of reinforcing the core purpose of data protection law, namely to protect human dignity and ensure individuals have control over the processing of their data. Discussions around the public good must return to these core principles, placing the affected individuals (ie, data subjects) at the centre of any discourse on fairness and the public interest.

From this perspective, the fairness principle is crucial for adopting a human-centred approach to the application of data protection frameworks. It puts the expectations and agency of data subjects at the heart of data practices, respecting the choices of vulnerable individuals and their values. It also recognises that different groups of people may hold different values (for example, migrants in culturally diverse regions like the Mediterranean). Fairness in data protection is therefore closely linked to the human dignity and should be treated as more than just a checklist for legal compliance; it should place individuals at the heart of data processing activities, guaranteeing that data is processed ethically by balancing fundamental rights and freedoms to prevent harm, discrimination, or exploitation.

As fairness is inherently contextual, consideration must be given to the specific circumstances under which data is collected and processed. In humanitarian

[58] In the US, the concept of fairness in data privacy can be traced back to the Fair Information Practice Principles (see G González-Fuster, *The Emergence of Personal Data Protection as a Fundamental Right of the EU* (Cham, Springer, 2014) 33–34). Providing information and addressing informational power imbalances between those whose data is processed and those processing it is also significant in the EU. For instance, the European Parliamentary Research Service, 'The Impact of the GDPR on AI' (2020) www.europarl.europa.eu/thinktank/en/document/EPRS_STU(2020)641530 refers to 'informational fairness', a concept closely linked to transparency (see C de Terwangne, 'Article 5 – Principles Relating to Processing of Personal Data' in C Kuner, L Andrew Bygrave, C Docksey, and L Drechsler (eds), *The EU General Data Protection Regulation (GDPR): A Commentary* (Oxford, Oxford University Press, 2020)). See also Recital 60 of the GDPR. It is worth noting that informational fairness is also linked to accountability, which is particularly challenging in opaque decision-making processes, especially in the context of humanitarian action where multiple parties process the same data. Furthermore, with the AI applications being incredibly offered in this context, the uncertainty of their outcomes, and the multiplicity of their purposes add to this challenge. This provides a new dimension to the principle relating to the explicability of automated decisions (see also European Parliamentary Research Service, 'Artificial Intelligence at EU Borders – Overview of Applications and Key Issues' (2021)).

[59] See D Clifford and J Ausloos, 'Data Protection and the Role of Fairness' (2018) 37 *Yearbook of European Law* 130, doi.org/10.1093/yel/yey004.

[60] Fairness is highly relevant in the context of power imbalances, particularly in migration and refugee response settings. For example, individuals on the move often experience significant power imbalances when dealing with authorities, governments, NGOs, or corporations that collect their data. In these contexts, fairness plays a crucial role in mitigating these imbalances, ensuring that data processing serves the interests of the data subjects rather than those of the data controllers.

settings, individuals' data is often collected in challenging situations, such as during humanitarian aid efforts. Those involved are in vulnerable positions, and their expectations about how their data will be used are closely tied to the services they require. For example, migrants may expect their data to be used solely for essential services such as medical care, shelter, or food, and not for purposes beyond these immediate needs, such as for artificial intelligence (AI) training or for building digital capital for organisations.

When data are used to train AI algorithms without clear and informed consent regarding this use – which differs from the original purpose of data collection – the fairness principle must be considered alongside the purpose limitation principle. Fairness requires that data subjects are not exploited through the misuse of their personal information. This is an even more crucial issue in the context of advanced technologies, such as the integration of AI into humanitarian aid settings, which makes the repurposing of data more complicated, in ways that migrants neither expect nor benefit from.

Lawfulness alone is not sufficient to guarantee fairness, particularly in humanitarian contexts where people often have little choice or control over how their data is collected or processed. Fairness therefore requires a dynamic consideration and ongoing assessment of whether data processing practices are aligned with the evolving needs and expectations of individuals, ensuring that their data is not used for unforeseen or uncommunicated purposes.[61] The question of whether the data subjects who provide information to international organisations foresee and expect their data to be shared with donors, as well as with individual consultants hired for a certain period to conduct evaluations of interventions by UN agencies, remains a critical one.

It is also important to consider whether data subjects can have a say in how their data is processed in order to receive benefits from these organisations in humanitarian settings, and whether they can choose not to have their data shared with other stakeholders, such as donors or evaluation departments, who use that data for research purposes in order to inform future UN agency programmes and report to donors on how the funding was used.

Fairness also plays a key role in addressing discriminatory practices that may arise from the use of personal data,[62] particularly in migration contexts where profiling is often used by immigration authorities to approve or reject visa applications. These digital systems can sometimes result in biased outcomes that unfairly disadvantage certain groups of migrants. Ensuring fairness in these contexts is essential to preventing unjust or discriminatory practices that put

[61] For example, data shared with UN agencies for the purpose of obtaining support or benefits from humanitarian interventions or programme initiatives involving women's rights NGOs may later be shared with evaluation departments of these respective UN agencies, which employ individual consultants to analyse the data and evaluate the programmes.

[62] See P Hacker, 'A Legal Framework for AI Training Data – from First Principles to the Artificial Intelligence Act' (2021) 13 *Law, Innovation and Technology* 1257.

migrants in vulnerable and unfair positions. The fairness principle can provide a safeguard for vulnerable groups when there are no available rules to protect vulnerable groups.[63]

In data protection law, fairness is an overarching principle[64] that includes recognising individuals' reasonable expectations, taking into account the possible adverse consequences of data processing and the potential effects of existing power imbalances between data subjects and data controllers.[65] Addressing power imbalances is particularly important in the context of migration. For example, immigration authorities may use digital profiles to approve or reject visa applications, and this process can involve discriminatory practices.

In the IOM (2010) Data Protection Guidance, the concept of fairness is reflected in the principle of lawful and fair collection, which states that 'personal data must be obtained by lawful and fair means with the knowledge or consent of the data subject'. In this respect, the IOM Guidance also considers gender sensitivity as a fairness issue.[66]

It is also important to note that fairness can provide an external constraint on transparency by making it clear that transparency does not simply consist in writing down all information and treating data protection rules as a checklist. Instead, it requires considering the effect of processing activities on power imbalances. As such, different needs and layers of vulnerability and barriers, such as language and digital literacy, should be considered when providing information to individuals on the move, as they are likely to find it complex and inaccessible.

It has been noted[67] that people's vulnerability should also be considered when assessing the validity of consent in the context of humanitarian action. This assessment requires an understanding of the social, cultural and religious norms of the

[63] In the context of migration, this principle is argued to be jeopardised because the EU interoperability system could make data from the existing data systems accessible to a broader number of authorities, other than those bodies collecting and using the data in the first place. See C Blasi Casagran, 'Fundamental Rights Implications of Interconnecting Migration and Policing Databases in the EU' (2021) 21 *Human Rights Law Review* 433.

[64] The fairness principle is set out in Art 5(1)(a) of the GDPR as one of the bedrock principles of the EU data protection, alongside lawfulness and transparency. However, fairness is a highly relevant and common concept used in the national data protection laws of many non-EU countries (eg Turkey and Morocco), and the Council of Europe's Convention 108+ also places this principle at the heart of its framework. See also CJ Hoofnagle, B van der Sloot and FZ Borgesius, 'The European Union General Data Protection Regulation: What It Is and What It Means' (2019) 28 *Information & Communications Technology Law* 65,doi.org/10.1080/13600834.2019.1573501.

[65] The added value of the fairness principle lies in truly putting the focus on the individuals and groups of individuals themselves in an effort to cater for their needs and expectations. Notably, these expectations can differ depending on different vulnerability layers or even factors such as culture. See also G Malgieri and J Niklas, 'Vulnerable Data Subjects' (2020) 37 *Computer Law and Security Review* 105415, doi.org/10.1016/j.clsr.2020.105415.

[66] It provides that fairness requires ensuring that 'collection methods are gender, culture and age sensitive'.

[67] See Kuner and Marelli (n 7).

group to which data subjects belong as well as ensuring that each data subject is treated as the owner of their personal data.[68]

Finally, fairness can offer an opportunity to shape the data processing environment by shifting away from an individual-centric approach.[69] This shift could be particularly relevant in the context of humanitarian action and when exploring whether and how the fairness principle can be used when addressing challenges faced by vulnerable groups collectively. Treating, for example, refugees as vulnerable data subjects, adopting a vulnerability-aware lens arguably aligns with the purposes of the fairness principle. Notably, we argue that a gender-sensitive lens among other vulnerability layers[70] should be brought when assessing and addressing any potential risks and adverse impacts that are needed to ensure fairness of data processing.

Building on the fairness principle, the UK Information Commissioner's Office's Age-Appropriate Design Code (AADC) is grounded in the UNCRC and reflects a rights-respecting, risk-based and proportionate approach.[71] It also adopts a needs-based and vulnerability-aware approach that recognises that children have different layers of vulnerability, with some being more vulnerable than others and therefore having additional needs.[72] Similarly, the Netherlands introduced the Dutch Code for Children's Rights to offer comprehensive child-rights guidelines for digital innovators.[73] The AADC explicitly refers to equality legislation

[68] As emphasised by the IOM, organisations should adopt an inclusive approach when applying data protection rules in practice, carefully considering relevant vulnerability factors such as illiteracy, disability, age, gender and sexual orientation. See IOM, 'IOM Data Protection Manual' (2010), https://publications.iom.int/system/files/pdf/iomdataprotection_web.pdf. These factors become even more significant in humanitarian contexts, where women and children are already vulnerable, as addressed by different stakeholders previously. See, eg, P Molnar, 'Territorial and Digital Borders and Migrant Vulnerability Under a Pandemic Crisis' in A Triandafyllidou (ed), *Migration and Pandemics: Spaces of Solidarity and Spaces of Exception* (Cham, Springer International Publishing, 2022) 45–64; A Farrés Jiménez, 'Embedding Gender in International Humanitarian Law: Is Artificial Intelligence Up to the Task?' (2021), www.justsecurity.org/77970/embedding-gender-in-international-humanitarian-law-is-artificial-intelligence-up-to-the-task; UN – IBC Gender and IBC LMPDR, 'Joint Advocacy Brief on the Impacts of COVID-19 on Refugee and Migrant Women and Girls and the Importance of Including Their Specific Needs and Rights in COVID-19 Recovery Plans' (2022), https://eca.unwomen.org/en/digital-library/publications/2022/03/joint-advocacy-brief-on-the-impacts-of-covid-19-on-refugee-and-migrant-women-and-girls-and-the-importance-of-including-their-specific-needs-and-rights-in-covid-19-recovery-plans.

[69] See also O Lynskey, 'Delivering Data Protection: The Next Chapter' (2020) 21 *German Law Journal* 80.

[70] See F Luna, 'Elucidating the Concept of Vulnerability: Layers Not Labels' (2009) 2 *International Journal of Feminist Approaches to Bioethics* 121, doi.org/10.3138/ijfab.2.1.121.

[71] See UNICEF, 'The Case for Better Governance of Children's Data: A Manifesto' (2021), www.unicef.org/globalinsight/reports/better-governance-childrens-data-manifesto.

[72] See ICO, 'Age Appropriate Design: A Code of Practice for Online Services' (2020), https://ico.org.uk/media/for-organisations/uk-gdpr-guidance-and-resources/childrens-information/childrens-code-guidance-and-resources/age-appropriate-design-a-code-of-practice-for-online-services-2-1.pdf.

[73] The Dutch Code sets out guiding principles for designers and developers to embed children's rights in their digital products and services, and explicitly recognises the vulnerabilities of children. See S van der Hof, K Pothong and S Livingstone, 'The Dutch Approach to Realise Children's Rights in a Digital World: Code Voor Kinderrechten' (2022) Digital Futures Commission-5Rights Foundation, https://digitalfuturescommission.org.uk/blog/the-dutch-approach-to-realise-childrens-rights-in-a-digital-world-code-voor-kinderrechten.

in this context, including the Equality Act 2010, which considers 'gender-related' protected characteristics.[74]

Here, we highlight the importance of a common approach towards empowering data subjects, irrespective of whether their additional layers of vulnerabilities are covered in relevant equality laws. Adopting a similar vulnerability-aware, human rights-based approach and making Data Protection Impact Assessments (DPIAs) a requirement in data protection frameworks could help to address the needs of migrants.[75] Even though references to DPIA can be found in other available recommendations and policy frameworks, DPIAs should be included in the laws of all countries in the Mediterranean region.[76]

Based on these different considerations and the multifaceted nature of the concept of fairness, we can conclude that fairness is far from a straightforward principle in practice. This is particularly relevant when discussing a unified approach in the Mediterranean region. For instance, migrants in the Mediterranean come from diverse cultural, social, and political backgrounds, rendering fairness in data processing an even more complex issue. What constitutes fair data processing for one group may not be applicable to another, since cultural values and expectations regarding privacy can vary significantly. Overall, fairness, therefore, must be adaptive and sensitive to these differing needs, ensuring that data processing practices are tailored to the specific values and expectations of the individuals and communities involved.

2.5. Conclusion

It is important to distinguish between lawfulness and transparency, and fairness,[77] as otherwise one risks oversimplifying the nuanced and contextual nature of fairness. In the face of growing humanitarian aid demands, strengthening the application of fairness within existing legal frameworks may be a more effective way to ensure that the data of affected individuals is handled ethically and in line with their expectations.

Although this is not an easy task, we argue that it is crucial to recognise that fairness is an obligation for data controllers in both EU and non-EU countries.

[74] The AADC is an excellent example of how the data protection authorities can take an intersectional approach and explicitly require organisations to consider international human rights laws and non-discrimination/equality laws. However, this can be challenging as different countries in the region might rely on different jurisdictions.

[75] This practice would also align with the principles of equality, fairness, non-discrimination, empowerment, agency, and autonomy of women and girls in all processes relating to the building, interpreting, or implementing data protection laws and policies within the Mediterranean region.

[76] See, Joint Statement by the Council and the Representatives of the Governments of the Member States meeting within the Council, the European Parliament and the European Commission, The European Consensus on Humanitarian Aid (OJ C 25/1, 30.1.2008).

[77] See n 59.

Therefore, a human-centred, human-rights-respecting,[78] culturally sensitive and intersectional approach is needed to operationalise fairness and ensure it works for all data subjects, not just for some groups of individuals. To achieve this, there is a need for multistakeholder and interdisciplinary approaches, especially with regard to potential tensions in relation to values and competing interests that may arise when data is processed in humanitarian settings.

A key component of fairness is ensuring that data processing aligns with the reasonable expectations of individuals, rather than just legal requirements (eg lawful bases for data processing). Therefore, achieving fairness in data protection is critical, ensuring that data processing is carried out in an ethical manner,[79] putting data subjects at the heart of data processing considerations, and respecting their rights and expectations. Although discussions about public interests have already arisen in relation to individuals' level of control and agency over their data processing, as well as the balance between processing data for the public good and protecting individuals' right to data protection, the fairness principle has remained under-explored in these discussions.

In the Mediterranean context, where individuals or groups of individuals might face various and intricate vulnerabilities, the fairness principle is crucial for protecting personal data and preventing its misuse or exploitation for purposes beyond data subjects' expectations and that lawfulness principle, as well as preventing legal basis being used as a mere checklist.

Against this background, this chapter has critically examined the complexities surrounding data processing in humanitarian contexts, particularly the need for a distinct legal basis for data sharing. Humanitarian organisations operate in exceptional circumstances, often requiring rapid, large-scale data processing to protect and assist individuals in situations marked by violence, disaster and vulnerability. However, the existing legal frameworks, such as the GDPR, while providing a robust structure for lawful processing, may not fully accommodate the specific operational and ethical challenges faced by these organisations. This chapter has argued that, rather than generalising the purpose of the processing, the underutilised principle of fairness should be foregrounded in discussions on data protection within humanitarian action.

The principle of fairness, as set out in data protection law, provides a crucial lens through which to assess whether data processing practices respect the rights and dignity of individuals, particularly those in vulnerable situations which follow

[78] See Council of Europe, 'Artificial Intelligence and Data Protection' (2019), https://edoc.coe.int/en/artificial-intelligence/8254-artificial-intelligence-and-data-protection.html; A Mantelero and MS Esposito, 'An Evidence-Based Methodology for Human Rights Impact Assessment (HRIA) in the Development of AI Data-Intensive Systems' (2021) 41 *Computer Law & Security Review* 105561, doi.org/10.1016/j.clsr.2021.105561; A Mantelero, *Beyond Data – Human Rights, Ethical and Social Impact Assessment in AI* (The Hague, Springer, 2022), https://link.springer.com/content/pdf/10.1007/978-94-6265-531-7.pdf.

[79] See CD Raab, 'Information Privacy, Impact Assessment, and the Place of Ethics' (2020) 37 *Computer Law & Security Review* 105404, doi.org/10.1016/j.clsr.2020.105404.

natural or man-made disasters. In this light, we argue that the concept of the 'public good' presents significant risks if not carefully aligned with fairness and purpose limitation principles.

While the public good may justify data sharing in the broader interest of society, this justification can easily lead to overreach, where individuals' personal data is used in ways that they did not anticipate or consent to, thereby undermining their autonomy and privacy. The chapter has highlighted the potential dangers of humanitarian exceptionalism, where the urgency of crises is used to justify excessive data sharing without adequate safeguards or accountability to individuals whose data are collected.

Rather than advocating for a new legal basis, this chapter supports strengthening the application of fairness within existing legal frameworks and proposes that the EU has a role to play in downstreaming this principle, among other data protection principles. Fairness, with its focus on balancing power dynamics and respecting the expectations of data subjects, offers a vital safeguard against the misuse of personal data in humanitarian contexts. In particular, this approach is crucial in the Mediterranean region, where diverse cultural, social, and political factors influence the vulnerabilities and expectations of individuals, especially migrants and displaced persons. A context-sensitive, human-centred approach to fairness is essential to ensure that the processing of personal data serves the best interests of these individuals, rather than merely fulfilling organisational or public objectives prioritising data controllers' own interests.

Ultimately, the principle of fairness is not merely a complement to lawfulness or transparency; it is a critical component of ethical and value-sensitive approaches in data protection and governance. It demands that humanitarian organisations place the needs and expectations of vulnerable individuals at the centre of their data management practices, ensuring that data is processed in ways that are both lawful and fair. As such, fairness must be rigorously applied to prevent the exploitation of personal data, particularly in situations where individuals have limited agency over how their information is used. In conclusion, this chapter calls for a recalibration of the humanitarian data governance framework, one that places fairness at its core to protect the dignity and rights of those most in need of assistance.

3

Contractual Solutions to Protect Human Rights in Critical Areas of International Cooperation

ALESSANDRO MANTELERO

3.1. Introduction

Cooperation between the northern and southern shores of the Mediterranean Sea has a long tradition and saw an important turning point with the Barcelona Process, which also includes attention to the protection of human rights.[1] On 28 November 1995, in Barcelona, the EU and 12 Mediterranean countries (Algeria, Cyprus, Egypt, Israel, Jordan, Lebanon, Malta, Morocco, the Palestinian Authorities, Syria, Tunisia and Turkey) signed the new Euro Mediterranean Partnership (EMP) as a framework for political, economic, cultural and social ties between the Mediterranean countries. The EMP has been complemented by other initiatives such as the European Neighbourhood Policy (ENP), adopted by the EU in 2004, and the creation of the Union for the Mediterranean (UfM) in 2008.

Against this background, the 'euphoria of the 1990s … was replaced in the next decade by scepticism over the ramifications of the stability-security nexus'.[2] The changed geopolitical scenario and the emergence of a more fragmented and conflictive space have also been combined with an EU-centric approach, with a view driven by the contingent interests of EU countries rather than a long-term view of the area and its development.[3]

[1] See also L Bartels, 'A Legal Analysis of Human Rights Clauses in the European Union's Euro-Mediterranean Association Agreements' (2004) 9 *Mediterranean Politics* 368, doi.org/10.1080/1362939042000259933; I Zamfir, *Human Rights in EU Trade Agreements* (Bruxelles, European Parliamentary Research Service, 2019), www.europarl.europa.eu/RegData/etudes/BRIE/2019/637975/EPRS_BRI(2019)637975_EN.pdf.

[2] C Kourtelis, 'A quarter-century of studying Euro-Mediterranean relations: A systematic literature review' (2024) 29 *Mediterranean Politics* 165, 166, doi.org/10.1080/13629395.2022.2129189.

[3] EuroMeSCo, 'Annual Conference 2023. From the Euro-Mediterranean Partnership to a Euro-Mediterranean Geostrategic Alliance' (2023) 17–18, www.euromesco.net/wp-content/uploads/2023/11/Report-AC-2023-1.pdf.

The same notion of the European Neighbourhood Policy (ENP), which includes the Southern Neighbourhood, has been criticised because of the lack of homogeneity of the EU's neighbourhood in general and, with regard to the Mediterranean region, because of the heterogeneity of the current scenarios. This has also led to a situation where international cooperation in this area has been characterised by a series of emergencies in the last decades, mainly from the perspective of the EU countries and their economic and geopolitical interests. At the same time, the countries of North Africa and the Middle East have experienced increasing fragmentation and the establishment of authoritarian regimes.

Cooperation between the EU and third countries in this area has continued, but in many cases EU-funded projects operate in scenarios where the protection of human rights is limited. This has raised concerns about the concrete and effective protection of these rights in the contexts where projects are developed and by the local partners involved in field work.

These issues are the focus of this chapter in relation to the increasing role of digital technologies in cooperation projects, both in terms of digital solutions for the development of the individual project (eg, digital ID to support the distribution of aid, participatory platforms for smart cities projects, smart education solutions, etc) and tools for accountability (data collection to prove the effectiveness of the results achieved, data analysis to provide reports on the results of the initiatives taken, etc).

Irrespective of the impact of geopolitical tensions on Euro-Mediterranean cooperation, which is not analysed here, nor their causes, these tensions undermine the possibility of achieving a common level of state-based human rights protection in this region. While the EU's recent extensive regulation of the digital ecosystem[4] and the presence of established human rights practices, reinforced by judicial bodies and independent authorities, actively support a human rights-oriented approach to the digital society, other parts of the Mediterranean region present more challenging scenarios.

In the absence of a specific common legal framework and effective enforcement to protect human rights, international cooperation based on the development of local projects in non-EU Mediterranean countries should therefore build on internal mechanisms to ensure human rights compliance. These mechanisms may be project-specific (eg contractual clauses, ad hoc technical solutions and policies) or general, covering a group of activities or projects carried out by a single funding entity (eg general policies, guidelines, standard contractual clauses, technical standards).

Irrespective of the solutions adopted, whether project-specific or not, the multiplicity of actors involved (funding agencies, funded entities, local partners and

[4] The adoption of the General Data Protection Regulation (GDPR) in 2016 was followed by a new wave of regulatory instruments focused on the digital environment, such as the Artificial Intelligence Act, the Digital Services Act, the Digital Markets Act, the Data Governance Act and the Data Act.

third parties) requires some form of contractual agreement that makes compliance with guidelines, policies, etc mandatory for all parties involved, in order to align their actions with existing approaches to the protection of human rights. A similar approach to the international context has already been adopted in other cases, such as the standard contractual clauses and binding corporate rules used for cross-border data transfers[5] and the contractual principles adopted for the implementation of human rights in business.[6]

Integrating human rights into the contractual framework that links all the different actors in the cooperation project chain places human rights at the heart of the design of cooperation projects and of the development strategies from the outset. This helps to establish clear roles and responsibilities for the promotion and protection of human rights, leading to appropriate risk management strategies and allocation of responsibilities between the parties involved.

However, as existing practice shows, the creation of contractual obligations that provide a framework for the protection of fundamental rights is not in itself sufficient to ensure full compliance with these obligations. Specific instruments for monitoring compliance, such as audits, periodic inspections or at least self-assessment procedures and accountability obligations, need to be put in place. Three main components are therefore crucial in establishing a system of rights protection based on private agreements rather than on state law: (i) a contractual framework; (ii) clearly defined expected levels of protection; and (iii) a system for monitoring compliance.

Against this background, this chapter aims to fill a gap in the human rights literature on contractual instruments for promoting and protecting human rights in critical contexts, by proposing a decentralised and non-state-based approach. The main objective is to identify a set of tools for human rights protection that are applicable and adaptable to different contexts, and to outline the different strengths and weaknesses of these instruments to be considered in order to design the most appropriate response to the absence of effective human rights protection.

3.2. A Contract-based Framework for the Effective Protection of Human Rights

Within the general context described in the introduction, it is necessary to examine the differing characteristics of the possible instruments available to establish

[5] For a description of the various possible solutions, see https://ec.europa.eu/info/law/law-topic/data-protection/international-dimension-data-protection_en.

[6] See United Nations, 'Guiding Principles on Business and Human Rights' (2011), www.ohchr.org/sites/default/files/Documents/Publications/GuidingPrinciplesBusinessHR_EN.pdf.

an appropriate framework for the protection of human rights in the cooperation projects. In addition, the design of this framework, based on contractual agreements, should take into account the needs of each individual project and the context in which the related activities are carried out.

Three main tools can be used to establish this framework, either at a general or project-specific level: (i) contractual clauses; (ii) policies; and (iii) technical tools. Contractual clauses can set out key obligations to protect human rights, while policies can provide a more detailed framework in terms of expected safeguards, their implementation and compliance monitoring. Finally, technical tools can support the adoption of the best technologies to ensure an adequate level of protection of human rights and freedoms and to prevent their infringement in technology-driven contexts.

In order to be effective and applied, both policies and technical tools need to be specifically referred to in the contractual agreements between funding agencies, the funded entity (hereinafter also referred to as 'the contractor') and its local partners.

All three strategies can be developed at a general level, which is the same for all cooperation projects managed by the same funding agency, or they can be adapted to the specific needs of individual projects. The different solutions and their implementation have both strengths and weaknesses, and a combination of different tools is also possible, depending on the specific case.

Using contractual clauses as standard clauses applicable to all cooperation projects managed by the same funding agency facilitates the implementation of human rights protection (eg by referring to specific international instruments), and compliance and monitoring obligations can be set in a uniform way, without distinction for all contexts. This reduces the cost of implementation, as standard clauses can be reused in all contexts, and can increase the transparency of the adopted instrument, as the set of clauses used can be made publicly available, including explanatory notes to facilitate their interpretation and use.

However, standard contractual clauses also have some limitations that need to be taken into account when adopting and using them. First, because of their general application, they cannot address the specific needs of a given project or take into account the development context. In addition, a general standard may undermine more ambitious human rights goals that are achievable in some specific projects or contexts. Finally, such clauses usually cannot set out detailed requirements on human rights and they refer to other instruments, both binding and non-binding, such as international conventions, policies and guidelines.

With regard to the use of policies to protect human rights, general policies applicable to all cooperation projects managed by the same funding agencies offer the same advantages as standard contractual clauses in terms of cost reduction and transparency, but have a wider scope because they can provide a detailed description of the expected objectives in terms of human rights protection. Moreover, because of their soft law nature, general policies can be easily revised in the light of the technological developments and changes in the contexts in which cooperation projects are implemented, without the need to amend the contractual agreements that refer to them.

On the other hand, general policies suffer from the lack of a project-specific approach and therefore need to be adapted to the context in their implementation, with the risk of partial and erroneous application. Moreover, as they are drawn up by the funding agencies or the contractors (ie the funded entities), they may reflect the views of these entities on the implementation of human rights, neglecting important contextual and local concerns. In this respect, as they are not negotiated with local partners, they may also be seen as a top-down exercise and, as such, less likely to be fully embraced by the partners than co-designed contextual policies.

Finally, it is possible to implement general technical standards focusing on the technologies used in the cooperation projects and their impact on human rights, making it possible to define a minimum level of protection where technological elements play a key role (eg media and communications, electronic cash and payments, identity management systems, etc). The definition of these standards can benefit from best practices already adopted worldwide and, by establishing common rules, facilitate interoperability between different projects and the different local implementations of each project.

However, the adoption of general technical standards may face difficulties in their updating process or in their contextual implementation, due to the limited availability of certain technologies or the skill level of the users, which may hinder the effectiveness of these standards. As with general policies, technical standards imposed by funders and contractors may not have local legitimacy and may conflict with existing practices or local standards.

The same balancing test of the strengths and weaknesses of the three types of contractual-based solutions considered here can be done at the project level. Again, the three options can be combined into a more articulated solution to protect human rights.

Project-specific contractual clauses, which are designed for a single project and detailed in its legal agreement, can provide a better protection of human rights as they are tailored to the needs of the project and its development context. They can also take advantage of available local resources and capacities for human rights protection (eg existing binding provisions, human rights bodies, local professional skills) and can pay greater attention to human rights compliance requirements and potentially affected rights and freedoms in relation to different project elements and development stages. Finally, this contextual dimension facilitates forms of co-design with local partners, taking into account their specific needs and views in drafting the agreement.

On the other hand, this focus on an individual project can create complexity for funding agencies and contractors in terms of the variety of clauses used and the need to personalise each contract, whereas uniform standard clauses for all projects can lead to more efficient results and reduce the effort required. Moreover this variety may lead to differing approaches to human rights requirements and monitoring in similar projects, due to the range of parties involved in drafting the clauses and the potentially different outcomes of negotiations. Finally, the contract-specific nature of these clauses may limit their disclosure and the sharing of the solutions adopted.

Specific policies focused on a particular cooperation project reduce the risk of partial or incorrect applications of general policies, as they are focused on the specific case and context of use, and are the result of a co-design process. Moreover, their project-specific nature and co-design facilitate the inclusion of contextual human rights practices, better address relevant local issues and ease compliance for local partners. On the other hand, as with contractual clauses, the personalisation of policies has a negative impact in terms of increased complexity and a potential reduction in transparency.

Finally, it is also possible to tailor the technical solutions available to enhance human rights protection in relation to the specific project, based on individual agreement. This provides a better outcome than a standardised approach, as it takes into account relevant contextual factors, such as available technologies and user skills, which also increases local acceptance and integration with existing practices or local standards. In addition, this approach makes it easier to update technical solutions in line with technological and societal changes, as these solutions are centred on the specific project. However, this customisation increases the costs in case of managing different projects and reduces technical interoperability.

This overview of the role that different contract-based instruments can play in establishing a human rights framework – based on specific clauses, policies or technical standards – demonstrates the possibility of creating an enabling environment in terms of rights protection in contexts where state-based protection may be ineffective or incomplete. The different options outlined can be combined not only at each level (general or project-specific), but also in a cross-cutting manner, for example by adopting general policies that are further implemented through project-specific contractual clauses.

3.3. Contract-Based Solutions and their Implementation by Subcontractors

Looking at the implementation of the instruments discussed in the previous section, and taking into account the existing experience of contractual agreements already in place, the whole 'cooperation chain' has to be considered. More specifically, cooperation projects involve not only the funding agencies and the funded organisations (contractors), but usually also subcontractors, ie local organisations active in the implementation of the contractor's strategies and in the development of the projects in the local context.

Although cooperation projects can be implemented in a variety of scenarios, from a legal point of view they can be classified according to two key criteria: the international dimension of the relations between the parties involved; and the nature of these parties.

In funded projects within the context of Euro-Mediterranean cooperation, we generally find a layered organisational model comprising three types of actors: (i) an EU funding agency; (ii) a contractor (funded organisation) implementing the project and often involving (iii) one or more subcontractors in the project development (often local entities). This multilayered structure relies on a set of obligations defined in a contract between the funding agency and the contractor, and in subcontracts between the latter and local partners. This makes it possible to rely on contractual clauses to ensure human rights compliance in project development, with different levels of granularity and forms of duty allocation decided by the parties.[7]

In terms of the territorial reach, which has implications for applicable laws, such relationships – especially in the case of subcontractors – have an international dimension that should be carefully considered in relation to legal compliance and human rights protection.

These elements need to be contextualised within two main types of relationship: partnerships with local governments; and partnerships with local private entities, such as NGOs. The main difference between these two scenarios relates to the public power that government bodies can exercise, which can lead to a power imbalance and demands relating to project management and development, including data processing. This raises concerns when there is a conflict between local government attitudes and the principles and values enshrined in the EU's fundamental rights instruments.

In such cases, as has been shown in the context of data protection,[8] certain technical measures can be helpful, especially for the information and communications technology (ICT)-based part of the projects (eg, data encryption, end-to-end encrypted messenger apps, use of so-called burner phones, data compartmentalisation,[9] remote data storage on protected servers accessed via secure virtual private network connections), as well as organisational measures in

[7] For example, funding agencies may require funded organisations to adopt project-specific human rights policies, either defined by the funded bodies or co-designed with the local entities. On the other hand, a funding agency can set some general policies and ask funded organisations to adopt them as an obligation under the funding agreement and to require subcontractors' compliance with these policies. Different combinations of the solutions discussed in the previous section are thus possible for involved parties according to their interest and based on a balancing exercise that considers the strengths and weakness outlined above.

[8] European Data Protection Board, 'Recommendations 01/2020 on Measures That Supplement Transfer Tools to Ensure Compliance with the EU Level of Protection of Personal Data' (2020), https://edpb.europa.eu/our-work-tools/our-documents/recommendations/recommendations-012020-measures-supplement-transfer_en.

[9] This is the practice of storing data collected from fieldwork concerning individuals separately from identifying information.

the documentation of the project findings (eg, placing sensitive/confidential data in separate annexes to limit their sharing and circulation).

However, these solutions may only have a limited effect in mitigating potential risks. It is therefore crucial to conduct a preliminary assessment of the risks inherent in this type of partnership, with a focus on the local context. In carrying out this assessment, it is also possible to draw on the expertise of local partners and to establish a relationship with local human rights bodies, human rights defenders and experts.

While a contract-based approach to human rights can be more easily adopted in the relationship between EU funding agencies and contractors, more critical issues arise in the implementation of contractual clauses protecting human rights in agreements between contractors and subcontractors. These clauses usually refer to general criteria, such as reliable, honest and careful data processing in the case of data protection, or to general legal requirements. There is therefore a lack of granularity at this level of contractual agreement, which raises concerns about both the proper formulation of human rights protection obligations and the accountability of subcontractors in this regard.

With regard to data protection, which plays a crucial role in the use of digital technologies in cooperation projects, contractors are often based in the EU and therefore need to comply with the GDPR when developing projects in non-EU countries.[10] Local subcontractors process data by cooperating with contractors, primarily acting as data processors or joint controllers. They must therefore follow GDPR-compliant instructions from the controller, or fulfil obligations under the joint controllership agreement.

Different considerations apply to international organisations, or national/local organisations that are not based in the EU and operate outside the EU. The former may have their own independent data protection rules,[11] while the latter – although committed to comply with the GDPR as data processors – are also subject to local law. In both cases, therefore, specific contractual obligations should be set out in the EU cooperation agreement to ensure that subcontractors operate within the framework of the EU regulation.

As regards human rights other than data protection, it should be stressed that the Charter of Fundamental Rights and national provisions are binding on beneficiaries of EU funds (contractors) based in EU countries. They must therefore act in accordance with these principles and reflect them in their agreements with local partners, while taking into account the specificities of the local legal framework. In this respect, the contractual solutions discussed above can also contribute to the effective implementation at subcontractor level of the rights and freedoms enshrined in EU and national law, including data protection.

[10] GDPR, Art 3.1 ('This Regulation applies to the processing of personal data in the context of the activities of an establishment of a controller or a processor in the Union, regardless of whether the processing takes place in the Union or not').

[11] See eg, ICRC, 'ICRC Rules on Personal Data Protection' (2019), https://shop.icrc.org/icrc-rules-on-personal-data-protection-pdf-en.html.

As in the case of data protection, contractual clauses can be used to commit local partners to an approach aimed at protecting fundamental rights, including audit procedures and the provision of appropriate assessment tools and specific policies where required by the context. However, the use of these clauses may be limited by binding local provisions (eg, legitimisation of disproportionate inspection powers by government agencies, mandatory disclosure of data, etc). In such cases, the adoption of effective technical risk prevention measures may be included as a specific obligation in contracts.[12]

Finally, in terms of policy strategy, although contract-based instruments play an important role in the examined contexts, contract clauses, policies and standards often create unidirectional obligations regarding human rights in the relationship between the contractor and the subcontractors (local partners) involved in the project.

Even where the contractor remains fully responsible for the fulfilment of the partners' obligations, the mere establishment of such obligations may not be sufficient to ensure the full commitment of the organisation to a human rights-oriented strategy. Human rights may be seen primarily as a matter of legal compliance with contractual agreements, rather than as a common framework underpinning the combined strategies of all actors involved in the project.

It is therefore important to go beyond this command-and-control logic (embedded in various solutions such as checklists, inspections, audits) and to adopt a different approach based on the active participation of both the contractor and its local subcontractors in the human rights due diligence process. Contractors are thus required to assist their project partners in meeting human rights standards, not only through training and monitoring, but also through co-designing the most appropriate solutions. To this end, both contractors and subcontractors can be held accountable for meeting human rights standards, and active collaboration in developing context-specific solutions can be encouraged, thereby reducing the competence/awareness gap that may exist among local partners.

3.4. Legal Zoning and Human Rights-Oriented Design

While human rights instruments provide a universal framework to safeguard individual and collective rights and freedoms, it is worth noting the underlying

[12] For a similar approach in the context of cross-border personal data transfers, see EDPB, 'Recommendations 01/2020 on measures that supplement transfers tools to ensure compliance with the EU level of protection of personal data' (2020), https://edpb.europa.eu/system/files/2021-06/edpb_recommendations_202001vo.2.0_supplementarymeasurestransferstools_en.pdf, and European Commission, Annex II of Commission Implementing Decision (EU) 2021/914 of 4 June 2021 on standard contractual clauses for the transfer of personal data to third countries pursuant to Regulation (EU) 2016/679 of the European Parliament and of the Council [2021] OJ L 199/31. See also J Bjørn Aslak, E Kozyri, D Johansen and JP Rui, 'The third country problem under the GDPR: enhancing protection of data transfers with technology' (2023) 13 *International Data Privacy Law* 225,doi.org/10.1093/idpl/ipad013.

tensions that characterise this universal approach.[13] This should be taken into account in the contractual-based protection of these rights and in the way general and project-specific tools are implemented and combined.

From a policy and regulatory point of view, while human rights provide a broadly applicable common framework, the nuances of its implementation and the limited theoretical and practical elaboration of the most innovative applications of digital technology[14] suggest a differentiated approach. This means that when a cooperation project is developed in different contexts, it may require a legal zoning process.

This process considers the various human rights scenarios that the project has to deal with, including relations with local governments and human rights protection bodies. A single project may therefore have context-specific developments in different areas with regard to the protection of human rights, thus creating a zoning effect, with similarities and differences to be considered and coordinated by the project manager.

This zoning effect on the whole project plan needs to be reflected in specific contractual agreements on human rights protection obligations. These should refer to each zone and emphasise the role of coordination tools such as policies, standards, data management plans, and assessment tools.

In this context, local partners can play an active role in project development, both in understanding the local situation and facilitating dialogue with relevant stakeholders to improve the level of protection. Moreover, this contextual approach can facilitate the adoption of different solutions, taking into account their feasibility and technical implementation.

The focus on the specific context in which the cooperation activities are implemented is relevant not only in terms of the zoning effect, but also in relation to the existence of potential contextual limiting factors in project design and development. In this respect, the lack of an adequate level of human rights protection and the presence of state actors who violate human rights are the main limiting factors. However, even in a more favourable environment, competing interests (eg, technical efficiency, economic interests) or inherent constraints (eg, limited expertise, lack of awareness, etc) may adversely affect human rights-centred design.

Various tools are available to support human rights-oriented project design and development, which can counteract these limiting factors in

[13] This is evident in the contextualisation of these rights and freedoms (based on different processes, such as appropriation, colonisation and vernacularisation), and in the debate on universalism and cultural relativism in human rights.

[14] See, eg, Council of Europe – Committee of Ministers, Recommendation CM/Rec(2020)1 of the Committee of Ministers to member States on the human rights impacts of algorithmic systems; Council of Europe – Consultative Committee of the Convention for the Protection of Individuals with regard to Automatic Processing of Personal Data, *Report on Artificial Intelligence Artificial Intelligence and Data Protection: Challenges and Possible Remedies*, T-PD(2018)09Rev (2019), https://rm.coe.int/artificial-intelligence-and-data-protectionchallenges-and-possible-re/168091f8a6.

different ways. They can be classified as either recommendation-based or assessment-based tools.

The recommendation-based tools, which include questionnaires and checklists, are awareness-raising and monitoring instruments that aim to provide general recommendations useful to project managers at the design stage.[15] The assessment-based tools are assessment instruments that can be incorporated in a human rights due diligence process to ensure accountability and provide context-specific evidence of human rights safeguards.[16] The two types can be combined, and questionnaires and checklists are often used in the planning and scoping stage of Human Rights Impact Assessment (HRIA),[17] as well in the collection of relevant data.

Various recommendation systems and assessment models are used in human rights-oriented project design and development, but in the digital context the most important tools relate to data management and Data Protection Impact Assessment (DPIA) for data protection and HRIA for artificial intelligence (AI), where DPIA can also be a section of HRIA.

In a context characterised by the increasing use of AI, protecting personal information and safeguarding of human rights are currently the two most significant issues for digital-focused projects, due to the potential risks and complexity of addressing them. Unauthorised access to sensitive information, disproportionate use of personal data, the risk of discrimination, AI-based decision-making systems that impact on human rights are just some of the possible threats associated with data processing and the use of AI.

Adequate risk management systems that focus on the specific operations and potential prejudice to rights and freedoms associated with each project must therefore be developed. This will prevent adverse consequences by adopting a procedural approach that creates a safe environment for the use of digital solutions in funded cooperation projects.

[15] For an example of a human rights checklist, see the Digital Rights Check realised by the Deutsche Gesellschaft für Internationale Zusammenarbeit GmbH and The Danish Institute for Human Rights, available at https://digitalrights-check.toolkit-digitalisierung.de.

[16] See, eg, The Danish Institute for Human Rights, 'Guidance on HRIA of Digital Activities' (2020), www.humanrights.dk/publications/human-rights-impact-assessment-digital-activities; A Mantelero, *Beyond Data – Human Rights, Ethical and Social Impact Assessment in AI* (The Hague, Springer, 2022) ch 2, https://link.springer.com/content/pdf/10.1007/978-94-6265-531-7.pdf; Government of Canada, Algorithmic Impact Assessment, https://canada-ca.github.io/aia-eia-js.

[17] In this chapter the international terminology (Human Rights Impact Assessment) is used, although in the EU context the reference is to Fundamental Rights Impact Assessment. As pointed out by the European Union Agency for Fundamental Rights (https://fra.europa.eu/en/about-fundamental-rights/frequently-asked-questions#difference-human-fundamental-rights), referring to human rights or fundamental rights depends on the perspective adopted, but is equivalent in terms of safeguarded interests. Here we prefer to refer to HRIA for two main reasons. First, HRIA is a methodology established at global level and known as such. Second, focusing the analysis on the development of EU projects at international level, human rights represent the most appropriate framework. For an example of an HRIA methodology focused on AI, see UNDP, 'Human Rights Impact of AI Assessment Toolkit' (2025), https://www.undp.org/eurasia/publications/human-rights-impact-ai-assessment-toolkit.

3.5. Conclusions

Despite the attempt to promote Mediterranean cooperation, the main achievements in this field are characterised by a fragmentation of the initiatives and increasing difficulties in the dialogue between the Mediterranean countries. This has not stopped the interaction and the cooperation between states, and even more so in the context of the EU's European Neighbourhood Policy. However, due to the geopolitical issues outlined in the introduction, the concrete cooperation initiatives have not been supported by a common legal framework for the protection of human rights.

In the absence of a state-based framework, it is possible to promote human rights protection in critical contexts in the Mediterranean region by relying on binding agreements between the various actors involved in cooperation. As in the case of data protection in relation to transborder data flows, appropriate contractual, policy and technical solutions, both general and contract-specific, can be adopted to endure an adequate level of protection of human rights.

This chapter, by outlining some of the possible solutions to achieve this objective and the related issues to be faced in their implementation, has provided a first response in the direction of a bottom-up Mediterranean dialogue on common safeguards for human rights, starting from the perspective of the actors directly involved in cooperation, thus bridging the gap that exists at the state level.

4

Maritime Security in the Mediterranean Sea

LILIAN MITROU

4.1. Maritime Security and the New Threats

Sea and maritime traffic are of essential importance for Mediterranean countries and their societies. The *Mare Nostrum* represents a crossroad between continents, civilisations and people, while more than 70 per cent of the EU's external border are maritime.[1] Over 80 per cent of global trade is seaborne, about two-thirds of the world's oil and gas supply is either extracted at sea or transported by sea, and up to 99 per cent of global data flows are transmitted through undersea cables.[2] In this respect it has become essentially important to know 'what is happening at sea' and more specifically to maintain a high level of vigilance and ensure that maritime activities are carried out safely and securely.

The threats and challenges stemming from the marine environment are multiple and various: from violence threats as piracy or terror (such as the attack on the *Achille Lauro* in 1985) and threats of marine resources (environmental damages and degradation and/or pollution of the sea's ecosystem) to threats to sovereignty and the law, such as illegal fishing, smuggling activities, trafficking of arms and narcotics, and human trafficking. The growing occurrence of maritime accidents, especially in the Mediterranean, emphasises the need to monitor and detect irregularities at sea and manage emergency issues and search and rescue activities in an efficient way.[3] The EU defines this necessity as maritime domain awareness

[1] M Fantinato, 'Governance of International Sea Borders: Regional Approaches and Sustainable Solutions for Maritime Surveillance in the Mediterranean Sea' in A Carpenter, TM Johansson and JA Skinner (eds), *Sustainability in the maritime domain: towards ocean governance and beyond* (Cham, Springer Nature, 2021) 170.

[2] See Council of the European Union, 'Council conclusions on the Revised EU Maritime Security Strategy (EUMSS) and its Action Plan' (2023) 5.

[3] See M Reggiannini et al, 'Remote Sensing for Maritime Traffic Understanding' (2024) 16 *Remote Sening.* 557, doi.org/10.3390/rs16030557. See also B Sengül, F Yılmaz and Ö Ugurlu, 'Safety–Security Analysis of Maritime Surveillance Systems in Critical Marine Areas' (2023) 15 *Sustainability* 16381, doi.org/10.3390/su152316381.

(MDA), ie the effective understanding of activity associated with the maritime domain that could impact the security, safety, economy, or environment of the EU and its Member States.[4]

Cross-border crimes and steady increases in irregular migration have an intrinsic transnational nature and a serious impact on Mediterranean states.[5] The need to guarantee safety and security of the seas has been translated into a need to establish and enhance maritime surveillance mechanisms. The emergence of new threats in the Mediterranean Sea has contributed to reshaping the notion of maritime security.

In this chapter we discuss the concept and the various aspects of maritime security. The progressive digitalisation of the maritime sector opens up new scenarios with regard to security, including cybersecurity. The digital environment, coupled with the growing presence of geopolitical conflicts and challenges in the Mediterranean area, also brings new risks, while offering new means to face them. This chapter analyses these new multidimensional threats, the 'digitisation of security' especially in the context of border control and migration, and the implications for fundamental rights and freedoms.

Emphasis is put on the use of tools like drones and artificial intelligence (AI)-enabled surveillance and analysis technologies. The chapter provides also an analysis of search and rescue operations as well as disaster and accident management. As we discuss maritime security in the Mediterranean sea we focus on the European maritime space and the respective legal framework. Because the scope of provisions that refer to maritime security and safety is wide, the analysis is limited to highlighting the issues pertaining to the conflict and the balance to be struck between the goals of maritime security and fundamental rights, such as the right to the protection of personal data.

4.2. Maritime Security: More than the Absence of Danger?

Security, in a nutshell, is the absence of danger. It is identified in strict correlation with (the notion and definition of) threats and risks that have to be faced. On a generic level it could be defined as 'the condition (perceived or confirmed) of an individual, a community, an organisation, a societal institution, a state, and their assets (such as goods, infrastructure), to be protected against danger or threats such as criminal activity, terrorism or other deliberate or hostile acts, [and] disasters (natural and man-made)'.[6]

[4] Council of European Union (n 2) 3.

[5] Fantinato (n 1) 190.

[6] L Mitrou, 'Attacks against Information Systems: Technical Definitions' in I Iglezakis, P Jougleux, L Mitrou and TE Synodinou, *The Legal Regulation of Cyber Attacks*, 2nd edn (Alphen aan den Rijn, Kluwer Law International 2020) 9–18.

4.2.1. Maritime Security: A Buzzword filled *ad libitum*?

Maritime security, for some authors a buzzword filled *ad libitum* is a broad concept that encompasses both traditional and non-traditional or transnational security issues. This term refers to a different variety of different security challenges, ranging from threats to state sovereignty and defence[7] to the shipping industry and maritime transportation sector, in the context of which security efforts are concentrated on ensuring the passage of goods and the safety of crews and passengers. 'Maritime security' as a term occupies a grey area, as there is no mutually or multilaterally agreed definition of it, a situation complicated by the absence of a clear distinction between maritime security and safety.[8] The meaning and content of 'maritime security' depend on the region and the security challengers, and form part of national policies, doctrines, military transformation, geographic location and geopolitical conditions. In the context of the Mediterranean this become obvious in the connection between border and irregular migration control.

It is noteworthy that EU official documents do not include a definition of 'maritime security'. The definition adopted by the European Maritime Surveillance Agency (EMSA) is a quite descriptive one – measures taken for protection against unlawful acts, such as piracy, armed robbery, terrorism and maritime violence – while the Revised EU Maritime Security Strategy indicatively refers to areas of the maritime domain that are covered by maritime security: security and defence, including cybersecurity critical infrastructure, environmental protection, fishing trade and shipping, energy, transport and tourism.

Authors have emphasised the need to create the preconditions to provide a timely and accurate warning of an impending threat, offering a response for removing or neutralising that threat by repelling, capturing or eliminating the perpetrators.[9] In this perspective, maritime security is intrinsically related to warning and prevention. Maritime security across EU borders entails the overall good governance of the maritime domain and the effective management of its external sea borders.[10]

[7] Maritime security, on the other hand, is frequently defined as a condition of a maritime environment that is free from various threats to territorial sovereignty and the enforcement of national and international laws aimed at ensuring the realisation of a country's national interest which stands between traditional and non-traditional security frameworks, as well as the efforts to realise maritime security beyond national borders. See C Bruwer, 'Transnational organised crime at sea as a threat to the sustainable development goals: taking direction from piracy and counter-piracy in the Western Indian Ocean' (2019) 28 *African Security Review* 172.

[8] C Bueger, 'What is maritime security' (2015) 53 *Marine Policy* 159.

[9] Fantinato (n 1) 176.

[10] European Commission – High Representative of the Union for Foreign Affairs and Security Policy, 'Joint Communication on the update of the EU Maritime Security Strategy and its Action Plan. 'An enhanced EU Maritime Security Strategy for evolving maritime threats' JOIN(2023) 8 final (2023), https://oceans-and-fisheries.ec.europa.eu/publications/joint-communication-update-eu-maritime-security-strategy-and-its-action-plan-enhanced-eu-maritime_en.

4.2.2. New Risks and Maritime Cybersecurity

In this context maritime cybersecurity[11] has become a very important issue both nationally and internationally. Until recently, information systems security and – even more recently – cybersecurity seemed not to be a big issue for the maritime sector. The dominant perception regarded the whole shipping environment as isolated from the outside world, sitting within an 'air gap' inaccessible to malicious hackers and not menaced by cyber threats. Recent cyber-attacks have shown that ships, maritime companies, ports and maritime terminals are far from immune from emerging cyber threats.[12]

There are several factors that make the maritime industry and activities particularly vulnerable to cyber incidents and attacks. The maritime domain is a complex ecosystem with many interdependencies and organisations of different sizes, operational scope, and information and communications technology (ICT) complexity. Vessels are nowadays equipped with digital systems such as access control, power management, cargo handling, etc. The cyber threat also increases due to the interconnectedness of the maritime industry with the rest of the supply chain and the dependence on digitalisation and automation.[13] Vessels and ports rely heavily on data and their management, and on the digitalisation of information, systems and procedures.[14] Ships may be accessed, supported, managed and monitored remotely, while connectivity can lead isolated cyber events to have global effects.[15]

A cybersecurity incident (corruption, loss or compromise of information systems or other infrastructure) may result in shipping-related operational, safety or security failures.[16] Cyber-attacks may affect the ship's safety, including that of personnel and passengers, and lead not only to business disruptions and property

[11] The definition adopted by the Cybersecurity Act (Art 2(1) of Regulation (EU) 2019/88) is quite descriptive, as 'cybersecurity' means the activities necessary to protect network and information systems, the users of such systems, and other persons affected by cyber threats, defined as 'any potential circumstance, event or action that could damage, disrupt or otherwise adversely impact network and information systems, the users of such systems and other persons' (Art 2(8)).

[12] The vulnerability of the maritime industry to cyber-attacks is stressed by the fact that since September 2020, the industry's largest companies (Maersk, CMA CGM, COSCO) were hit. All attacks took place within a short period of time, starting in 2017 with the Maersk ransomware attack.

[13] See EP Kechagias, G Chatzistelios, GA Papadopoulos and P Apostolou, 'Digital transformation of the maritime industry: A cybersecurity systemic approach' (2022) 37 *International Journal of Critical Infrastructure Protection* 100526.

[14] Kouroupis and Sotiropoloulos mention that smart shipping and maritime technology entail intelligent decision-making technology, intelligent routing technology, marine communication network security technology, route planning technology, autonomous navigation technology, etc. K Kouroupis and L Sotiropoulos, 'Cyber Challenges amid the Digital Revolution in Maritime Transport Juridical Tribune' (2024) 14 *Review of Comparative and International Law* 321.

[15] Kechagias et al (n 13).

[16] See IMO, 'Guidelines on maritime cyber risk management' MSC-FAL.1/Circ.3/Rev.3 (4 April 2025).

damage but also to loss of life.[17] Consequently, the EU Maritime Security Strategy (EUMSS) Action Plan covers maritime cybersecurity, aiming to reinforce and improve security management, protection and resilience against cyber threats in the maritime transportation and ports.[18]

At the same time, research has identified different perceptions and approaches within the maritime industry with regard to cybersecurity threats and a lack of awareness of them.[19] However, it seems that underestimating the new cybersecurity threats and neglecting the new challenges and requirements is no more acceptable, not only in respect of operational needs but also from a legal perspective. The maritime industry is classified in the critical infrastructure.[20] The so-called NIS2 Directive[21] significantly broadens the scope of entities that are required to comply with the provisions, and establishes new requirements and obligations forcing their addressees to focus on compliance.

4.3. The Digitalisation of Maritime Security

The needs of maritime security called for new means and have endorsed the adoption of new techniques to ensure that maritime activities are carried out in a lawful, secure and safe way. Nowadays, the maritime industry is characterised by digitalisation aiming to boost the performance of maritime assets and allowing continuous and interactive monitoring of key technical and operational parameters.[22] The maritime sector adopts new digital technologies such as the Internet of Things, cloud computing, data analytics, robotics, and various other innovations, forming a new landscape. As the maritime industry advances, the optimisation of operations and processes transform the vessels to 'digital ships' and ports to 'digital ports'.[23]

[17] Kechagias et al (n 13).

[18] I Progoulakis et al, 'Digitalization and cyber physical security aspects in maritime transportation and port infrastructure' in TM Johansson et al (eds), *Smart Ports and Robotic Systems: Navigating the Waves of Techno-Regulation and Governance* (Cham, Springer International Publishing, 2023) 227–48.

[19] A decisive element refers to the so-called 'human factor' and especially a lack of awareness due to ill-trained staff.

[20] ENISA, 'Critical Information Infrastructures and Services: Maritime' (2018), www.enisa.europa.eu/topics/critical-information-infrastructures-and-services/maritime.

[21] Directive (EU) 2022/2555 of the European Parliament and of the Council of 14 December 2022 on measures for a high common level of cybersecurity across the Union, amending Regulation (EU) No 910/2014 and Directive (EU) 2018/1972, and repealing Directive (EU) 2016/1148 (NIS 2 Directive).

[22] Progoulakis (n 18).

[23] MA Ben Farah, E Ukwandu, H Hindy, D Brosset, M Bures, I Andonovic, and X Bellekens, 'Cyber security in the maritime industry: A systematic survey of recent advances and future trends' (2022) 13 *Information* 22.

4.3.1. From Patrolling to Intelligence-driven Surveillance

At the same time, there has been a consolidation of the deployment of technological instruments in the security domain, identified as trend of 'techno-securitisation'.[24] The past two decades have seen a rapid growth in data and data-driven tools aimed at promptly identifying irregularities at sea.[25] The digitalisation of surveillance has also been enhanced to address the particularities of maritime activities, which have been (and remain) difficult to monitor given their geographic isolation from land, lack of distinct borders, and vast scales – attributes that create or compound an already complex legal regime.[26]

The character of surveillance has been changed accordingly to enable effective situational awareness over activities at sea that may impact maritime security and facilitate respective sound decisions and actions. The growing availability and variety of data and its processing is offered as a solution to deal with the complications of sea monitoring, such as the lack of direct access.

Maritime surveillance is focused on the localisation of the vessels and conducted through a diverse instrumentarium of data-generating sensors, including vessel monitoring systems (VMS), automatic identification systems (AIS), ship and coastal radars, air and space synthetic aperture radars (SAR), optical systems in ports and coasts, and vessel traffic services (VTS). Surveillance systems in the Mediterranean areas, such as the Aegean Sea, tend to move intelligence-driven operations to patrolling the sea with various types of vessels and air units, increasingly combined with 'smarter' systems, such as radars, satellites, and coordination centres.[27]

Another important feature is the integration of existing surveillance systems and their interoperability. As noted by Papadaki and Markellou, the needs of maritime surveillance operations call for the integration of data collected from land-based, naval, and aerial equipment. These technologies may refer to satellites, unmanned aerial vehicles (UAVs) or remotely piloted aircraft systems (RPAS) or drones, radars, scanners (seismic, magnetic), CCTV, cameras (smart, infrared, high-resolution optical), the fusion of data collected from those sources, and the performance of data analytics (such as predictive analytics).[28]

[24] See D Papadaki and M Markellou, 'The Andromeda Galaxy: Legal and Ethical Aspects of Technology-Aided Maritime Border Surveillance Operations' in B Akhgar, D Kavallieros and E Sdongos (eds), *Technology Development for Security Practitioners* (Cham, Springer International Publishing, 2021) 299–313.

[25] B Sengül, F Yılmaz and Ö Ugurlu, 'Safety–Security Analysis of Maritime Surveillance Systems' (2023) 15 *Sustainability* 16381.

[26] See J Hancock, R Hui, J Singh and A Mazumder, 'Trouble at Sea: Data and digital technology challenges for maritime human rights concerns' in *FAccT '24: Proceedings of the 2024 ACM Conference on Fairness, Accountability, and Transparency* (2024) 988–1001, doi.org/10.1145/3630106.3658950.

[27] See H Dijstelbloem, R Van Reekum and W Schinkel, 'Surveillance at sea: The transactional politics of border control in the Aegean' (2017) 48 *Security Dialogue* 224.

[28] Papadaki and Markellou (n 24).

These monitoring processes, designed to increase effectiveness and decrease operational costs, are – mostly – holistic and comprehensive, implying – beyond simple collection – understanding and preventing events. The goal is to achieve a certain level of situational awareness that enables properly information 'at the right time, about the operational environment and the threats that accompany it'.[29]

4.3.2. Identification and Monitoring of Vessels (and People?)

A key tool for detecting maritime traffic is the AIS. Since 2004, it has been compulsory for all passenger vessels and all commercial vessels over a certain size to carry it.[30] Although AIS was initially used as a short-range system to avoid collisions along busy maritime lanes, it has been developed into a global apparatus to increase maritime domain awareness, its coverage and purposes extended to respond to the various vulnerabilities in the global maritime traffic. The development and transformation of AIS indicates the significance of the integrated and multi-purpose use of various technologies, such as radars or remote sensing technologies.

Copernicus[31] forms another part of the extensive monitoring infrastructure. By providing satellite images relevant for fisheries control, customs, law enforcement and marine pollution, Copernicus enhances the qualitative shift of monitoring of coasts and sea, thus extending the physical jurisdictional border outwards. Data gathered through satellite observation are combined with a wide range of other information, originating from different internal and external sources.

Information is collected in a quite extensive manner by unmanned aircraft systems (UAS), including unmanned aircraft vehicles (UAVs). Being easily concealed and remotely controlled, UAVs enable enhanced surveillance and the transfer in real time of the data they collect. Due to their longer endurance and capability to operate in harsh environments, drones can quickly provide data that offer a more accurate picture, especially of the of the EU's border zones, for a longer period of time, and in a continuous way compared to manned aircraft and satellites.

By enhancing performance in border patrolling and increasing the operational capacity of surveillance systems, UAVs are considered a valuable element of the so-called smart borders or technological borders. Deploying UAVs in the

[29] See A Andreou, 'e-Securing the EU Borders: AI in European Integrated Border Management' (2023) 2 *Journal of Politics and Ethics in New Technologies and AI*, doi.org/10.12681/jpentai.34287.

[30] The IMO has made it compulsory. See L Pezzani and C Heller, 'AIS Politics: The Contested Use of Vessel Tracking at the EU's Maritime Frontier' (2019) 44 *Science, Technology, & Human Values* 881.

[31] European Union's Earth Observation Programme (COPERNICUS), previously known as Global Monitoring for Environment and Security (GMES).

Mediterranean has been suggested as an ideal solution: they can detect even small vessels[32] and provide information with regard to the type of vessel, its 'behaviour', speed, position and direction in particular maritime areas.[33] They are also able to receive AIS signals from ships that enable the detection, identification and categorisation of vessels of interest according to their needs and follow these vessels upon detection. As noted, the size and speed of the vessel serve as indicators that may reinforce or refute a presumption of having detected a vessel carrying unauthorised migrants.[34]

Ship identification and tracking is combined with remote sensing tools to monitor the specific activities performed by vessels and to foresee their potential behaviour and effects.[35] New radar technologies give the opportunity to their operators to have a clearer view of the approaching unknown small vessels while improving significantly the operational capabilities, as well through the provision of automatic alerting procedures, classification of alerting and self-learning capabilities. Increasing technological surveillance is therefore an inherent characteristic of the enhanced controls of the EU's external maritime borders.

4.3.3. Warning Systems and Artificial Intelligence

One of the aims of this collection of a quite vast amount of data is developing 'warning systems' and 'watchlists',[36] especially for cases that are connected with cross-border unlawful acts and illegal immigration, in order to trigger appropriate reaction capabilities. In this context AI systems are introduced to counterbalance the physical and technical border deficiencies, analysing and evaluating information gathered by multiple sources, conducting risk assessments for individuals and groups, and predicting potential threats. AI technologies enhance situational awareness especially with regard to border control.[37]

As noted in the Frontex study of 2020, the use of AI in the context of border control could entail a range of applications including biometric scanning, facial recognition and document authenticity validation. AI could be utilised to improve

[32] Csernatoni notes that the Council of the European Union and the Commission as well as Frontex, EMSA, but also national border and coast guard agencies, have been major stakeholders in the promotion and use of drones. See R Csernatoni, 'Constructing the EU's high-tech borders: FRONTEX and dual-use drones for border management' (2018) 27 *European Security* 175.

[33] EMSA, Appendix 1 to the tender specifications: Service and Technical Requirements, in Invitation to tender no. EMSA/OP/01/2018. Lisbon, Portugal. See www.emsa.europa.eu.

[34] However, Jumbert underlines that this is possible insofar as it fits with a pre-defined (stereo)typical case of migrants crossing the sea. See MG Jumbert, 'Control or rescue at sea? Aims and limits of border surveillance technologies in the Mediterranean Sea' (2018) 42 *Disasters* 674.

[35] Reggiannini et al (n 3).

[36] See Art 15 of Commission Implementing Regulation (EU) 2021/581 of 9 April 2021 on the situational pictures of the European Border Surveillance System (EUROSUR).

[37] Andreou (n 29).

automated border control systems to detect potential threats, such as face presentation and morphing attacks.[38] Technologies such as sensors, UAV swarms, thermal cameras, laser radars, CCTV, and biometric recognition and identification of persons are used.

These technologies could ameliorate the development of situations that have to be managed and, in some cases, allow the prevention of unlawful activities even before the conventional border check. In this context border management will largely become AI-centred. AI-based systems and tools are also used for the prediction of the intensity, the timespan and the direction of cross-border illicit activities and refugee/migrant flows,[39] and provide 'early warnings' so to forecast potential malfunctions of the existing systems and enhance the managerial readiness of border authorities.[40]

4.3.4. Connecting the Dots …

A prerequisite for an effective maritime security policy is the ability to share information and connect the dots between various data and information sources. The Regulations ruling Frontex provide for its competences to collect operational data, combine information from different sources, establish a communication network to provide analytical tools and exchange information with other EU agencies such as Europol.[41]

An interoperable and security-focused system used to surveil maritime territory is the so-called Common Information Sharing Environment (CISE) initiative. Aiming to make European and EU Member States surveillance systems interoperable to give all concerned authorities access to data they need to conduct missions at sea, CISE has been conceived an integral part of the EUMSS. By integrating existing surveillance systems CISE facilitates the rapid and real-time exchange and sharing of information between various authorities that are responsible for different aspects of maritime security (maritime safety, security and prevention of pollution by ships, fisheries control, marine pollution preparedness and

[38] Frontex, 'Artificial Intelligence-based capabilities for the European Border and Coast Guard. Final report' (March 2021), www.frontex.europa.eu/assets/Publications/Research/Frontex_AI_Research_Study_2020_final_report.pdf.

[39] Recently the ITFLOWS project resulted in the generation of migration flow predictions in the EU in the phases of reception, relocation, settlement and integration of migration, drawing on multiple sources of information and with a focus on human rights. These insights have been provided by an evidence-based ICT enabled solution (the EUMigraTool) and models (www.itflows.eu).

[40] In their study, İşleyen, Uçar and Balo tested an algorithm based on simulated annealing to face the problem of identification of irregular migrant boats crossing the Aegean Sea. According to their findings this algorithm identified all 'targets' in the least possible time for all 50 different scenarios tested and holds the potential to significantly enhance the rapid response to illicit activities at sea. See SK İşleyen, U Uçar and F Balo, 'A New Solution Approach for Maritime Surveillance Operation: The Case of Aegean Sea' (2019) 1 *Mathematical Problems in Engineering*, doi.org/10.1155/2019/8575219.

[41] See S Gandhi, 'Frontex as a hub for surveillance and data sharing: Challenges for data protection and privacy rights' (2024) 53 *Computer Law & Security Review* 105963.

response, marine environment, customs, border control, general law enforcement and defence). By bringing added value and complementarity to existing maritime data systems and services while avoiding duplication, the use of CISE ensures the effectiveness and cost-efficiency of maritime surveillance activities and enables the various authorities to conduct missions at the Mediterranean Sea.[42]

In this context is enshrined the EUROSUR system, which was adopted in 2013 as a framework for information exchange and cooperation between EU Member States, Frontex and other EU agencies. Its objectives are multiple: it aims not only to prevent cross-border crime and prevent irregular migration but also to contribute to protecting migrants' lives. EUROSUR covers most aspects of border management, including land, maritime and air border surveillance.[43] Its objectives, scope and functioning are regulated in a quite detailed manner by the Commission Implementing Regulation (EU) 2021/581 on the situational pictures of the European Border Surveillance System (EUROSUR).[44] This Regulation also provides for the automation of processing operations of satellite images in the context of EUROSUR, allowing machine-to-machine interconnections and automated decision support tools.

4.4. Monitoring for Safety, Search and Rescue

New technologies are also offered as solutions, which can increase the velocity, efficacy and cost-effectiveness of responses to natural or man-made disasters that can endanger people's health, safety and lives. Moreover, technologies introduced to monitor and ensure the situational awareness at sea are often simultaneously deployed for search and rescue operations or responses to emergency situations, such as vessel accidents at sea.

The so-called search and rescue (SAR) obligation refers and binds anyone at sea, irrespective of the maritime jurisdiction in which the boat is located, the nationality of the people on board, and the circumstances in which they are found.[45] Providing assistance to save life at sea is a legal obligation. In consideration of the vulnerability of humans at sea, a number of international legal instruments

[42] The development of the maritime CISE was proposed in 2009 and has since been refined through various interoperability and security research projects, and supported by subsequent Commission Communications and Council Conclusions. See www.emsa.europa.eu/cise.html.

[43] As in the case of CISE, the EUROSUR Fusion Services enable EU Member States access to space-based surveillance systems and in general to advanced technologies that they could not alone afford.

[44] This Regulation is to be conceived and implemented in combination with Regulation (EU) 2019/1896 of the European Parliament and of the Council of 13 November 2019 on the European Border and Coast Guard and repealing Regulations (EU) No 1052/2013 and (EU) 2016/1624.

[45] Jumbert (n 34).

provide for the commitment to provide search and rescue in cases of vessels and people in distress.[46]

4.4.1. Use of Surveillance Technologies for SAR Operations

Effective disaster response requires preliminary mapping and observation of the scene of disaster to ensure the safety of first responders, and proper planning of SAR activities and risk mitigation. This is especially the case for SAR actions in areas too dangerous or remote for rescue agencies to otherwise.reach. Detection technologies, in combination with the deployment of human or non-human resources (SAR vessels, first responders) are key factors for a successful completion of rescue missions, especially when physical contact with persons in distress is necessary for their rescue.[47]

In particular, tools based on aerial surveillance, radars or sensors are portrayed as efficient solutions for spotting vessels in danger and providing SAR, where needed. Location, speed and direction are essential indications when locating with precision a vessel identified or reported to be in distress.[48] The use of drone footage to detect and collect information about people present on vessels in distress allows SAR vessels to better prepare for and conduct rescue operations, including for approaching distress incidents in a safe way for the people concerned.[49] The technical capabilities and effects that UAVs offer are of utmost importance for conducting SAR activities. Due to longer endurance, faster response times and the ability to operate even in harsher weather conditions, tools such as drones are deployed to enhance searching capabilities and assist searching operations in sea areas that are far from land with reduced or non-existent communication coverage or possibilities.

UAVs may be heterogeneous thus incorporating attachments, devices and software, which themselves have specific capabilities, thus enabling more and multiple applications. During and/or after natural or man-made disasters, aerial surveillance is expected to monitor and assess the spread and extent of phenomena/risks, monitor and assess damages, identify SAR needs, and support effective and efficient emergency preparation, response and recovery.

In the Mediterranean Sea, SAR is conflated with maritime security and detection of illegal activities, including irregular migration and environmental

[46] See the provisions of the 1974 Convention on Safety of Life at Sea (SOLAS Convention), the 1979 Search and Rescue Convention (SAR Convention) as well as the 1982 United Nations Convention on the Law of the Sea (UNCLOS).

[47] See P Loukinas, 'Drones for Border Surveillance: Multipurpose Use, Uncertainty and Challenges at EU Borders' (2022) 27 *Geopolitics* 89.

[48] Jumbert (n 34).

[49] Loukinas (n 47).

security.[50] EU Member States have to report SAR operations as these incidents are often related to irregular migration. Technologies such as drones and sensors are discussed and deployed for both security and humanitarian aims, thus amounting to a dual use, in the sense that the same tools simultaneously have different purposes.

These technologies are better suited to supporting and enhancing SAR operations, by alerting, locating and sharing potentially vital information with relevant users. This users circle includes authorities that are primarily oriented to security. Contributing to 'ensuring the protection and saving the lives of migrants' is one the objectives of EUROSUR.[51] Indeed, the collected information may prove crucial in distress incidents, taking also into account that migrating by sea is associated with particular risks, such as the risk of drowning or facing bad weather conditions with – often unseaworthy – vessels.[52]

Although authorities have attempted for years to keep separate border patrolling and SAR, the tensions between maritime border control and legal obligations to rescue people in danger is unavoidable and they have had profoundly transformative effects for European politics of unauthorised migration and asylum.[53] Some authors point out that SAR purposes and operations, and in general the use of 'humanitarian framing', may serve as a powerful legitimating factor for the deployment of surveillance instrumentaria.[54] However, it cannot be neglected that tools such as UAVs gradually and progressively used for joint and multipurpose operations can advance the SAR capabilities of both state and private actors, having an undeniably positive impact on the security and safety of migrants.[55]

4.4.2. Emergency Preparedness and/or Monitored Safe Evacuations

The safety of passengers forms a central objective with regard to the maritime security. The emergency preparedness, ie the existence of emergency response plans for abandoning a vessel in case of events, either human-induced or caused by nature or technological failures, is mandated by the International Convention for the Safety of Life at Sea (SOLAS) and is of crucial importance for the safety

[50] ibid.

[51] See Art 1 of Regulation (EU) No 1052/2013 establishing the European Border Surveillance System (Eurosur). According to Rec 2, 'EUROSUR should considerably improve the operational and technical ability of the Agency and the Member States to detect such small vessels and to improve the reaction capability of the Member States, thereby contributing to reducing the loss of lives of migrants'.

[52] Jumbert (n 34).

[53] Dijstelbloem et al (n 27).

[54] Jumbert (n 34) is referring to 'humanitarian legitimacy'.

[55] See R Koslowski and MB Schulzke, 'Drones along Borders: Border Security UAVs in the United States and the European Union' (2018) 19 *International Studies Perspectives* 305.

management. Beyond the 'traditional' methods, such as the sounding of general emergency alarms and safety announcements[56] the interest is oriented to the use of new technologies to enhance mustering and evacuation of passengers. The introduction of new tools is considered for facing the challenges of evacuation situations that are dynamic and to enhance preparedness in emergencies, where the behaviour of passengers in panic is unpredictable.

In general, the technology most typically used for safety management in such cases consists of CCTV systems to coordinate evacuation incidents. However, there has more recently been a shift of the relevant research to real-time evacuation tools and strategies, based on mobile applications and two-way communication mechanisms.[57]

Recently, in the context of research projects, new integrated systems have been developed that are built on real-time monitoring and location support for passengers. Based on a complex of apps installed on mobile devices (smartphones, smartwatches etc), CCTV and sensors on board, such systems aim at assisting passengers and crew for safe and efficient evacuation.

One of the main components of such systems is that they provide dynamic and personalised navigation to the identified exits for each passenger based on his/her real-time location. Other applications, such as smart wristbands, allow the unique identification of each passenger and the measurement and tracking of the passengers' biometric information and vital signals to calculate their stress levels.[58]

4.5. Security, Safety and Fundamental Rights

4.5.1. Data Processing (and Protection) as Exception?

Maritime surveillance is not primarily oriented towards identifying individuals. However, the potential for direct or indirect identification of an individual during maritime monitoring activities raises the issue of sufficient protection of their personal data. UAVs, especially drones carrying a combination of monitoring

[56] The safety information provided by traditional means is considered as static and difficult to understand especially under stressful conditions, and in conditions of low visibility (eg fire, or evacuation at night). See D Drakoulis et al, 'The architecture of EVAGUIDE: a security management platform for enhanced situation awareness and real-time adaptive evacuation strategies for large venues' B Akhgar, D Kavallieros and E Sdongos (eds), *Technology Development for Security Practitioners* (Cham, Springer International Publishing, 2021) 461–75.

[57] Such systems were initially developed to support evacuations in large facilities, such as malls, stadiums etc. in case of evacuation incidents.

[58] P Liston et al, 'Acceptability and Usability of Location-Support Technologies for Cruise Ship Evacuations' in M Rauterberg, F Fui-Hoon Nah, K Siau, H Krömker, J Wei and G Salvendy, *HCI International 2022 – Late Breaking Papers: HCI for Today's Community and Economy* (Cham, Springer Nature, 2022) 337–52.

devices (sensors, visual recording, detection and radio-frequency equipment, etc), may provide a greater amount of higher-quality data, including biometric data, while conferring ubiquity, immediacy and responsiveness.[59]

These features make drones extremely powerful surveillance tools, and so raise serious questions with regard to compliance with the fundamental right to respect for private and family life (Article 8 of the ECHR, Article 7 of the EU Charter of Fundamental Rights) and the right to protection of personal data (Article 8 of the Charter). Several privacy and data protection risks may arise, ranging from interference with location privacy to a lack of transparency. In any event, the difficulty in knowing which data processing equipment are on board, for what purposes personal data are being collected, and by whom, is obvious.[60]

Data processing activities conducted or assisted by drones are subject to the requirements of the existence of a legal ground for processing (Articles 6 and 9 GDPR) and the application of data protection principles as embedded in Article 5 GDPR (lawful purposes, concrete demonstration of necessity and appropriateness, transparency). In the context of maritime and sea-border security, and considering the multipurpose use of UAVs, it seems quite easy to justify there being no other instruments at the disposal of maritime and border authorities that could be regarded as less interfering. However, the extent of data and the intrusiveness of the on-board equipment in conjunction with potential subsequent uses may have a serious impact on privacy and data protection.

The framework regulating the activities of EUROSUR, including the use of 'situational pictures', reflects the conception of the EU with regard to a functional balance between surveillance for safety and security, and the privacy and data protection rights of people in vessels. According to Article 13 of the EUROSUR Regulation, personal data can only be processed in the national situational pictures. No personal data can be processed in the European situational picture and the common pre-frontier intelligence picture, except for ship identification numbers.[61]

The EUROSUR data processing/protection architecture is based on the rationale that personal data are not necessary for risk analysis purposes[62] and consequently on the 'exceptional' character of both the indirect identification of natural persons[63] and the processing of respective personal data. However, as such

[59] Csernatoni (n 32).

[60] Article 29 Data Protection Working Party, 'Opinion 01/2015 on Privacy and Data Protection Issues relating to the Utilisation of Drones' (2015).

[61] See European Union Agency for Fundamental Rights, 'How the Eurosur Regulation affects fundamental rights' (2018), https://fra.europa.eu/sites/default/files/fra_uploads/fra-2018-eurosur-regulation-fundamental-rights-impact_en.pdf. The FRA indicates the differences in understanding the categorisation of data as personal, with more than half of the EU Member States that responded to EUROSUR questionnaire not considering ship identification numbers as personal data.

[62] ibid 10.

[63] Identification may be achieved based on reasonable means. As the FRA noted in 2013, photos and videos attached to an incident and posted within the EUROSUR system may allow for the

processing cannot be excluded, if processing of personal data is exceptionally required, these have to be deleted as soon as the purpose for which they have been collected has been achieved.[64]

However, concerns are not stilled: as noted by critical commentators, despite the data protection obligations set out in the EUROSUR Regulation, the system itself and the large-scale collection of data increase the risk of misuse of personal information. The risk of secondary use increases, as cooperation between maritime surveillance actors is encouraged and enhanced.[65]

4.5.2. 'High-risk' AI-driven Surveillance?

Surveillance becomes more intrusive due to the further development and conjucted use of facial recognition systems and AI systems that perform predictive analysis. AI tools that profile and identify people on the move, and predict migration flows, are increasingly used in the field of border and migration management. It is worth mentioning that the use of algorithms to analyse the collected data to classify behaviours from 'raising alerts' or 'non-raising alerts' is common.[66]

Beyond implications upon the rights to privacy and data protection, the use of AI systems may have a substantial impact on other fundamental rights and freedoms, such as non-discrimination. Attention has to be paid to the fact that such detection and identification activities in combination with profiling capabilities and use of sophisticated or even biased algorithms may be focused on specific groups, which in turn may lead to categorised targeting and discrimination against persons belonging to particular groups.

The use of biometric categorisation of natural persons, such as travelers on a vessel, based on biometric data to deduce or infer their race or their religious beliefs is considered an unacceptable risk and consequently is prohibited by the Artificial Intelligence Act (AIA).[67]

According to Recital 60 of the AIA:

> The accuracy, non-discriminatory nature and transparency of the AI systems used in [the contexts of migration, asylum and border control management] are

identification of individuals, either directly or via software, or via a combination of data, depending on factors such as the weather, the distance, the light, and the potential of the deployed technologies, such as the resolution of an image. See European Union Agency for Fundamental Rights, 'Fundamental rights at Europe's southern sea borders' (2013), https://fra.europa.eu/sites/default/files/fundamental-rights-europes-southern-sea-borders-jul-13_en.pdf.

[64] See Art 40 of Implementing Regulation (EU) 2021/581 of 9 April 2021 on the situational pictures of the EUROSUR.

[65] Papadaki and Markellou (n 24).

[66] ibid.

[67] Regulation (EU) 2024/1689 of the European Parliament and of the Council of 13 June 2024 laying down harmonised rules on artificial intelligence and amending Regulations (EC) No 300/2008, (EU) No 167/2013, (EU) No 168/2013, (EU) 2018/858, (EU) 2018/1139 and (EU) 2019/2144 and Directives 2014/90/EU, (EU) 2016/797 and (EU) 2020/1828 (Artificial Intelligence Act).

> [therefore] particularly important to guarantee respect for the fundamental rights of the affected persons, in particular their rights to free movement, non-discrimination, protection of private life and personal data, international protection and good administration.

Considering the vulnerable position of individuals in such situations and especially their dependency upon the output of the systems and the outcome of the action of the competent public authorities, the European legislator has classified such systems as high-risk.[68] In the context of maritime security, AI systems 'intended to be used by or on behalf of competent public authorities or by Union institutions, bodies, offices or agencies to assess a risk, including a security risk, a risk of irregular migration'[69] are relevant.

The development and deployment of high-risk systems are subject to specific requirements, such as the establishment of risk management and quality assessment systems, data governance to ensure quality, accuracy and representativeness of data, technical documentation, record keeping, and human oversight.[70] However, 'given the specificities of the areas of … migration, border control', the requirement of human oversight of the functioning of AI should not apply where EU or national law considers the application of that requirement to be disproportionate.[71] Under the same rationale, the registration obligation 'should be fulfilled in a secure non-public section of the EU database'.[72] Although the security interest is 'easy enough to understand', disproportionate limitations of transparency may result in a lack of public scrutiny and accountability.

4.5.3. Is Privacy a 'Luxury Right' when Lives are at Stake?

Natural or man-made disasters may endanger people's lives, health and safety, thus affecting many vital and/or other substantial interests and rights of different persons, their groups and the society in general. On the other side, the – unquestionable – need to increase the efficacy and effectiveness of emergency responses on fatalities may raise ethical and legal concerns, as the measures taken for the protection of the lives may interfere with the fundamental rights of the victims or those, including first responders, not directly suffering from the disaster but involved at the scene.

[68] See Art 6 AIA. Civil society organisations have criticised this approach, arguing that such systems should fall under the category of prohibited risks. See E Chelioudakis, 'Unpacking AI-enabled border management technologies in Greece: To what extent their development and deployment are transparent and respect data protection rules?' (2024) 53 *Computer Law & Security Review*, doi.org/10.1016/j.clsr.2024.105967.

[69] As mentioned in Rec 60 'for assessing certain risks posed by natural persons entering the territory'.

[70] See Arts 8–17 AIA.

[71] See Rec 73 AIA, in conjunction with Art 14.

[72] See Rec 131 AIA.

The new, technology-based ways to cope with incidents at sea bring fresh challenges for various aspects of privacy, such as bodily privacy as well as privacy related to behaviour and activities in public spaces. In this context the link between privacy and identity, and therefore to the dignity of a person, is obvious.

The incident/disaster management cycle has to take into consideration that the response has to be not only timely and effective, but also lawfully conducted, culturally sensitive and gender-appropriate.[73] Ethical management of disasters is indeed a complex issue, as 'an emergency sometimes requires taking decisions which can be morally difficult'.[74] Does the 'technologising of care' meet the requirements derived from humanitarian principles? Is the use of drones a threat to dignity, or is it regarded as *salus ex machina*?

Principally, it is expected and legally required to ensure privacy and dignity also to individuals suffering from the most extreme conditions. As individual life is of crucial importance, protecting it might override people's fundamental rights as well as those of others. The right to privacy can be limited in accordance with the law and whether it is necessary in a democratic society for the protection of health or for the protection of the rights and freedoms of others.[75] The exercise, laid down in Article 8 of ECHR and Article 52 of the EU Charter, aims to find the right balance between the right to privacy of those involved in the disaster, and the necessity to protect their lives.

The legal ground of 'vital interests of data subject or another natural person'[76] that may legitimate the processing of personal data addresses exactly such SAR and/or emergency situations. In relation to 'vital interest' the EU legislator conceives an interest that is 'essential for the life' of an individual.[77] In real emergency situations it is the vital interest that is the appropriate legal ground of data processing, as it cannot be manifestly based on another legal basis, such as consent.[78] Recital 46 GDPR affirms that processing 'may serve both important grounds of public interest and the vital interests of the data subject as for instance when processing is necessary for humanitarian purposes'.

Furthermore, the explicit legal obligation to report and share information about vessels and people in distress may constitute a legal ground for processing, but the collection and use of data for the purposes of SAR operations should be dealt with in a way that ensures respect for the purpose limitation principle as laid

[73] See also ch 2.

[74] See M Prieur, 'Ethical Principles on Disaster Risk Reduction and People's Resilience' (Council of Europe, 2012).

[75] See Art 8(2) ECHR.

[76] See Arts 6(1)(d) and 9(2)(c) GDPR (Regulation (EU) 2016/679 of the European Parliament and of the Council of 27 April 2016 on the protection of natural persons with regard to the processing of personal data and on the free movement of such data, and repealing Directive 95/46/EC).

[77] See Rec 46 GDPR.

[78] See G Sartor, 'Article 6-Lawfulness of processing' in V Papakonstantinou, P De Hert, G Hornung and I Spiecker gen. Döhmann, *General Data Protection Regulation: Article-by-Article Commentary* (Baden-Baden, Nomos Verlagsgesellschaft 2023) 278–314.

down in GDPR (Article 5 § 1b), ie that data must be collected for specified, explicit and legitimate purposes and not further processed in a manner that is incompatible with those purposes.

Concerning the – quantitively and qualitatively – extensive collection of personal data for better managing evacuation operations and tailored evacuation assistance in vessels, the legal assessment is based on different considerations. Even if (informed!) consent of passengers to the use of apps and the respective collection of data is likely to be invoked as legal basis, this is not the case with regard to the crew members due to the imbalance of powers.

The major privacy concern, however, is the potential multiple use of location or behaviour data of both passengers and employees; especially for purposes that do not relate at all to the need to deal with emergency situations. Another issue that arises concerns the implications of the use of apps designed to infer – based on biometrics analysis – information about a person's emotional features and/or state. Beyond interferences with the right to privacy and data protection, the use of such AI-based systems has to comply with the conditions and requirements derived from the AIA, taking into account that 'human dignity requires acknowledging the complexity and richness of human identity, experience, values, and emotions'.[79]

4.6. Some Final Remarks about Maritime Security in the Mediterranean Sea

The *Mare Nostrum* is gradually acquiring the features of a digital *Mare Nostrum*, in multiple senses: maritime security is also at risk due to challenges and threats, respectively supported or provoked by technology. At the same time, the use of technological means, including AI systems, to pursue security and safety objectives is becoming a critical component of maritime security strategy and armature.

In this perspective, data and different modes of surveillance are significant factors to achieve and ensure maritime domain awareness. Data enables a better understanding and management of risks. In other words, it allows us to know – in an accurate, coherent and timely manner – what is going on 'out there at sea' so as to search, track and intervene responsively and effectively within maritime areas of operations.

States have considered the sea significant in terms of protecting their military, economic and political power, and sovereignty.[80] The maritime domain is complex, the maritime security and safety challenges interconnected, and they

[79] Council of Europe, Explanatory Report to the Council of Europe Framework Convention on Artificial Intelligence and Human Rights, Democracy and the Rule of Law, Rec 53.

[80] See L Otto, 'Introducing Maritime Security: The Sea as a Geostrategic Space' in L Otto (ed), *Global Challenges in Maritime Security. Advanced Sciences and Technologies for Security Applications* (Cham, Springer, 2020) 1–12.

cannot be assessed and faced separately from other – mainly but not only – public interests, expectations and goals.

Given the geographic isolation from land, lack of visible distinct borders and vast scale, activities in maritime spaces have been always difficult to monitor.[81] In addition, the multi- and cross-jurisdictional territory and the complexity of legal framework intensify the difficulties in achieving both maritime security and keeping track of the way these – principally legitimate – security objectives are pursued.

In the geostrategic space of the Mediterranean Sea, the balance between security goals and respect of fundamental rights – undeniably – proves to be sometimes delicate. However, the core European human rights instruments and secondary EU law provide for specific and strict conditions for lawful interference with those rights: necessity, proportionality, transparency, oversight and effective remedies.

[81] Hancock (n 26).

PART II

Digital Services and Mediterranean Cross-Country Cooperation

5

Tourist Data: Towards a Mediterranean Data Space

MARIA SAMANTHA ESPOSITO* AND
ALESSANDRO MANTELERO**

5.1. Introduction to Data Spaces

Data spaces respond to the central role that data increasingly plays in our digital societies, as well as to the current asymmetries in the digital economy[1] and their geopolitical consequences. However, a data space is not a mere socio-technical concept describing practices of data sharing and data stewardship[2] that facilitate the circulation of data within a specific sector or industry.

A data space is the outcome of a data governance strategy, such as that adopted by the EU. This strategy leverages a common level of protection for relevant rights and freedoms, as well as common technical standards.[3] In this view, and in the EU context, the common legal framework ensuring an adequate level of protection to rights and freedoms is the precondition[4] for data pooling and is also the way to combine the EU's attention to fundamental rights[5] with innovation, in line with the idea of responsible innovation. This architecture therefore reinforces the 'third

* Author of section 5.2.

** Author of sections 5.1, 5.3 and 5.4.

[1] Regarding tourism, see P Minoia and S Jokela, 'Platform-Mediated Tourism: Social Justice and Urban Governance before and during Covid-19' (2022) 30 *Journal of Sustainable Tourism* 951, doi.org/10.1080/09669582.2021.1922426.

[2] See also Ada Lovelace Institute, 'Exploring legal mechanisms for data stewardship' (2021), www.adalovelaceinstitute.org/wp-content/uploads/2021/03/Legal-mechanisms-for-data-stewardship_report_Ada_AI-Council-2.pdf.

[3] See also ch 6 on health data spaces.

[4] See also European Commission, 'Commission staff working document on Common European Data Spaces' (2024) 4, https://digital-strategy.ec.europa.eu/en/library/second-staff-working-document-data-spaces.

[5] See also the European Declaration on Digital Rights and Principles for the Digital Decade, 2023/C 23/01, PUB/2023/89, OJ C 23, 23 January 2023, 1–7, https://eur-lex.europa.eu/legal-content/EN/TXT/?uri=OJ:JOC_2023_023_R_0001.

way' approach adopted by the EU, between the market-driven view and the state-driven approach adopted by other countries.[6]

Against this background, it is clear that the lack of a regulatory precondition consisting of effective legal harmonisation is a barrier to the creation of data spaces, undermining the trustworthy and secure environment in which the operators can share their data. In this respect, the state of the EU regulation on digital society raises some concerns about its effective harmonised implementation across Member States. At the same time, it is possible that the creation of these data spaces and the benefits they bring will become a driving element to promote common practices with regard to data processing and data governance.

These brief considerations also suggest the challenges associated with the extension of these data spaces outside the EU, such as in the context of the Mediterranean region. The presence in this area of EU and non-EU countries creates obstacles to the definition of a common level of protection of the relevant rights and freedoms, which, as mentioned above, is a precondition for the creation of data spaces. However, as discussed in the following pages, the lack of a common legal framework does not exclude the possibility of achieving similar or partial results in the field of data spaces by adopting other strategies focusing on interoperability (eg, common taxonomy, governance instruments, interoperable data processing standards), data portability, and bottom-up approaches based on common principles and values.

In this context, this chapter investigates one of the most challenging and economically relevant areas of the Mediterranean digital space: the processing of tourist data. While in other sectors relevant to the Mediterranean region and discussed in this book, such as humanitarian action or migration,[7] the role of governmental and non-governmental international bodies facilitates the creation of common practices and policies, tourist data represents a highly fragmented sector. In addition, the Mediterranean area is the first global tourist destination, but the EU lacks a specific competence on tourism, which leaves more room for manoeuvre in the design of the digital space, not relying on the EU/non-EU dichotomy, but on a proper Mediterranean perspective.

The tourist data sector can therefore be a case study for outlining a more inclusive and Mediterranean-centred data strategy to create common data spaces for this sector, giving more voice to the interested countries and defining more flexible solutions, that are not solely based on alignment with the EU model. Moreover, a more gentle approach by the EU and its member states when promoting their common policies and regulatory views would prevent their initiatives from being perceived as a form of new regulatory and market-based colonialism, which could exacerbate the existing tensions in the region.

[6] See A Mantelero, 'The AI Act: a geopolitical tool to foster human rights and ethics' in D Brasioli et al (eds), *Routledge Handbook of Artificial Intelligence and Geopolitics* (Abingdon, Routledge, 2025).

[7] See ch 2.

Finally, it is worth noting that, despite the significant digitalisation of the tourism sector, the legal literature on data and society has largely ignored this area. This leaves policymakers, industry representatives and citizens without an adequate legal analysis to support their initiatives in this crucial field.

This chapter outlines the main characteristics of tourist data in terms of their nature and the main actors involved in data processing. Based on this preliminary analysis in section 5.2, section 5.3 focuses on the main challenges in designing a common data space for the Mediterranean area. It discusses the bottom-up nature of the tourism digital landscape in the Mediterranean, the structural constraints and the recent EU initiative on the common European data space for tourism. Based on the analysis of these challenges and constraints, section 5.4 outlines possible strategies to face them from a Mediterranean perspective, namely from a multilateral perspective where Mediterranean countries can shape their own data space rather than simply adopting a given regulatory model.

5.2. Tourist Data: Nature and the Main Actors Involved in Data Processing

Data and data analysis play an increasingly central role for the tourism industry in the development and management of innovative services. This process has been made possible by the widespread integration of information and communication technologies in the different segments of the tourism industry (ie tourist destinations, online services, smart tourism devices and services). The use of such technologies aims not only to improve the interaction between local administrations involved in the tourist offer, but also to enrich the tourist experience through personalised solutions and access to real-time information.

In this context, 'smart tourism' describes the use of information and communication technologies (ICT) to develop innovative tools and approaches in the tourism sector.[8] This idea builds on the concept of smart cities, where

[8] Smart tourism can be defined as the 'tourism supported by integrated efforts at a destination, to find innovative ways to collect and aggregate/harness data derived from physical infrastructure, social connections, government/organizational sources and human bodies/minds in combination with the use of advanced technologies to transform that data into enhanced experiences and business value-propositions with a clear focus on efficiency, sustainability and enriched experiences during the trip': see U Gretzel et al, 'Smart tourism: foundations and developments' (2015) 25 *Electronic Markets* 179. See also U Gretzel et al, 'Smart Tourism Challenges' (2015) 16 *Journal of Tourism* 41; World Tourism Organization (UNWTO), 'Guidelines for Institutional Strengthening of Destination Management Organizations (DMOs). Preparing DMOs for new challenges' (2019) 11, www.unwto.org/global/publication/unwto-guidelines-institutional-strengthening-destination-management-organizations-dmos-p, according to which a smart destination is based on the interaction of five elements: management, innovation, technology, accessibility and sustainability.

various integrated digital technologies, such as the Internet of Things (IoT), Artificial Intelligence (AI) and cloud computing, enable the management of urban resources.

This approach has gradually been adopted by tourism destinations, giving rise to so-called smart tourism destinations (STDs), a growing environment where different stakeholders[9] work together to improve the quality and efficiency of their services based on ICT.[10] Within a data-driven logic, these tools enable the administrations of tourist destinations and tour operators to gain valuable insights from collected data, improve their strategic view and planning capabilities, and create a stronger interaction with tourists' experience though personalised services, virtual reality, and real-time information.

From the perspective of data spaces, these various data-driven approaches must be contextualised within the legal framework for the protection of individual rights and freedoms, which, as mentioned above, is the first condition for the creation of trustworthy data spaces. In this respect, privacy and data protection issues play a key role[11] and are addressed in different ways in the Mediterranean region, but with a common core that also has a reference in Convention 108 of the Council of Europe.[12]

5.2.1. Data Sources and Nature of Data

When dealing with the tourism data space, it is first necessary to consider the specific characteristics of the industry and the data to be processed. In terms of data sources, relevant information for the tourism ecosystem comes from various sources along the entire tourism value chain. They can be grouped into three main clusters: user-generated content (UGC) created by tourists; location-based information; and service-related information.

UGC is information voluntarily shared by users through online platforms before, during and after travel. Reviews, photos and comments posted on social networks or specialised sites provide valuable insights into travellers'

[9] Destination management organisations (DMOs) should play a relevant role in coordinating such stakeholders; see also UNWTO (n 8) 12, where DMO is defined as 'the leading organizational entity which may encompass the various authorities, stakeholders and professionals and facilitates partnerships towards a collective destination vision'.

[10] See, eg, DZ Jovicic, 'From the Traditional Understanding of Tourism Destination to the Smart Tourism Destination' (2019) *Current Issues in Tourism*, www.tandfonline.com/doi/abs/10.1080/13683500.2017.1313203; R Baggio and G Del Chiappa, 'Real and Virtual Relationships in Tourism Digital Ecosystems' (2014) 14 *Information Technology & Tourism* 3–19, https://doi.org/10.1007/s40558-013-0001-5.

[11] See also MD Masseno and C Santos, 'Smart Tourism Destinations Privacy Risks on data protection – A first approach, from a European Perspective' (2018) 1 *Revista Eletrônica Sapere Aude* 126; CM Hall and Y Ram, 'Protecting privacy in tourism – a perspective article' (2019) *Tourism Review* 77.

[12] Sixteen Mediterranean countries are parties to Convention 108: Albania, Bosnia and Herzegovina, Croatia, Cyprus, France, Greece, Italy, Malta, Monaco, Montenegro, Morocco, Slovenia, Spain, Tunisia, Turkey and the United Kingdom.

preferences, habits and experiences. UGC can also include details of geographic location, spending capacity, reasons for travel and, in some cases, even household information.[13]

Location-based information mainly relates to the use of wearable devices and technologies that can collect information about the tourist's location via GPS, Wi-Fi, and Bluetooth features. This information is used both for specific applications, such as digital maps or virtual tours, and to improve the efficiency and overall quality of services offered through data mining and predictive analytics. In addition, information about tourist flows or main routes in a given space, such as a city, can be collected without relying on personal devices, using urban sensors such as those used for traffic monitoring.

Finally, service-related information includes digital transactions, such as reservations, online purchases, and the use of electronic tickets to access museums or public transport, which generate information relevant to the tourism sector,[14] not only for the provision of services and, in some cases, to comply with legal obligations, but also to optimise the services offered.[15] In this context, the same hospitality facilities can be transformed into data gathering tools that reveal tourists' habits (eg IoT systems for controlling lights, heating, air-conditioning, music; interactive devices for selecting dishes from restaurant menus[16]).

Having defined the macro-categories of data that can be included in the tourism data space, from a legal point of view and with the aim of establishing common rules to ensure the trust of both data subjects and operators in the future data space, it is important to look at the data governance rules, taking into account both the nature of the data processed and the operators involved in data processing.

The datasets generated by the different sources mentioned above contain both personal and non-personal data. For example, personal information may be collected when booking a hotel or a flight, or when renting a vehicle. Mobility data, when associated with a specific individual, must also be considered as personal data (eg data collected by car, bike or scooter rental companies) and can provide

[13] See also PwC et al, 'EU guide on data for tourism destinations' (2022) 8, https://smarttourism-destinations.eu/digital-library; Masseno and Santos (n 11) 255; HCM Senefonte et al, 'PredicTour: Predicting Mobility Patterns of Tourists Based on Social Media User's Profiles' (2022) 10 *IEEE Access* 9257–70; M Hort et al, 'Tourists Mobility on Social Media' (2018) 1 ff, https://computd.nl/wp-content/uploads/2019/12/Tourists_Mobility_on_Social_Media-1.pdf.

[14] See also A Mantelero, 'Data protection, e-ticketing, and intelligent systems for public transport' (2015) 4 *International Data Privacy Law* 311.

[15] For example, the recent EU Regulation (EU) No 2024/1028 introduced a requirement for online platforms that facilitate short-term accommodation rentals to periodically submit certain data to the relevant public authorities, including the number of guests and overnight stays for each unit. These measures aim to improve the transparency of the sector and promote sustainable tourism by regulating access to and provision of such services, as well as encouraging more effective management of tourist flows.

[16] See, eg, Inamo Restaurant, www.inamo-restaurant.com, and Hotel Lugano Dante, https://luganodante.com/it/hotel. On this topic, see also Masseno and Santos (n 11) 256–57.

information not only about tourists' itineraries in a given area and the most visited attractions, but also details about their preferences and social interactions.[17]

Special categories of personal data are also processed in the tourism sector,[18] not only in the case of medical tourism, but also in the context of more general services, such as health data or information revealing religious beliefs collected in order to offer personalised menus,[19] or information needed to assist passengers with reduced mobility. In addition, special categories of data may be inferred from information that is not classified as such. This is the case of mobility data collected by car rental companies or by geolocating smartphones and smartwatches, which may, in certain circumstances, reveal information about users' health conditions or religious/political orientations (eg mobility data showing regular visits to hospital centres or presence in a church or public space during a political meeting).[20]

In a more limited number of cases, biometric data can also be collected in the context of tourist activities (eg, facial recognition or fingerprint scanning systems, used to manage access to accommodation facilities[21]), but the limitations of the use of this category of data and the difficulties of including it in data spaces, due to the critical balancing test between data protection and economic interests, renders this category marginal in the current debate on data spaces.

Other datasets collected in the tourism sector do not directly identify individuals but make it possible to single them out and influence decisions about them.[22] This is the case of online profiling in relation to tourism services by online platforms that provide personalised offers and suggestions, in some cases combined with traditional profiling based on fidelity programmes.

Finally, it is worth noting that non-personal data also play a significant role in the tourism context. For example, information about a city, such as its streets, monuments and attractions, can be used to create virtual reality experiences.[23] In addition, data on the flow of people in specific areas, collected through sensors

[17] See also Autorité de Protection des Données (APD), Decision No 130/2024, 11 October 2024; Garante per la Protezione dei dati personali, 7 November 2013, No 499, Web Doc No 2911484.

[18] Even in the tourism sector, the mishandling of such data has led to negative consequences for those concerned, such as in case of discrimination; see PP Verhaeghe et al, 'Ethnic discrimination on the shared short-term rental market of Airbnb: evidence from a correspondence study in Belgium' (2023) 109 *International Journal of Hospitality Management* 103423; S Clemence, 'Black Travelers Say Home-Share Hosts Discriminate, and a New Airbnb Report Agrees' *The New York Times*, 13 December 2022, www.nytimes.com/2022/12/13/travel/vacation-rentals-racism.html.

[19] See also S Lučić, 'Protection of personal data in the tourism sector' (2023) 1 *Hotel and Tourism Management* 199. The COVID-19 pandemic has also highlighted how accommodation and transportation companies may be obliged to collect health data for reasons of public interest.

[20] See Mantelero (n 6) 311.

[21] See, eg, J Wang, 'You Can Now Check In With A Facial Scan At Marriott In China' (2018) *Forbes*, www.forbes.com/sites/jennawang/2018/07/24/you-can-now-check-in-with-a-facial-scan-at-marriott. See, also, Garante per la Protezione dei dati personali, 18 June 2015, No 360, web doc no 4170232.

[22] See Article 29 Data Protection Working Party, 'Opinion 4/2007 on the concept of personal data' WP 136 (2007) 14.

[23] L Edwards, 'Privacy, security and data protection in smart cities: a critical EU law perspective' (2016) 2 *European Data Protection Law Review* 28.

installed in streets and parks as well as inside museums, airports and train stations, are particularly useful for improving the organisation of spaces and tourist activities and services. These data, together with those collected by smart city traffic or air quality sensors, which are shared in aggregate form by public administrations for statistical purposes in the context of open data strategies,[24] can be further used for broader purposes, including the development of strategies for tourism activities.[25] Similarly, information on tourism flows, processed through data transmitted by accommodation facilities in a given destination, can play an important role in the development of tourism policies and business strategies.[26]

5.2.2. Actors Involved and Legal Bases

The complexity of the digital tourism ecosystem, due to its variety of data sources and the nature of the data, is also reflected in the variety of actors involved and purposes that drive them to play an active role in this ecosystem, as well as their future involvement in a more structured data space.

In this respect, public authorities and public administrations, both local and national, are interested in using tourist data to plan and allocate resources, improve the management of public services, such as public transport, and organise tourist activities, such as cultural events.[27] Similarly, private sector operators, such as restaurants and travel agencies, use this information to personalise their offers, optimise the scheduling of activities and provide additional services based on customer preferences.[28] Online booking platforms also use this type of data to modulate offers and adjust prices to demand. In addition, technology companies that develop software and digital solutions for tourism rely on this data to create tools that improve operators' efficiency, such as augmented reality applications or AI-based systems. Finally, tourists themselves benefit directly from this information by being able to make more informed choices about destinations and activities.[29]

[24] See also C Longhi, J-B Titz and L Viallis, 'Open Data: Challenges and Opportunities for the Tourism Industry' in MM Mariani et al (eds), *Tourism Management, Marketing, and Development: Volume I: The Importance of Networks and ICTs* (New York, Palgrave Macmillan US, 2014) 57–76, doi.org/10.1057/9781137354358_4; D Ordóñez-Martínez, JM Seguí-Pons and M Ruiz-Pérez, 'Toward Establishing a Tourism Data Space: Innovative Geo-Dashboard Development for Tourism Research and Management' (2024) 7 *Smart Cities* 633,doi.org/10.3390/smartcities7010026.

[25] See PwC (n 13) 6.

[26] Such data includes, for example, information collected and shared on short-term housing rental activities offered through online platforms, as required by EU Regulation (EU) 2024/1028.

[27] See PwC et al (n 13) 7.

[28] See M Kędzior and M Sadowska, 'General Data Protection Regulation: Opportunities and Risks of the Implementation of GDPR in Tourism' (2019) 25 *ACC Journal* 71; JF Fondevila Gascón et al, 'Social Media and Tourism: Case Study in Catalonia' (2016) 16 *Revista Científica Hermes* 115, 118; Massero and Santos (n 11) 253.

[29] See also Fondevila Gascón et al (n 28) 118.

This range of actors and interests, together with the complexity and variety of data flows in the tourism sector, call for careful data management in compliance with data protection regulations. This is key to harnessing the potential of information and developing tourism data spaces, while ensuring that the rights and freedoms of travellers are respected. In this context, the legal basis for data processing is the key element of the current digital ecosystem and the stepping stone for building the future data space.

The main legal bases that may justify the processing of personal data in this context are: the consent of the data subject; the necessity of processing for the performance of contractual or pre-contractual obligations; the fulfilment of legal obligations; and the legitimate interest of the data controller.[30] These legal bases are recognised, with some nuances, in the Mediterranean countries, with some exceptions regarding legitimate interest.

The most commonly used basis is the necessity of processing data for the performance of a contract or preliminary activities requested by the data subject. This includes, for example, the collection of identification and contact data necessary to complete a reservation for a hotel guest, a travel agency customer or a transportation company. The collection of banking data may also be justified when necessary to secure a reservation or to complete an online purchase, such as the data processing necessary to provide the user with a quote for a service.

On the other hand, data requested by the operator for activities of its own interest,[31] such as customer satisfaction questionnaires or periodic newsletters informing subscribers of new services and related offers, cannot be considered indispensable for executing the contract. In these cases, and in a broader context, an important legal basis for the processing of personal data is the consent of the data subject. This is particularly relevant for data collected with the aim of improving the management and efficiency of tourism services (as in the case of the use of personal information obtained through feedback questionnaires), as well as for monitoring purchasing habits and preferences in order to personalise offers.[32] Consent may also be essential for the processing of special categories of data (eg, data relating to health conditions collected to fulfil specific customer requests in accommodation facilities), as in the case of the General Data Protection Regulation (GDPR), where no other exceptions to the processing prohibition in Article 9 can usually[33] be applied in the tourism sector.

In these situations, tourism operators need to obtain the consent of data subjects before collecting personal data, taking care to list separate requests

[30] Art 6(1)(a), (b), (c) and (f) GDPR.

[31] Article 29 Data Protection Working Party, 'Opinion 06/2014 on the notion of legitimate interests of the data controller under Article 7 of Directive 95/46/EC' WP 217 (2014) 18 and 47.

[32] See EDPB, 'Guidelines 1/2024 on processing of personal data based on Article 6(1)(f) GDPR' (2024) 17; Article 29 Data Protection Working Party 2014 (n 31) 26.

[33] For example, during the COVID-19 pandemic accommodation facilities were required to collect data on guests' health, such as body temperature or vaccination status, in order to fulfil legal obligations justified by public health interests.

if the processing has different purposes. However, since consent must be free, specific, informed and unambiguous,[34] critical issues related to its validity may also arise in the context of tourism destinations. These issues include, for example, the freedom of the users to give consent when access to a service (eg booking a guided tour, admission to a museum) depends on consent for marketing purposes.[35]

The complexity increases with the widespread use of IoT devices, both those owned by tourists and those available at tourist destinations. In the case of IoT devices, the ability of data subjects to give consent[36] is often limited by the design of the system, which lacks an interface for user interaction and often by default collects and transmits large amounts of data to other devices in a network.[37] In some cases, the user may not even be aware of the presence of such devices and the processing of data, as in the case of sensors installed at cultural sites to monitor traffic or visitor flows.[38]

Given these limitations of traditional consent-based protection,[39] exacerbated by the device-based nature of IoT tools used in the tourism sector, effective lawfulness of processing can be ensured primarily through impact assessment and the data protection by design and by default approach.[40]

Looking at the other applicable legal bases, the processing of travellers' data may be justified by the need of the tour operator, as data controller, to satisfy a legitimate interest, provided that this interest overrides the rights and freedoms of the user. This includes, for example, the processing of personal data for direct marketing purposes or extrajudicial debt collection under certain circumstances.[41] The use of video surveillance and geolocation systems for reasons of security of

[34] See also Art 5 of the Council of Europe's Modernised Convention for the Protection of Individuals with Regard to the Processing of Personal Data (Amending protocol to the Convention for the Protection of Individuals with Regard to the Processing of Personal Data, adopted by the Committee of Ministers at its 128th Session in Elsinore on 18 May 2018).

[35] See also Art 7(4) GDPR; Article 29 Data Protection Working Party, 'Guidelines on consent under Regulation 2016/679' WP259rev.01 (2018) 6.

[36] Given the pervasive nature of data collection through such devices, the legal basis required to justify processing in this context is, in most cases, consent. See also Article 29 Data Protection Working Party, 'Opinion 8/2014 on the on Recent Developments on the Internet of Things' WP 22, (2014) 17.

[37] See, eg, AD Thierer, 'The Internet of things and Wereable Technology: Addressing Privacy and Security Concerns Without Derailing Innovation' (2015) 2 *Richmond Journal of Law & Technology* 60; SR Peppet, 'Regulating the Internet of Things: First Steps Toward Managing Discrimination, Privacy, Security, and Consent' (2014) 93 *Texas Law Review* 140.

[38] See WK Hon et al, 'Twenty Legal Considerations for Clouds of Thing' (2016) Queen Mary University of London, School of Law, Legal Studies Research paper no 216/2016, 23. See, also, Edwards (n 23) 28.

[39] See A Mantelero, 'The future of consumer data protection in the E.U. Re-thinking the "notice and consent" paradigm in the new era of predictive analytics' (2014) 30 *Computer Law & Security Review* 643; G von Westphalen, 'Individual Human Autonomy: The Rule of Law v. the Rules of Smart Technologies and their Inherent Manipulations' in A De Franceschi and R Schulze (eds), *Digital Revolution – New Challenges for Law* (Munich, Nomos, 2019) 108.

[40] See also V Mayer-Schönberger and Y Padua, 'Regime Change? Enabling Big Data through Europe's Data Protection Regulation' (2016) XVII *Columbia Science & Technology Law Review* 332.

[41] See Rec 47 GDPR; Article 29 Data Protection Working Party 2014 (n 31) 25.

persons or business assets is also justified by the legitimate interest of the owner (eg use of cameras to monitor access in a hotel or GPS systems in rented vehicles).

However, legitimate interest is often considered insufficient under data protection laws to justify the processing of special categories of data, for which the data subject's consent or another legal basis is required.[42] Moreover, processing involving invasive profiling activities or online tracking practices for advertising and marketing purposes is unlikely to be considered justified under this legal basis.[43]

Finally, the processing of tourists' data may be required to fulfil legal obligations imposed on the data controller. This is the case with information (such as first name, last name, date of birth, home address, and ID number) that accommodation operators must collect in order to notify public authorities and local governments of the presence of guests, for security reasons, or for the payment of tourist taxes. Similarly, the collection, storage and transmission of information required for bookkeeping and issuing invoices is justified.

5.3. Tourist Data, Governance Background: Key Principles and Challenges in an EU–Mediterranean Space

Despite the increasing use of data in the tourism sector, and despite the variety of processing operations and actors involved, as described in the previous section, there is a lack of specific policies and regulatory initiatives centred on tourist data at regional level. The localisation of tourist attractions and their strong link to the local socio-economic context make tourism strategies mainly a bottom-up process, from local to wider dimensions.

Municipalities and regional areas are the entities most involved in the development and exploitation of tourism, while the national and supranational levels focus more on coordination or common issues such as consumer protection, safety and security, and infrastructure development. The bottom-up approach and fragmentation are therefore the main characteristics of this data space.

In addition to these elements, two other features must be taken into account: the quality of the data and the reliability of the information provided. The technological and data management fragmentation,[44] the diversity of practices and the

[42] See eg, Art 9 GDPR and Council of Europe, 'Explanatory Report to the Protocol amending the Convention for the Protection of Individuals with regard to Automatic Processing of Personal Data' (2018) para 46.

[43] See Article 29 Data Protection Working Party, 'Guidelines on Automated individual decision-making and Profiling for the purposes of Regulation 2016/679' WP251rev.0 (2018) 16.

[44] See Council of the European Union, 'European Agenda for Tourism 2030, Council conclusions adopted on 01/12/2022' (2022) ('the tourism ecosystem is composed of several economic sectors, which have their own specific sectoral approaches, where over 99% are micro, small and medium-sized enterprises').

lack of common governance are some of the main factors in the Mediterranean area that have a negative impact on these two key requirements.

Against this background, the EU has recently outlined its initial strategy for a tourism data space.[45] This forms part of a broader EU strategy to promote the creation of 'a genuine single market for data, open to data from across the world', with the aim of overcoming legal and technical barriers to data sharing. This strategy is based on the following three key elements: (i) data sharing tools and platforms; (ii) data governance frameworks; and (iii) data availability, quality and interoperability.

The data space strategy responds to the increasing pressure on the EU in recent years in the field of digital services, where non-EU players have achieved a dominant position in the digital market while EU industry still plays a limited role in the digital economy. As data availability is crucial to the development of this sector and new industrial initiatives, the EU has recently adopted a more market-oriented approach to data sharing.[46] The main justification for this approach is based on the EU regulatory framework, which would make it possible to combine the free flow of data with the protection of fundamental rights.[47]

However, the key elements of EU data spaces and their potential openness to non-EU players underestimate the fact that, with the exception of the GDPR, the recent rush of EU rule-makers to regulate the digital society has resulted in many laws being put on the table, but it will take years to effectively implement this framework. This may become even more difficult in a global geopolitical scenario characterised by increasing fragmentation and the weakness of the EU digital industry.[48]

Moreover, the relevant shortcomings that a mature piece of legislation such as the GDPR still faces (eg, cumbersome cooperation procedures, diversity in the organisation of the Supervisory Authorities, etc) and its problem of effective enforcement[49] clearly show the existing tension between the regulatory level and its concrete implementation. Finally, the tension between the approach of the GDPR and more recent regulatory initiatives on data sharing (Regulation (EU) 2025/327 on the European Health Data Space)[50] not only shows a partial change

[45] European Commission, 'Communication from the Commission. Towards a Common European Tourism Data Space: boosting data sharing and innovation across the tourism ecosystem' [2023] C 263/01, https://eur-lex.europa.eu/legal-content/EN/TXT/?uri=oj:JOC_2023_263_R_0001. See also European Commission, Directorate General for Internal Market, Industry, Entrepreneurship and SMEs, *Transition Pathway for Tourism* (2022), https://data.europa.eu/doi/10.2873/344425.

[46] See also European Commission, 'Communication from the Commission to the European Parliament and the Council. Data Union Strategy. Unlocking data for AI' COM(2025) 835 final (2025).

[47] See also Art 1 GDPR.

[48] See n 6.

[49] See also European Commission, 'Communication from the Commission to the European Parliament and the Council. Second Report on the application of the General Data Protection Regulation' (2024), https://eur-lex.europa.eu/legal-content/EN/TXT/?uri=COM%3A2024%3A357%3AFIN&qid=1721897017650.

[50] See also EDPB and EDPS, 'Joint Opinion 03/2022 on the Proposal for a Regulation on the European Health Data Space' (2022), www.edpb.europa.eu/our-work-tools/our-documents/edpbedps-joint-opinion/edpb-edps-joint-opinion-032022-proposal_en.

in the EU digital policy framework, but may also raise serious concerns for the development of future data spaces, in terms of the conflict between data protection and other competing interests.[51]

These observations should lead to a consideration of the main precondition for data spaces, namely a harmonised legal framework where both personal and non-personal data, including sensitive business data, are secure, and fundamental rights are protected. This precondition might suggest going beyond the simplistic EU/non-EU dichotomy and focusing more on concrete conditions for the creation of data spaces outside of an EU-centric perspective based on GDPR adequacy decisions.

While it is true that some non-EU countries, including some in the Mediterranean region, provide a low level of protection of individual rights and data, this does not prevent the creation of data spaces based on mechanisms that do not focus solely on the regulatory framework provided by specific hard law instruments. Moreover, this approach is not uncommon in digital societies.[52]

The EU has specifically included the tourism sector in the data space initiative,[53] based on its wide array of new implemented digital regulations.[54] However, the lack of a similar legal framework for digital societies in non-EU Mediterranean countries and the considerations on its effectiveness expressed above limit the mere extension of this model beyond the EU borders and call for different strategies for the Mediterranean region.

The second pillar of the data space, ie the establishment of common technical standards, is also critical because of its dependence on the technological infrastructure. In this respect, the digital divide of small and medium enterprises (SMEs) and micro-enterprises in tourism has led many operators to outsource part of their data-driven activities to global/regional platforms, such as reservation management, and websites providing information on structures and prices, etc. While at the individual level this has a limited impact in terms of tourist data, the resulting global data collection – as is common in the case of online platforms – has significant added value for these platforms in terms of trend monitoring and forecasting, as well as individual and group profiling.

Given the role that major ICT players have in some segments (eg booking services), the creation of a tourist data space needs to take into account their position and to involve them in data space building, which also contributes to reducing the existing power imbalance between them and the rest of the small

[51] See also ch 6.

[52] See, eg, LA Bygrave, *Internet Governance by Contract* (Oxford, Oxford University Press, 2015).

[53] See European Commission (n 45). See also Council of the European Union (n 44), where the Council invites the Commission to 'support Member States and tourism stakeholders in implementing interoperable data-sharing practices'.

[54] For a list of those relevant in tourism sector, see European Commission (n 53) 6–8.

fragmented actors. On the one hand, they should share aggregated data, such as in the EU short-rent regulation, to provide added-value information to the other actors in the ecosystem and facilitate a broader view of relevant trends. On the other hand, their access to data space information should be managed so as not to increase their power, given their resources in terms of data analysis and value extraction.

There is therefore an issue of data stewardship and democratisation of the sector. Data spaces should facilitate the integration of small players, destination management organisations[55] (DMOs) and communities, in order to promote an alternative model to large platforms, which have shown their critical issues in terms of consumer protection, exploitative approach and massification of the tourist experience. In this sense, the valorisation of the Mediterranean environment and its outstanding socio-cultural resources can be better guaranteed by local initiatives than by globalised players, and so too citizen participation in the use of local resources for tourism purposes.

5.4. A Strategy for the Mediterranean Region

Based on the considerations expressed in the previous sections, what is the possible future scenario for a tourism data space in the Mediterranean region? There are some significant constraints both in terms of legal framework and technological infrastructure. Despite the presence of non-EU Mediterranean countries with data protection laws in force, some of which are also party to Convention 108 of the Council of Europe, there is a clear gap in regional harmonisation and, to some extent, effective protection of privacy and personal data between the two shores of the Mediterranean.

Technical harmonisation may be easier to achieve than the legal harmonisation, but even here there is a need for specific agreement on standards. On the other hand, the existing fragmentation facilitates the growing power of digital platforms, which fill the lack of technical standards and infrastructure with their proprietary solutions.

The two main building blocks that enable data spaces are data interoperability and data governance. Data interoperability is necessary to create the infrastructure for data space and to share and process data for the purposes associated with it. We can identify five main elements of this building block: (i) common semantics, data formats and interfaces (APIs); (ii) technologies that enable data exchange and sharing; (iii) a system for identifying participants and data assets; (iv) procedures

[55] A DMO is an entity formed through public–private partnerships between local authorities, the private tourism sector, and local communities. Its primary goal is the development and promotion of the specific tourist destination, maximising its attractiveness to tourists and ensuring a high-quality tourism experience. See also n 9.

for tracking data sharing and verifying compliance; and (v) value extraction technologies (AI, data analytics, interfaces, etc).

Data governance comprises several elements, namely: (i) policies for the data space; (ii) a governance infrastructure; and (iii) an identity and authorisation management. While the last two elements are contextual and depend on choices made when building the data space, the relevance of the first element (policies) is strictly related to the existing legal framework. The existence of an effective and detailed legal framework for data governance, covering all the relevant aspects such as personal data protection, data sharing, and cybersecurity, reduces the need for detailed policies.

Against this background, a centralised approach based on contractual tools, relying on existing legal and technological frameworks, is the main way for the Mediterranean EU states to set up the building blocks of the tourism data space, through various agreements that define the respective roles, and the rights and responsibilities of the data space participants.

However, for the reasons mentioned above, this model is not easily replicable throughout the Mediterranean region. It could be adopted at national level by some countries, but a regional data space involving EU and non-EU countries faces significant legal and technical barriers, exacerbated in some cases by the geopolitical situation. A Mediterranean data space should therefore be designed around a different decentralised architecture, based on data portability, citizen engagement, certifications, open-source solutions, and interoperability.

A bottom-up and decentralised approach makes it possible to use legal tools, such as the data subject's consent and data portability, to fill the gap created by the lack of a common legal framework, and not to limit the possible implementation of a Mediterranean data space to the EU adequacy model.[56] However, while consent and data portability may enable tourists to share their data within a data space, the rules for the functioning of this space need to be defined. Also in this case, instead of a centralised scheme, it is possible to use some soft law instruments that are open to new partners, such as codes of conduct and model templates that can build on existing best practices. The latter can also facilitate the development of reference taxonomies.

This new approach may not only facilitate the interaction between EU and non-EU entities and trust in projects, but also create a data space that is modular and scalable; not a single basket, but a searchable structure composed of different data sub-sets following specific local policies. Moreover, given the diversity of the Mediterranean region, sub-sets should also be considered where a horizontal analysis leads to a combination of datasets relating to different contexts that are not easily comparable.

[56] To date, Israel and the UK are the only states with non-EU Mediterranean territories to benefit from an adequacy decision.

In this scenario, citizen engagement, certification, and open-source solutions can play an important role in creating this common data space. A key element of the proposed bottom-up approach is the active role of the data subject. This means that it is crucial to present the benefits of data sharing while implementing appropriate transparency rules and procedures, as well as protecting the rights of individuals with regard to data processing. In this respect, several non-EU Mediterranean countries already have data protection rules in place, although better enforcement and protection is needed in several cases. However, also in line with the EU model, it is possible to rely on contractual agreements or consent for data transfer, in accordance with the proposed bottom-up approach.

Finally, to give coherence to this structure, it is necessary to combine the aforementioned harmonisation through contract templates, codes of conduct and best practices, with solutions regarding the technical pillar of the data space. Here, certifications and open-source technologies can facilitate the adoption of common solutions and also reduce the effort and cost of implementation, enabling the modular approach mentioned above, where clusters of municipalities, tourism operators and service providers can join forces and share the data space.

As in other fields, the richness and diversity of the Mediterranean region represents a resource in the case of tourist data, but also a challenge to strengthen interaction and cooperation. However, this complexity can also become an opportunity to critically rethink the EU approach and to stimulate different and complementary ways of enhancing collaboration between countries in this area characterised by common interests and interconnected relationships involving people and material and immaterial goods.

6

Health Data Sharing in the Mediterranean Context

MARIA BELÉN ANDREU MARTÍNEZ* AND CHAWKI GADDES**

6.1. Increased Protection for Health Data on both Shores of the Mediterranean

The issue of protecting health data and transferring it outside national borders is a challenge shared by countries on both sides of the Mediterranean. Although the Mediterranean is a natural frontier that should act as a barrier confining peoples to their national territory, since ancient times it has served as a bridge between these different shores, enabling an exchange of culture and common influences. Today, it continues to serve as a bridge between different national legal spaces that have converging orientations on issues as important as respect for human rights and the protection of the national sovereignty of States in a dematerialising world.

Emin Maalouf wrote in 'Le Périple de Baldassare' (2000) that 'A good captain turns the Atlantic into the Mediterranean; a bad captain turns the Mediterranean into the Atlantic'. It is therefore up to decision-makers and intellectuals on both sides of the Mediterranean to bring the two shores of this lake closer together around common issues and therefore common standards, including, in today's digitalised world, those relating to the exchange of personal data between these national areas.

The flow of people across this space necessarily leads to the exchange of personal data between these different legal spaces. Whether for tourism, study and research, business, health or migration purposes, people see their personal data accompany them and pass the legal protection of their national space to that of the host country. Among this personal data is a category that is described as sensitive, and which includes personal health data.

It has been noted that the countries on both sides of the Mediterranean have instituted a legal system for the protection of health data that guarantees the preservation of the rights of the persons concerned (6.1) coupled with a system

* Author of sections 6.3 and 6.4.
** Author of sections 6.1 and 6.2.

for the transfer of these data to other areas that subjects them to fairly restrictive conditions (6.2). There are also instruments to be envisaged for future collaboration in the exchange of health data between the two shores of the Mediterranean (6.3).

In relation to the first section, the legal regimes for the protection of personal data set up in the countries on the southern shore of the Mediterranean have been inspired by those that preceded them in European countries. These data are thus included in a specific category, that of sensitive data, which leads to the application of a significantly restrictive processing regime.

6.1.1. Health Data: Sensitive Data

All data protection regimes create a specific category of personal data known as sensitive data. Sensitive data is subject to a specific, more stringent protection regime based on the risks incurred by the data subjects as a result of its processing. The EU General Data Protection Regulation (GDPR) identifies 'risks to the rights and freedoms of natural persons' for the processing of such data.[1]

On the southern shore of the Mediterranean, not all legal frameworks for the protection of personal data address health data in the same way. Algeria's data protection law, drafted after the adoption of the GDPR in 2016, defines what health data is.[2] Algeria is the only country south of the Mediterranean to have determined the meaning of 'health data'. No other national legislation has included a definition of health data.

The Algerian definition is clearly inspired by Article 4(15) of the GDPR. The distinctive elements of the concept of health data are found in the text of the law and revolve around the physical or mental situation of the person concerned. The difference from the GDPR is that Algerian law has omitted to include 'the provision of healthcare services'.

Revisions to national laws in southern countries, which are expected to bring them closer to the European regulation, will likely include a definition of health data in the near future. Currently, the legal frameworks of the southern Mediterranean countries include health data in the category of sensitive data.

[1] See Rec 75 GDPR ('Risks to the rights and freedoms of natural persons, of varying degrees of probability and seriousness, may arise from the processing of personal data which is likely to result in physical or material damage or psychological harm, in particular: where the processing may give rise to discrimination').

[2] See Art 3 ('For the purposes of this Act … "Data relating to health" means any information concerning the physical and/or mental state of the person concerned, including his or her genetic data'). All the articles cited in the footnotes have been translated into English by the authors.

Article 1 of the 2008 Moroccan law defines sensitive data[3] and expressly includes health data, but the law does not include a definition of health data. Neighbouring Algeria has also included health data as sensitive data in the definition included in Article 3 of the 2018 law.[4] The Tunisian Organic Law of 2004 reserves an entire section for the processing of health data, but does not define it in any of its provisions. Instead, it includes health data in the broad category of sensitive data.[5] On the other hand, the Egyptian law of 2020, while not defining health data, does include it in the category of sensitive data.[6] The Lebanese law of 2018 dealing with the protection of personal data is silent on this category of data, and the Syrian law of 2024 simply lists health data as one of those considered sensitive[7] without providing any further details.

6.1.2. Health Data still Subject to a Binding Authorisation Processing Regime

The inclusion of personal health data in the category of sensitive data will make the processing of such data in southern Mediterranean countries subject to a heightened protection regime. Some countries apply a general prohibition on the processing of such data, similar to that introduced by Article 9 of the GDPR.[8]

This is the case in Article 14 of the Tunisian law,[9] Article 18 of the Algerian law,[10] Article 12 of the Egyptian law,[11] and Article 13 of the Syrian law.[12]

[3] See Art 1 ('For the purposes of this Act, the following definitions shall apply: 3. "sensitive data": personal data revealing … or relating to his health, including his genetic data').

[4] See Art 3 ('For the purposes of this Act … "sensitive data" means personal data … relating to his health, including his genetic data').

[5] See Art 14 ('The processing of personal data relating, directly or indirectly … to health … is prohibited').

[6] See Art 1 ('In the application of the provisions of this Personal Data Protection Law ("Law"), the following terms shall have the meaning ascribed to them: … "Sensitive Personal Data": shall mean data which discloses psychological, mental, or physical health, or genetic').

[7] See Art 1 ('Sensitive personal data: For the purposes of this Act, the following terms and concepts shall be understood to mean: … any data which provides information about the individual's psychological, mental, physical or genetic state of health').

[8] See Art 9 ('Processing of special categories of personal data. 1. The processing of personal data revealing … data concerning the health or data concerning the sex life or sexual orientation of a natural person shall be prohibited').

[9] See n 8.

[10] See Art 18 ('The processing of sensitive data is prohibited').

[11] See Art 12 ('The Controllers and Processors, whether a natural or juristic person, are prohibited from collecting, transferring, storing, saving, Processing or disclosing Sensitive Personal Data except by virtue of a license issued from the Center').

[12] See Art 13 ('The controller or processor, whether a natural or legal person, shall be prohibited from processing sensitive personal data without the authorisation or declaration of the Authority').

The Moroccan law is the only one that does not introduce a derogation to limit the processing of health data.

This prohibition is not absolute and may be overridden by subjecting the processing of such sensitive data to more restrictive conditions. Article 9(2) of the GDPR, which establishes a similar prohibition, provides for a number of exceptions (consent, legal obligation, vital interests of a person, legitimate activities, public nature of the data, defence of a right in legal proceedings, public interest, preventive and occupational medicine, public health interest or for archival purposes in the public interest, scientific or historical research or statistics). This is the case for the laws of the southern Mediterranean countries.

The difference from the derogations introduced by the GDPR is that the laws of the southern Mediterranean countries make such processing subject to authorisation by the data protection authority, a procedure that disappeared in the European area with the introduction of the accountability principle. However, France's Data Protection Act still requires prior authorisation for the processing of health data, except in certain specific situations. Article 65 lists six situations in which the processing of health data does not require prior authorisation from the Commission nationale de l'informatique et des libertés (CNIL).[13]

In countries south of the Mediterranean, data controllers are generally required to submit an application for authorization, or at least a prior declaration.This is the case in Article 21[14] of the Moroccan law, which requires authorisation, but allows certain health data processing operations to be subject to a simple declaration in Article 22.[15] Article 18[16] of the Algerian law makes all sensitive data subject to authorisation. This applies if, after examining the declaration, it is determined that the data to be processed 'poses a clear threat to the right to privacy and the fundamental rights and freedoms of individuals', as is the case with health data.

[13] See Art 65 Data Protection Act, which refers to studies carried out by staff responsible for monitoring; bodies responsible for health insurance; doctors responsible for medical information; regional health agencies; the state; and public persons responsible for the design, monitoring or evaluation of public policies in the field of health.

[14] See Art 21 ('1. the processing of sensitive data is subject to authorisation by law, which lays down the conditions. Failing this, it must be authorised by the National Commission').

[15] See Art 22 ('Notwithstanding the provisions of Article 21 above, the processing of data relating to health is subject to a declaration to the National Commission, where its sole purpose is: (preventive medicine, medical diagnosis, the administration of care or treatment or the management of health services … to select persons likely to benefit from a right, benefit or contract)').

[16] See Art 18(2) ('the processing of sensitive data may be authorised for reasons of public interest which are essential to guarantee the performance of the legal or statutory functions of the controller or where the data subject has given his express consent, in the case of a legal provision to that effect or with the authorisation of the national authority').

The Tunisian legal framework is laconic in this respect, even though the law reserves a specific section for the processing of health data, which provides for authorisation from the authority for the communication of health data, but not for other processing. On the other hand, Article 11 of Decree no 2007–3004 of 27 November 2007, setting out the conditions and procedures for declaration and authorisation,[17] states that the processing of health data is subject to a request for prior authorisation from the National Authority for the Protection of Personal Data.

The Egyptian law does not deal specifically with health data. However, Article 26[18] requires authorisation for the processing of sensitive data. Finally, the Syrian law does not impose any specific procedures for processing health data, but Article 5[19] requires authorisation to be obtained for any processing of sensitive data.

The legal frameworks of Europe and southern Mediterranean countries both indicate that the processing health data poses a significant risk to the rights of the individuals concerned. Faced with this major challenge, health data has been included in the category of sensitive data. This classification means that, as a matter of principle, the processing of such data is prohibited, which is an exception to the general theory of data protection that merely seeks to provide a framework for such processing.

This approach requires specific conditions and procedures to be implemented for such processing. Health data is therefore subject to a system of protection that makes it possible to guarantee the rights of the data subjects within the national territory, but requires specific measures to be put in place when the data migrates outside of national borders.

6.2. Communication and Transfer Abroad Subject to Restrictive Conditions

In the digital world, the sovereign borders of states cannot remain hermetic; they are technically porous. Cross-border data flows undermine the protection of health data provided by national legal systems.

[17] See Art 11 ('Authorisation must also be obtained from the national personal data protection authority before the following operations are carried out: … the processing of personal data which relates directly or indirectly to racial or genetic origins, religious beliefs, political, philosophical or trade union opinions or health').

[18] See Art 26 ('The Center shall issue Licenses, Permits, or Certifications, as follows: … 6. Issue Licenses or Permits for the control and Processing of Sensitive Personal Data').

[19] See Art 5 ('A. Taking into account the provisions of Articles 13 and 40 of this law, the controller undertakes to …: 4. obtain authorisation or a declaration from the authority for the processing of personal data').

Health data crosses national borders and the Mediterranean in both directions for a variety of reasons. For example, it is clear that the data hosting services offered by companies in countries north of the Mediterranean are more attractive to data controllers in the south. But the movement of people between the two shores is not only limited to the physical journey of the person concerned, but also to that of their personal data, including their health data. Finally, research in the field of health is increasingly established in a spirit of cooperation between the different programmes and teams, which necessarily leads to an exchange of health data between the two shores of the Mediterranean.

It should not be forgotten that the transfer of data is one of the concerns of data protection systems. This is highlighted in Recital 6 of the GDPR, which states that technology 'should further facilitate the free flow of personal data within the Union and their transfer to third countries and international organisations, while ensuring a high level of protection of personal data'.

For all these reasons, the legal systems of both Europe and the countries of the southern Mediterranean, which cannot be designed in isolation, impose specific conditions and procedures for transferring data outside their sovereign territory. This poses a major challenge, especially when it comes to hosting data abroad, but also when it comes to transferring data outside the national territory to partners or subcontractors.

6.2.1. Measures to Ensure that Transferred Health Data Continue to Enjoy Adequate Protection

The concern of national data protection bodies is to ensure that once personal health data has been transferred abroad, it continues to benefit from a protection regime that is at least equivalent to that in place at national level.[20] This is one of the fundamental principles of the GDPR, which devotes an entire chapter (Chapter V) to this subject,[21] with a separate article for each condition of transfer. The country of destination must either benefit from an adequacy decision,[22] or the transfer must be carried out in accordance with appropriate safeguards[23] or binding company rules.[24] Furthermore, Article 48 provides for transfers 'based on an international agreement'. Any transfer that does not comply with these rules will result in significant penalties for the data controller, as set out in Article 83(5) of the GDPR.

[20] See also Rec 101 GDPR ('transfers to third countries and to international organisations may only take place in full compliance with this Regulation').

[21] See also Art 12 Council of Europe's Convention 108 and Art 14 Modernised Convention for the Protection of Individuals with Regard to the Processing of Personal Data (Amending protocol to the Convention for the Protection of Individuals with Regard to the Processing of Personal Data, 2018).

[22] See Art 45 GDPR.

[23] See Art 46 GDPR.

[24] See Art 47 GDPR.

The legal bodies of the southern Mediterranean countries have also laid down similarly strict conditions for the transfer of data, accompanied by significant penalties for data controllers who fail to comply. Tunisia has also introduced a ban on the transfer of personal data to a foreign country when this is 'likely to harm public security or the vital interests of Tunisia'.[25] This is also the case under Algerian law.[26]

However, all the southern Mediterranean countries make the transfer of personal data conditional in principle, and impose significantly restrictive procedures for carrying out this operation. Morocco[27] and Algeria[28] make the transfer of personal data conditional on proof of 'sufficient' protection in the destination country. Tunisia[29] makes the transfer conditional on the destination country providing 'adequate' protection. Egypt[30] makes the transfer conditional on the destination country having put in place protection that 'meets' or 'exceeds' the requirements of its national law. Lastly, Syria[31] makes the transfer conditional on prior verification of the level of protection in place.

It is therefore clear that the transfer can only take place if the country of destination has implemented a level of protection that is at least equivalent to that provided for by the personal data protection law. This ensures that the transferred data is protected in the destination country to the same extent as in the country of origin.

The laws of countries south of the Mediterranean include certain provisions that specify the criteria for assessing whether data protection in the destination country is sufficient, adequate or similar. Article 43 of the Moroccan law[32] specifies that this assessment is made on the basis of the legal framework of the country of destination, the security of the data and its nature. As far as Algeria is concerned, Article 44[33] of the

[25] See Art 50 ('It is prohibited in all cases to communicate or transfer personal data to a foreign country when this is likely to affect public security or the vital interests of Tunisia').

[26] See Art 44 ('The communication or transfer of personal data to a foreign country is prohibited in all cases where such transfer is likely to harm public security or the vital interests of the State').

[27] See Art 43 ('The controller may transfer personal data to a foreign State only if that State ensures an adequate level of protection of the privacy and fundamental rights and freedoms of individuals with regard to the processing of which such data are or may be the subject').

[28] See Art 44 ('The controller of a processing operation may only transfer personal data to a foreign State with the authorisation of the national authority, in accordance with the provisions of this law, and only if that State ensures an adequate level of protection of the privacy and fundamental rights and freedoms of individuals with regard to the processing of which such data are or may be the subject').

[29] See Art 51 ('Personal data undergoing processing or intended for processing may be transferred to another country only if that country ensures an adequate level of protection').

[30] See Art 14 ('Transfer of Personal Data which is collected or prepared for Processing, to a foreign country, or its storage or sharing may only be undertaken if the level of data protection or security in the foreign country meets (or exceeds) the requirements stipulated under this Law, and subject to obtaining a relevant License or Permit from the Center').

[31] See Art 15 ('It is prohibited to transfer personal data that have been collected or prepared for processing or recorded or communicated to an Arab or foreign State unless the authority verifies the acceptable level of protection and authorises it').

[32] See Art 43(2) ('The adequacy of the level of protection provided by a State shall be assessed, in particular, in the light of the provisions in force in that State, the security measures applied there, the specific characteristics of the processing operation such as its purposes and duration, and the nature, origin and destination of the data processed').

[33] See Art 44 ('The adequacy of the level of protection provided by a State shall be assessed by the national authority in particular in the light of the legal provisions in force in that State, the security measures applicable there, the specific characteristics of the processing operation such as its purposes and duration, and the nature, origin and destination of the data processed').

law repeats the same Moroccan provision. Article 51[34] of the Tunisian law stipulates that the possibility of transfer shall be assessed in the light of the nature of the data to be transferred, the purposes for which it is to be processed and its duration, as well as the country of destination and the security measures put in place for the transfer. Article 14[35] of the Egyptian law delegates the determination of transfer conditions to a regulatory decree implementing the law. The Syrian law[36] simply makes the transfer of data conditional on the destination country having a law that provides similar protection for personal data on its territory.

The requirement for the protection put in place in the destination country to be at least equivalent to that in the country of origin of the personal data is subject to an exception in most southern Mediterranean countries relating to the transfer of health data. This is the case under Article 44[37] of the Moroccan law, which states that data may be transferred even if the country of destination does not have adequate protection for personal data when the purpose is to safeguard the life of the person concerned or the prevention, diagnosis or treatment of medical conditions. The same derogation with the same terms is transposed in Article 45[38] of the Algerian law. Article 15[39] of the Egyptian law recommends the same approach, as does Article 15[40] of the Syrian law.

[34] See Art 51 ('The transfer to another country of personal data undergoing processing or intended for processing may only take place if that country ensures an adequate level of protection assessed in the light of all the elements relating to the nature of the data to be transferred, the purposes of their processing, the duration of the processing envisaged, and the country to which the data will be transferred as well as the necessary precautions implemented to ensure the security of the data').

[35] See Art 14 ('The Executive Regulations of this Law shall set out the policies, criteria, regulations and rules necessary for transferring, storing, sharing, Processing or disclosing Personal Data across borders and the protection thereof').

[36] See Art 16 ('The controller or processor may, as the case may be, communicate personal data to another controller or processor outside the Syrian Arab Republic, with an authorisation from the authority, when the following conditions are met: … c. The level of legal and technical protection of personal data at the controller or processor located abroad is at least equal to the level determined in the regulations implementing this law').

[37] See Art 44 ('By way of derogation from the provisions of Article 43 above, the controller of a processing operation may transfer personal data to a State which does not meet the conditions laid down in the above article, if the person to whom the data relate has expressly consented to their transfer or: 1. if the transfer is necessary: a. to protect the life of that person; … g. for the prevention, diagnosis or treatment of medical conditions').

[38] See Art 45 ('By way of derogation from the provisions of article 44 of this law, the controller of a processing operation may transfer personal data to a State which does not meet the conditions laid down in the said article: 1 if the data subject has expressly consented to the transfer; 2 if the transfer is necessary: a. to safeguard the life of the data subject; … g. for the prevention, diagnosis or treatment of medical conditions').

[39] See Art 15 ('Notwithstanding Article (14) of this Law, if the explicit consent of the Data Subject or his representative is obtained, transferring, sharing, circulating or Processing Personal Data may take place without the required minimum level protection stipulated in the previous article, in the following cases: 1. to preserve the life of the Data Subject and provide him/her with medical care or treatment or the management of health services').

[40] See Art 15 ('b. It is permitted, in the case of the express consent of the person concerned or who represents him, to transfer or exchange or process personal data to a State which does not guarantee a level of protection indicated in the previous article, in the following situations: 1. the preservation of the life of the person concerned, providing him with medical care, treatment or the management of health services').

The laws of countries south of the Mediterranean establish a procedural condition for transferring data abroad. This generally involves requesting prior authorisation from the national supervisory authority. The Moroccan law does not contain a specific provision requiring authorisation for the transfer of data abroad, but the national data protection authority has put a specific authorisation request form online. Article 44 of Algeria's law[41] requires authorisation to be sought for any transfer of data abroad. Tunisia does the same in Article 52 of its law.[42] The same applies to Article 16 of the Egyptian law[43] and Article 15[44] of the Syrian law.

6.2.2. Obligation to Host Health Data on National Territory

Personal data may be transferred to another country for processing in the interests of the data subject. However, personal data is increasingly transferred simply for the purpose of hosting. Problems can also arise in this case regarding ensuring that the hosting provider used is in a country that provides similar protection conditions to those in place in the country of origin.

In general, data protection laws do not include specific provisions for this situation. However, these operations can not only infringe the rights of the individuals concerned, but also undermine the sovereignty of the relevant states. Indeed, citizens' data sheds light on their situation in various fields, providing strategic information also relating to the state. When sensitive data is involved, this can further increase the risk of data leaks and their use either by foreign states or by economic organisations.

National legislation in southern Mediterranean countries makes no specific provision for the use of the cloud abroad, and includes this as part of the transfer of data to a third country. However, Tunisia has taken a position on this specific treatment, motivated by the need to preserve national sovereignty, especially when

[41] See Art 44 ('The data controller may transfer personal data to a foreign State only with the authorisation of the national authority, in accordance with the provisions of this law, and only if that State ensures an adequate level of protection of the privacy and fundamental rights and freedoms of individuals with regard to the processing of which such data are or may be the subject').

[42] See Art 52 ('In all cases, it is compulsory to obtain authorisation from the Authority to transfer personal data abroad').

[43] See Art 16 ('Controller or Processor, as the case may be, may disclose Personal Data to another Controller or Processor outside the Arab Republic of Egypt by virtue of a License from the Center provided that the following conditions are met: 1. if there is conformity between the nature of work of each of the Controllers or Processors, or unity of the purpose for which they obtain the Personal Data; 2. if each of the Controllers, the Processors, or the Data Subject, have a legitimate interest in the Personal Data; and 3. the level of legal and technical protection of the Personal Data provided by the Controller or the Processor abroad shall not be less than the level of protection provided in the Arab Republic of Egypt. The Executive Regulations of this Law shall determine the necessary conditions, procedures, precautions, criteria, and rules in this regard').

[44] See n 36.

it comes to health data. Article 63[45] of the Personal Data Protection Bill 2018 prohibits any hosting of health data abroad, requiring data controllers to do so with national hosts.

This policy has not yet been enshrined in a positive applicable text, but it has necessitated the issue of a circular by the Head of Government in 2020,[46] which obliged all public structures to host the data they process exclusively on national territory. As part of this provision, the National Cyber Security Agency, in accordance with Article 12[47] of Legislative Decree 2023-17, is labelling national cloud providers as G-cloud for government hosting providers and N-cloud for hosting providers for private operators. A list of approved hosting providers is published on the Agency's website.

6.3. Convergence with the European Model for Building a Mediterranean Health Data Space

As has been explained above, there are common elements in the regulations from both sides of the Mediterranean in relation to health data protection. Although a definition of 'health data' has generally not been included in the southern Mediterranean countries' legislations (nor was it included in the old Directive 95/46/EC), greater protection of health data is instituted through its inclusion as sensitive data in these regulations.

In addition, international data transfers in both cases require a level of protection in the destination country equivalent to that of the country of origin, over and above any additional conditions that may be set, particularly in southern countries, such as the need to obtain prior authorisation.

These elements constitute an important starting point for a potential greater collaboration in the exchange of health data between the two shores of the Mediterranean Sea. Moving towards this greater collaboration, and even towards common data spaces that allow a flow of people (tourism, migration, studies, etc) together with their data (including health data), means knowing the current requirements for such transfers at European level, basically those imposed in the GDPR and the possibilities offered by the European Health Data Space (EHDS). Moreover, it is interesting to know what instruments are available to citizens in

[45] See Art 63 Personal Data Protection Bill of 8 March 2018 ('It is prohibited to host personal data relating to health outside Tunisian territory').

[46] Circular from the Head of Government number 24 of November 2020 ('Host websites and electronic service platforms in hosting centres on national territory').

[47] See Art 12 ('The Agency awards, renews and withdraws the "Government Cloud Service Provider (G-cloud)" label and the "National Cloud Service Provider (N-cloud)" label from hosting service providers after receiving the opinion of the Ministers for National Defence and the Interior').

order to manage their health data and share it with third parties, beyond the creation of a common data space.

6.3.1. The Demanding GDPR Regime Applied to International Transfers of Health Data in the Mediterranean Area

If we think of data transfers at the institutional level of public health services, today they have to comply with very strict requirements that certainly make them complex. Both European regulations and those of the southern Mediterranean countries include a requirement for an equivalent level of protection in the destination country.

With regard to north–south data flows, adequacy decisions based on Article 45 of the GDPR allow international transfers to be treated as intra-Community data processing. Currently, however, none of the countries on the southern shore of the Mediterranean area is in this situation.[48]

In order to benefit from this possibility, it is essential to continue working in the medium term on the following aspects: (1) further legislative approximation, which can undoubtedly benefit from the gradual reform of data protection regulations in the southern Mediterranean countries; and (2) the development, where appropriate, of other mechanisms establishing the practical effectiveness of the regulations themselves (existence of an independent supervisory authority, effective remedies and sanctions, etc)[49] which are taken into account in assessing the equivalent level of protection.

It should be noted that some of these countries, such as Tunisia and Morocco, have ratified the Council of Europe Convention 108 for the Protection of Individuals with regard to Automatic Processing of Personal Data, which places them in an advanced position in their commitment to data protection.

Indeed, these advances at a regulatory level facilitate the use of other options provided for by the GDPR for international transfers, such as legally binding and enforceable instruments between public authorities or bodies (international agreements), which Article 46(2)(a) of the GDPR regulates with the appropriate safeguards. Such agreements seem more feasible between countries for which, due to the importance of flows of people (in terms of migration, tourism or other) or cultural proximity (particularly with France), collaboration entails significant benefits for the parties.[50]

[48] https://commission.europa.eu/law/law-topic/data-protection/international-dimension-data-protection/adequacy-decisions_en.

[49] See Art 45(2) GDPR.

[50] The agreement between the Kingdom of Spain and the Kingdom of Morocco on cooperation in security matters and the fight against crime (concluded in Rabat on 13 February 2019) is an example of this, although it does not concern the field of health. Official Journal of the Spanish State No 83 of 7 April 2022, www.boe.es/eli/es/ai/2019/02/13/(2).

In any event, these instruments will have to incorporate the minimum guarantees to ensure a level of protection equivalent to that of the GDPR if they are to be signed by the European countries.[51] Compared with the adequacy decision, the international convention has the 'advantage' of having a more restricted scope (territorially, by sector, etc) in order to facilitate its adoption, and thus initiate the first steps towards collaboration on international data transfer between public authorities in certain northern and southern Mediterranean countries.

In the case of private entities (eg, private hospitals that are part of groups of companies; or pharmaceutical companies), the GDPR offers other possibilities, such as binding corporate rules based on Articles 46(2)(b) and 47,[52] or codes of conduct with binding and enforceable commitments.[53] In addition, data exports between individual controllers and/or processors may be carried out in accordance with standard data protection clauses approved by either the European Commission or a supervisory authority, pursuant to Article 46(2)(c)–(d) of the GDPR.[54] However, these instruments are limited in scope to specific actors and their usefulness is therefore secondary to an institutional collaboration between countries or to the construction of a future common data space in the Mediterranean area (even if limited to certain countries or sectors).

6.3.2. Opening Up the European Health Data Space to Third Countries

Beyond the general rules applicable to international data transfers, the possibilities offered by the new EHDS are of particular interest to the healthcare sector. The EHDS, in fact, addresses an internal problem of health data sharing within the EU. Despite the unifying function of the GDPR, its openness to national legislation (in particular, Article 9(4) for health data)[55] has led to a regulatory diversity that

[51] European Data Protection Board Guidelines 2/2020 on articles 46 (2) (a) and 46 (3) (b) of Regulation 2016/679 for transfers of personal data between EEA and non-EEA public authorities and bodies.

[52] See, for example, those approved for the Kumon Europe & Africa Limited, SA group (www.aepd.es/documento/ti-00002-2021-resolucion-aprobacion-bcr-e-kumon.pdf), although not for health, but for education.

[53] See Arts 46(2)(e) and 40 GDPR. See also Opinion 12/2024 on the draft decision of the French Supervisory Authority regarding the 'Code of Conduct for Service Providers in Clinical Research' submitted by EUCROF (18 June 2024): www.edpb.europa.eu/our-work-tools/our-documents/opinion-board-art-64/opinion-122024-draft-decision-french-supervisory_en; Code of Conduct regulating the processing of personal data in clinical trials and other clinical research and pharmacovigilance activities (10 February 2022): www.edpb.europa.eu/our-work-tools/accountability-tools/register-codes-conduct-amendments-and-extensions-art-4011_en?page=0 (the latter is at national level).

[54] Those approved by the European Commission are contained in Commission Implementing Decision (EU) 2021/914 of 4 June 2021, http://data.europa.eu/eli/dec_impl/2021/914/oj.

[55] It should not be forgotten that Member States retain competence for health policy and the organisation and delivery of health services and medical care (Art 168(7) TFEU).

poses obstacles to the exchange of data within the EU, particularly for secondary purposes (eg scientific research).

Regulation EU 2025/237[56] ('EHDS Regulation') aims to overcome these obstacles in order to create a common space (rules, infrastructures, standards and a governance system) enabling access to certain categories of electronic health data at EU level for primary use (provision of healthcare) and secondary use (policy-making and regulatory activities to support public sector bodies/scientific research related to health or care sectors, etc).[57]

Although it is a system designed for the access and exchange of health data at European level, the infrastructures envisaged for primary use (MyHealth@EU) and secondary use (HealthData@EU) allow third countries to be included as authorised participants, following approval by means of an implementing act of the European Commission.[58] In fact, it is firstly necessary to comply with the rules set out in the GDPR on international data transfers (Chapter V, as clarified the text of the EHDS Regulation). In addition, the legal, organisational, operational, semantic, technical and cybersecurity requirements set out in the EHDS Regulation for primary use (Chapter I) or secondary use (Chapter IV) must be complied with and, in the latter case, EU users must have access, under equivalent conditions, to the data available in data access bodies in third countries.

As can be seen, compliance with the GDPR rules on international data transfers is the gateway to the EHDS, but access as a participant in turn requires compliance with a number of additional requirements (legal, organisational, technical, etc) of the EHDS itself. These are quite demanding; currently, many European countries are not in a position to implement them. The system for primary use of health data is much more developed,[59] as it has its antecedents in the work of the eHealth network created by Article 14 of Directive 2011/24/EU,[60] while secondary use requires, among other things, the creation of data lakes, secure processing environments and the new governance framework, which few European countries have developed to date. This explains the different deadlines for the entry into force of this Regulation, which has also been extended to 10 years[61] for the third-country access provided for in Article 75(5).

The participation of third countries is more feasible for primary use, as the direct impact on people's healthcare (and therefore the political justification) is more obvious in this case. However, these third countries will need to make a firm

[56] Regulation (EU) 2025/327 of the European Parliament and of the Council of 11 February 2025 on the European Health Data Space and amending Directive 2011/24/EU and Regulation (EU) 2024/2847).

[57] See Art 1(1) EHDS Regulation.

[58] See Arts 24(3) and 75(5) EHDS Regulation.

[59] https://health.ec.europa.eu/ehealth-digital-health-and-care/electronic-cross-border-health-services_en.

[60] https://health.ec.europa.eu/ehealth-digital-health-and-care/eu-cooperation/ehealth-network_en.

[61] See Art 105 EHDS Regulation.

commitment to the technological development of the healthcare sector, including a previous implementation of tools such as electronic health records (EHR) or web portals for patients, as well as electronic identification systems, among others, insofar as the EHDS relates to 'electronic' health data, as defined in Article 2(2)(c) of the EHDS Regulation.

By contrast, certain elements of the EHDS Regulation may be useful for the future collaboration or participation of third countries:

- The exchange of data for primary use is limited to certain priority categories of data listed in Article 14(1) of the EHDS Regulation (although states may extend it). The complete EHR of individuals are therefore not concerned. This makes it possible to work *ex novo* on creating an infrastructure solely for this information (patient summaries, medical imaging studies, medical test results, discharge reports, etc), which, of course, must be digitised. This will subsequently allow for an external exchange, subject to compliance with legal requirements.[62]
- Some elements of standardisation are foreseen in the EHDS Regulation, which are necessary, inter alia, to ensure data interoperability, security and logging and, at the same time, may facilitate the work of third countries in exchanging information with the EU. For example, the European electronic health record exchange format (Article 15) and the harmonised software components that enable EHR systems to be placed on the market or put into service in the EU must comply with the provisions set out in Chapter III. This will encourage manufacturers to offer systems that comply with EHDS requirements.

On the other hand, it should be noted that the EHDS does not distinguish between public and private healthcare service providers, so that the latter can also access (in accordance with the requirements of the EHDS Regulation) the exchange system of health data for primary use.

6.3.3. Individual-level Instruments as the First Step in Health Data Sharing

In addition to the exchange of health data that may be carried out by healthcare service providers (public or private), the EHDS also incorporates a strong patient empowerment element, resulting in the recognition of a set of rights for the management of their electronic health data. We are particularly interested here in

[62] This is what has happened, for example, in a country with a decentralised healthcare system like Spain (with 18 different healthcare services, each with its own regulations and EHR systems). In collaboration with the Spanish Ministry of Health, a national health system's EHR has been launched, enabling a limited amount of health data, very similar to that covered by the EHDS, to be shared between the various regional health services. This in turn will enable this data to be shared at European level as part of the EHDS.

the provisions that complement the rights already included in the GDPR, such as the right of access or the right to data portability.[63]

Article 3 of the EHDS Regulation provides for a right to access (in addition to that already laid down in the GDPR) to at least the priority categories of electronic health data referred to in Article 14(1). Access must be immediate (through the electronic health data access services), free of charge, and in an easily readable, consolidated and accessible format. This right is supplemented by the possibility of downloading an electronic and free of charge copy in the European electronic health record exchange format.

This offers numerous possibilities for individuals to have and 'travel' with their health data in a north–south direction. However, leaving the possibility of using paper copies aside, electronic copying poses significant challenges. It is a copy in a format (European electronic health record exchange format) designed to be recognised and accepted throughout the EU. This raises a question as to what extent it will be exportable to third countries (not integrated into the EHDS) and also in relation to the technical resources that will be required. The autonomy envisaged for citizens to manage and share their data may in fact be an autonomy limited to the EU level (and to third countries that meet the corresponding legal and technical requirements). This is because the EHDS is a system designed to work at EU level.

The right of access is supplemented by the right to data portability, which is considerably improved in the EHDS Regulation, compared with the GDPR. This right allows citizens to give access to all or part of their electronic health data or to request that it be transmitted to another healthcare provider of their choice (in the European electronic health record exchange format, when located in another EU Member State) or transmit the electronic copy of the data to another healthcare provider.[64] Although the EHDS Regulation does not expressly state this, it refers to healthcare providers who are part of the EHDS. As a result, this right applies, a priori, to EU countries, although it also extends to third countries that may be part of this space.

In contrast to the rigidity that the EHDS can present in practice, where the data is held by a third party (data holder), and not by the data subject (who has a right of access, to data portability, etc), another more flexible way for European citizens to travel with their health data could be a Digital Wallet. Although the European Digital Identity Wallet ('EUDI Wallet') (Article 5a Regulation (EU) 910/2014, consolidated text), which can include electronic attestations of attributes, is not a priori designed to host EHRs, a specific wallet for health information could be envisaged.

This solution puts citizens in control of their data, enabling them to share it with third parties (eg healthcare providers) without the need for them to be connected

[63] In addition to those already recognised by the GDPR, access and portability rights are recognised for electronic health data; see Recs 8, 9, 14, and 15 EHDS Regulation.

[64] See Art 7 EHDS Regulation.

to a data space. The greater flexibility of this instrument derives precisely from this last aspect, ie the fact that it is not necessary to create a data space in order to allow the citizens to manage and transmit their health information to third parties. However, this solution does not grant total autonomy to the citizens to share their data either, as it might require the involvement of an identified third party and therefore require prior agreements (eg by means of an international agreement) in which the protection measures (for data to be read via the wallet) must be incorporated.[65]

6.4. Conclusions

There is still a long way to go to build a Mediterranean health data space, even if it is limited to certain actors or sectors. This possibility could be particularly useful with certain countries on the southern shore of the Mediterranean Sea, with which there is great geographical, cultural and linguistic proximity, as well as constant trade relations and a continuous flow of people. However, although the road ahead seems long (much like the development of the European health data space itself), there are various aspects that can be worked on in the meantime.

At a regulatory level, there are basic elements in common between the countries on both sides of the Mediterranean area, in terms of enhanced protection of health data as sensitive data and the requirement for an equivalent level of protection for their transfer to third countries. In the medium term, efforts can be focused on implementing the changes (both legislative and practical) needed to achieve a smooth exchange of data between the northern and southern shores of the Mediterranean Sea, through the recognition of an equivalent level of protection (in the EU case, the adequacy decision under Article 45 of the GDPR). In this regard, the countries that have already ratified Convention 108 of the Council of Europe may be in a more advanced position in this task.

In the near future, it should be possible to work on bilateral agreements (which, as far as European requirements are concerned, must incorporate adequate safeguards[66]) between countries on both shores of the Mediterranean Sea or with the EU to allow for a limited exchange of health data (for example, vaccination certificates, patient summaries, electronic prescriptions, etc).

This preliminary work, on the mutual recognition of equivalent levels of protection or on the development of instruments incorporating adequate safeguards, is also an essential prerequisite for moving towards a more fluid exchange of health data not only at the institutional level, but also at the individual level.

[65] It would also be necessary to comply with interoperability requirements which, to the extent that they are based on ISO standards and other international protocols used outside the EU, would facilitate this work.

[66] See Art 46(2)(a) GDPR.

Indeed, the EHDS, which is open to third countries, requires prior compliance with the requirements relating to international data transfers in the GDPR, in addition to the requirements (legal, technical, organisational, etc) of the EHDS itself. In parallel, progress should be made on this last point with a view to the possible (even partial) integration of the Southern Mediterranean into the EHDS or the construction of a specific Mediterranean space. The use of globally standardised formats and protocols will facilitate this work.

In the meantime, and in a complementary way, it is possible to promote the provision of tools (such as digital wallets) that allow citizens to manage and make available the health data of their choice to third parties. The latter possibility has the advantages of being quicker and more flexible to implement, since it does not require healthcare providers to be connected to a common exchange infrastructure. It is also less costly and could represent the first step in building a future Mediterranean health data space. However, as noted above, it is still necessary to respect certain legal guarantees (reflected in international agreements), so that data can be made available to third parties outside the national or EU space.

Finally, it is clear that none of the actions mentioned above can be carried out without a major prior effort to 'digitise health', starting with health records. In Europe, this effort will be imposed by the construction of the EHDS. In the countries on the southern shore of the Mediterranean Sea, it will require a political and financial commitment. This task will also have to be adapted to the social and cultural reality of each country, so as to leave no one behind and avoid creating digital divides in the health sector.

7

Technological Innovation and Advanced Data Management at the Local Level: Towards a Smart City Data Space?

JULIÁN VALERO TORRIJOS

7.1. Complexity as the Main Feature of Smart Cities

The focus on smart cities is currently one of the main expressions of technological innovation in the public sphere, especially at a local level. This kind of project aims to address some of the most relevant challenges raised by sustainability in the urban context to achieve better optimisation of resources and, consequently, a more efficient and more effective provision of services through the advanced use of information and communication technologies (ICT). This goal can only be achieved by analysing and processing the information generated as a result of the intensive use of electronic media, in particular, data associated with the provision and use of public and private services, spaces, and infrastructures.

The local government becomes the leading authority, as smart city projects are usually based on its competences. Smart city projects go far beyond the approach that underpins the digitalisation of public administration: it is not simply a matter of carrying out formalised actions in a formal environment,[1] and private stakeholders are also involved. In this environment, it is essential to link various sources of information, sometimes relating to actions of a material nature, ie outside the context of files, registers, and electronic notifications. Without this, the data coming from formalised administrative actions should be considered outside our focus since, as it will be analysed below, one of the axes from which the strategies

[1] J Valero Torrijos, 'From transparency and reuse of public sector information to data spaces' (2022) 3 *European Review of Digital Administration & Law* 35, 41–42.

of smart cities are articulated is, precisely, the exploitation of the largest possible volume of data regardless of their origin.

Given that we are dealing mainly with the use of information linked to the activity of public administrations – specifically, although not exclusively, local administrations – the legal approach that we seek to follow must be based on the three foundations of open government, which is the most advanced and current manifestation of the democratic basis that must define any initiative in the field of the public sector.[2] Consequently, in addition to an in-depth analysis of the legal implications of the socially demanded openness, the management of the data generated in smart city projects must be based on the following:

- Transparency, ie data accessibility as an advanced manifestation of transparency.[3]
- Participation of civil society, so that the point of view of citizens is not limited to a merely passive[4] and reactive position, ie that of mere users of services and, therefore, providers of information. On the contrary, citizens and private bodies play an essential role in improving the provision of services and, ultimately, they are legal subjects with rights that must necessarily be taken into account.
- Collaboration, so that companies, citizens, and associations can become key players in the process of modernising cities, including in the development of applications and services based on the accessibility and reuse of information generated in the provision of services directly or indirectly owned by a public entity.

7.2. Plurality of Actors in the Smart City Scenario: The Vital Role of the Local Government

From a subjective point of view and regarding the legal implications of this type of project, it is worth emphasising the complexity that the involvement of diverse and very heterogeneous subjects entails. On the one hand, there are numerous interests at stake that may even be contradictory and, therefore, generate conflicts with an undeniable legal dimension. This would make it difficult – if not directly

[2] Regarding this idea in smart city scenarios, see I Celeste Fonseca, 'Cities and Law, e-governance and rights: because we need a global digital transition strategy for the city' in I Celeste Fonseca (ed), *Smart cities and Law, e-governance and rights* (Milano, Wolters Kluwer-CEDAM, 2023) 20.

[3] AG Orofino, 'Openness of public data and transparency of administrative action' (2022) 3 *European Review of Digital Administration & Law* 54.

[4] L Sartori, 'Alla ricerca della smart citizenship' (2015) XXXVI *Istituzioni del federalismo: rivista di studi giuridici e politici* 927, 942–43.

impede – the opening of the data to facilitate its reuse, whether by companies for commercial purposes or by the different social agents for other purposes.

On the other hand, the plurality of activities and services involved also determines the diversity of applicable legal rules. Adopted for different purposes – e-government, data protection, environmental protection, open data, and re-use of public sector information – they are not always adequately aligned to pursue the objectives of smart city initiatives.

All of this in a context where the prominence of information and communication technologies requires additional efforts in terms of interoperability and information security. These two principles are of particular significance not only from a technological perspective but also from a legal and organisational perspective. In short, it is essential to design appropriate governance models that take into account all these dimensions[5] and the specific circumstances in which the smart city has to run.

One of the key tools to address this challenge is the law, as it provides the essential conditions for technological innovation in this type of initiative to be fully compatible with the integrity of legal safeguards and full respect for citizens' rights. Moreover, an appropriate regulatory framework – and interpretative guidelines in line with the social reality of the time in which it is to be applied – is a tool of great importance in guaranteeing the basic conditions of legal certainty that enable the essential public–private collaboration. Finally, it is necessary to undertake a proactive analysis of the regulatory context of smart cities in order to identify any legal barriers that may exist and, if necessary, to consider appropriate responses to address them.

It is therefore crucial to overcome the traditional perception of law as a barrier that tends to hamper technological innovation and thus hinder the success of smart city projects. The failures of the current legal framework should be addressed from a different perspective, which requires the adoption of a proactive, cross-cutting, comprehensive, and open vision. This will help to overcome the regulatory constraints that local governments may face and provide them with a truly alternative model of information and service management that will support their projects.

To this end, from a legal perspective, we consider it essential to provide interpretative criteria aimed at enabling local governments to adopt this vision, through an understanding of the legal framework that allows them to use the powers and tools granted to them by law. In short, the exercise of their competences to reinforce this vision, without prejudice to their ability to adopt unilateral decisions

[5] A comprehensive data governance is an essential precondition in smart city scenarios. Regarding this idea, see J Haberkern and T Schäffer, 'Towards Data Ecosystems in Smart Cities: Success Factors of Urban Data Spaces' in O Gusikhin, S Hammoudi and A Cuzzocrea (eds), *Proceedings of the 12th International Conference on Data Science, Technology and Applications* (Setúbal, SCITEPRESS, 2023) 555.

through administrative acts if necessary. There is still a long way to go in the field of public procurement, which, in the end and from the horizontal and strategic vision that must inspire any smart city project, would allow an adequate response to regulatory shortcomings and dysfunctions.[6]

Smart city projects are usually inspired by a management approach based on sustainability and efficiency in the use of available resources, particularly regarding environmental protection, mobility and, in general, local services. It is precisely the completion of this goal that determines why it must necessarily be based on the intensive use of information and communication technologies. More specifically, any project in this field needs to promote an advanced model of analysis and intensive exploitation of the information that is generated and, specifically, of the data associated with the provision and use of publicly owned services, spaces, and infrastructures.

The local government becomes the leading authority since smart city projects are articulated based on its competences, particularly in terms of the public services it provides and in terms of the use of the assets and infrastructures it owns. However, there are also several other players who are also called upon to play an influential role:

- Private entities that, through the suitable contract, are responsible for providing public services when the local government has opted for a private model of management.
- Companies in charge of developing the applications and IT systems used for the provision of services, except in those cases this function is carried out by local government staff.
- Entities that manage telecommunications networks through which information is transmitted and services are managed. These entities would usually be private companies although the municipality itself frequently owns and manages those networks.
- Interconnected objects and sensors that automatically and continuously provide a vast amount of data of potential interest for the better and more efficient provision of services and use of public resources. All of this is supported by Internet of Things (IoT) devices.
- Beneficiaries of the services, whose data are incorporated into the information systems, either by the public entity itself or by third-party service providers.
- Re-users who, by developing software applications, offer added-value services, free of charge or not, based on the data generated in the context of the smart city project.

[6] M Fernández Salmerón, 'Soluciones innovadoras y gestion avanzada en entornos urbanos: Problemas jurídicos derivados de la contratación pública en el desarrollo de "ciudades inteligentes"' (2015) XXXVI (4) *Istituzioni del federalismo: rivista di studi giuridici e politici* 975, 998–99.

Given this plurality of subjects, the main legal risk lies in the diversity of the interests pursued by them, which may be in conflict with each other. For instance, it is feasible that entities that provide the services may be unwilling to share the data they manage, as this could mean that other companies competing with them would have access to relevant information.

Similarly, from the users' perspective, it is understandable that they may be wary of the use of information related to their own activities, especially if adequate measures are not implemented to keep the data separate. Finally, telecommunications companies themselves may consider it in their interest to retain exclusive control over their customers' data in order to offer them, even with prior consent, personalised added-value services.

As a result, we are faced with different and even fragmentary interests that only the local government, as the body responsible for the smart city project, can redirect towards the unity that is essential to meet the needs of a context of technological innovation. It is therefore up to the local government to adopt an overall approach which may involve the exercise of unilateral powers and competences legally attributed to them. Nevertheless, beyond the technological dimension, this goal demands a management model based on the parameters of open government – transparency, participation, and collaboration – to reinforce not only the legal requirements but a solid democratic vision as well.

7.3. Diversity of Activities and Legal Frameworks

The large number of actors involved in smart city scenarios entails an added complexity to the associated density of the demanding use of technology and the exploitation of data. Many of the parties involved carry out a different activity consisting of the provision of relevant services to society and individuals. These services are ruled by different legal frameworks which are not always adjusted to the needs and specificities of a smart city. Moreover, the intense presence of technology in this context poses an additional challenge from the legal point of view, as, together with the regulatory diversity, it is also critical to ensure that the information generated by all the subjects involved can be made available under the requirements of open data. In other words, data should be readable in an automated manner according to criteria of technical, semantic, organisational, and legal interoperability.

In the context of smart city projects, we find a plurality of services of a heterogeneous nature from a legal perspective. On the one hand, there is a combination of private services such as energy supply or telephone services, which means that – at least potentially – a plurality of private providers may offer them. This is not the case, on the other hand, for public services owned by the local government, such as domestic water supply, street lighting or urban public transport. Sometimes it will be the municipality itself that will provide them all directly so that the capacity for control and decision-making by the local government is guaranteed.

In contrast, when an indirect management modality is chosen, although a private entity provides the service, the public ownership of the service would allow the municipality to act by unilaterally defining the conditions of the activity through the corresponding contract. As a result, the local government has an unquestionable competence when it comes to guarantee its control mechanisms in the handling of the data generated and the conditions under which they should be opened for re-use by third parties.

Against this scenario, it is essential to adopt a comprehensive digital transition strategy specific to the city, considering the various perspectives involved but with a prominent role of the municipality. As mentioned above, this challenge must be addressed considering the fulfilment of major global sustainability objectives. However, technology should be used as a suitable lever for the transformation of city management, particularly from an orientation based on the prominence of data, cloud computing, and the advanced use of artificial intelligence. The focus should be placed not only on better service provision, but also on the rights of those who live in the city with a special focus on the problems and challenges arising from the digital divide as regards access to services.

7.4. Advanced Data Management and its Access: Implications for the Smart City

From the perspective of sharing data generated in smart city environments, legal analysis takes on particular importance due to the uniqueness of their characteristics and the specific challenges they raise. The provision of appropriate solutions becomes an essential need to provide legal certainty to the investments and efforts being made by both local governments and service providers and, in general, the involvement of civil society in this area.

In this regard, it is necessary to focus first on the characteristics of the network of actors and services provided. The main distinguishing feature is their diversity and heterogeneity. This is an additional difficulty in facilitating a realistic, effective, and efficient approach to data access, especially from the perspective of re-users.

Whereas in simpler scenarios of data sharing, policies are usually defined by the data producer, in smart cities multiple stakeholders need to be involved in defining them.[7] Moreover, the prominence of information and communication technologies in this context requires additional efforts to ensure interoperability, which should encompass other dimensions beyond the technological, necessarily including the legal dimension.

[7] QH Cao, I Khan, R Farahbakhsh, G Madhusudan, G Myoung Lee and N Crespi, 'A Trust Model for Data Sharing in Smart Cities' in *2016 IEEE International Conference on Communications* (2016) doi.org/10.1109/ICC.2016.7510834.

Given these premises, the prominent role of the local government takes on special relevance when it comes to tackling the legal challenges inherent to data governance in smart cities.[8] In addition to promoting the regulatory reforms that fall within its competences, this role is even more important in promoting a management model based on an open government basis, using the powers legally conferred on local government and the legal instruments at its disposal to face the difficulties and challenges that may arise from the applicable rules.

Here, a network approach would be particularly well suited in order to bring all the stakeholders on board,[9] as issues related to access, interpretation and ownership of data are 'particularly pertinent to urban contexts, as they highlight important urban democracy gaps in the governance of cities due to a lack of civic engagement'.[10] In this sense, the accessibility of data in smart cities requires a number of unavoidable premises, so that data re-use can be enhanced, while respecting the requirements of the law. Specifically:

- A new model of document management should be promoted. Going beyond a simple commitment to the use of electronic means, although based on the stimulus offered by electronic administration, it must overcome the inflexibility and formalities that have traditionally driven the regulation of administrative action.
- The challenge of protecting citizens' data must be addressed by adapting the legal guarantees to the specific nature of the processing that the current state of technological development in smart city scenarios raises.
- Public procurement must be seen as a central tool for project management rather than as a mere limited and formal process for finding suppliers of goods and services.
- Finally, it is essential to adapt the project management model to the Open Government approach in order to reinforce its democratic and inclusive nature in the face of a potential fragmentation and disaggregation dynamics inherent to the diversity and complexity of smart city initiatives.

Although smart cities are based on the unavoidable technological modernisation of the administrative management of the different local services, the relevance of the principles of open government cannot be underestimated. Taking into consideration this dual requirement, smart cities must assume an explicit commitment to transparency through innovation. Specifically, it is a priority that the information generated during the provision of the various services, whether directly by the public administration or by private entities, is available according to re-use of

[8] A Mantelero, *Beyond Data. Human Rights, Ethical and Social Impact Assessment in AI* (The Hague, Springer, 2022) 81.

[9] A Cerrillo i Martínez, 'Los servicios de la ciudad inteligente' in C Barrero and JM Socias (eds), *La ciudad del siglo XXI: transformaciones y retos* (Madrid, INAP, 2020) 440–41.

[10] C Baibarac-Duignan and M de Lange, 'Controversing the datafied smart city: Conceptualising a "making-controversial" approach to civic engagement' (2021) 8 *Big Data & Society* 6.

public sector information and open data standards.[11] Finally, the goal would be that the data generated can be re-used to provide value-added services, and that such processing can lead to the improvement of the very services on which the smart city project is based.

It should be noted that the scope of the regulation on transparency and access to information usually covers only public entities or, where appropriate, private bodies linked to the public sector. Although public service providers are also affected by this regulation, they are only obliged in a very specific way, which may become a legal barrier to the re-use of information. Natural or legal private entities providing a public service – and in general the beneficiaries of public sector contracts – sometimes may not be obliged to provide information directly to other private parties, as is the case with re-users. On the contrary, any request for information that may be made to them must be processed through the public administration in charge of the service, without any legal reference to electronic means or interoperability conditions.

Therefore, on the basis on this kind of legal provisions, it can hardly be assumed that private parties have a great interest in offering direct and automated access to their information systems,[12] which once again highlights the importance of the obligations set out in the contract governing the provision of the public service. In this respect, there may even be a natural reluctance to open data because other companies with potentially conflicting interests, such as competitors in the market, could benefit from it. It is therefore of great importance to specify which data can be part of the activity involved in the provision of the public service and which, on the contrary, can be generated by the business know-how of the entity carrying out the activity. Despite the difficulty that this distinction often poses in specific cases, only the data in the first group could be subject to a contractual obligation to make them available to third parties.

Another challenge posed by the application of the rules on transparency and access is the large number of areas where access can be restricted. For example, it would not be possible to consider the re-use of data when third parties' rights or public interests are affected (eg, environmental protection, prevention and punishment of criminal and administrative offences, administrative functions of surveillance and control, public safety). However, even taking this major difficulty as a starting point, it should be noted that the application of such restrictions must be proportionate and justified. Partial access to data could be considered

[11] See A Abella, M Ortiz and C de Pablos, 'A model for the analysis of data-driven innovation and value generation in smart cities' ecosystem' (2017) 64 *Cities* 47, 51. For a more sceptical vision, particularly based on the lack of enough methodological studies, see FT Neves, MC Neto and M Aparicio, 'The impacts of open data initiatives on smart cities: A framework for evaluation and monitoring' (2020) 106 *Cities* 102860.

[12] See A Ferrer Sapena and E Sánchez Pérez, 'Análisis de las barreras para la explotación de los datos abiertos: estrategias y soluciones' in L Cotino and A Todolí (eds), *Explotación y regulación del uso del big data e inteligencia artificial para los servicios públicos y la ciudad inteligente* (Valencia, Tirant lo Blanch, 2022) 56.

unaffected by such restrictions, which leads us to conclude that the interpretation must necessarily be restrictive in order to facilitate data re-use.

Beyond these significant limitations, the local government itself can legally force the various entities involved in the smart city to adopt a management and operating model appropriate to the parameters of open data. In other words, any legal limitations can in no way be used as an obstacle if the local government assumes and exercises its responsibilities from a good governance perspective, taking into account the specificities of the smart city. In fact, regarding the private companies that provide public services, there would always be the possibility for the municipal administration to include this obligation in the contract. It is undoubtedly more difficult to extend these measures to the rest of the private sector bodies, whether they are service providers not linked to local authorities or the citizens themselves. In these cases, there would only be room to promote measures based on the voluntary opening of information systems, while respecting the requirements of the regulations on personal data protection.

On the other hand, the specific legal provisions on the re-use of public sector information do not always contemplate a legally enforceable obligation to provide access to their data in open and machine-readable formats. Although in some cases the effective application of this requirement will have to take place progressively – for example, when the specifications are renewed or, where necessary, the appropriate technological tools are implemented – the fact is that the municipality can go beyond the strict legal obligation, which also poses an additional requirement.

While the legislator itself frequently refrains from requiring the public sector to make an effective commitment to maintain access to data for a long period of time in order to facilitate its re-use, it is still true that such a commitment appears to be imperative. Otherwise, there will hardly be the necessary incentive to count on the collaboration of private sector re-users and society in general. It is no longer a question of limiting the problem to a reactive approach based on the liability of the local administration, since this would lead to an overly restrictive and distorted view of the legal tools. On the contrary the effective overcoming of the legal provisions can only be seen, once again, from a global and proactive vision of the smart city project, that is, in the confidence of the transformative potential that it can bring. However, as we will analyse below, this requires that a certain advanced governance model is actually adopted.

7.5. Proactive Management of Public Procurement as an Unavoidable Premise

Public procurement is an essential tool for achieving the objectives set out above, and its importance should be acknowledged as a major challenge from a legal perspective. The coherence and uniformity of criteria required by any smart city project must be achieved through mechanisms adapted to such requirements, hence the firm commitment to interoperability. Thus, in its multiple technical, organisational, semantic, and legal dimensions, the advanced management of information systems is crucial, ultimately forcing us to focus on a requirement of greater scope.

Specifically, as has been emphasised since the 2014 reform of the European regulation of public procurement, public procurement must become a strategic tool for the institutional leadership of public authorities, in this case, municipalities. Only with this vision can we face the singularity of smart city ecosystems, where instead of a single company in charge of providing services and making investments, it is imperative to create a collaborative dynamic in which not only other companies can participate, but even citizens and society itself play a prominent role. To achieve this goal, a more flexible and open institutional approach is paramount.

Based on this revised view of the role that public procurement innovation must play,[13] the importance of a proactive approach should not be underestimated by the local governments to ensure the effectiveness of legal guarantees. In this regard, the contractual instrument is essential to delimit what part of the information generated and managed by the service providers and, in general, by those collaborating with the project, is to be offered to third parties in accordance with the requirements of open standards. This requires a formalised specification, if necessary, through the contractual instrument, by the local government that is ultimately responsible for the services.

In the same way, this kind of proactive vision can overcome the limited scope of legislation on e-government, transparency, and the re-use of public sector information. Requiring private entities to comply with the existing standards in these areas when possible – or, failing that, by means of promotion measures – is a prerequisite for the success of smart city projects. Finally, given that a written record of the guarantees is legally required, the contract becomes the ideal legal instrument to establish the conditions and limits of the use of citizens' personal information, especially when it is made available to third parties to meet the needs of the services related to smart cities.

7.6. The Model of European Data Spaces and its Projection on Smart City Scenarios

The document 'A European strategy for data'[14] foresees the launching of a series of data spaces in strategic areas of special public interest. The aim is to facilitate

[13] See P Costa Gonçalves, 'Smart Cities e contratação pública' (2021) 2 *European Review of Digital Administration & Law* 127, 129–31.

[14] Communication from the Commission to the European Parliament, the European Council, the Council, the European Economic and Social Committee and the Committee of the Regions, COM(2022) 230 final.

the availability of large data repositories in these sectors, as well as the necessary tools and technical infrastructures to use and exchange data, as well as appropriate governance mechanisms.

According to the European Commission's 'Staff working document on Common European Data Spaces', data spaces are promoted with the aim of 'overcoming legal and technical barriers to data sharing combining the necessary tools and infrastructures and addressing trust issues through common rules'. These spaces require not only the implementation of appropriate infrastructures, but also the design of enabling governance frameworks, which poses significant legal challenges. Although there is no general legally binding definition of data spaces, they are considered to be ecosystems where data from the public sector, businesses and individuals, as well as research institutions and other types of organisations, are available and exchanged in a reliable and secure manner.

7.6.1. The Legal Structure of Data Spaces

In the absence of a general regulation on data spaces,[15] their specific structure will depend both on the particularities of the sector to which they refer and on the objectives pursued in setting them up. However, we can start from a general characterisation that will help us to outline their main implications from a legal perspective.

First, each participant must retain control over the data they provide to the common space, which implies the freedom to decide not only on their inclusion but also on their withdrawal. However, some nuances to this feature may result from the existence of legal obligations in this respect, as may be the case for public sector entities under the legal framework for public sector information re-use and public data.

On the other hand, it is essential to ensure conditions of technological neutrality, so that there is no dependency on a specific tool or solution. This premise allows data spaces to move from one environment to another and to use different infrastructures. In this respect, the various environments must be built based on parameters that allow them to be interoperable, so that they can be interconnected and data migration between different infrastructures can be facilitated.

Likewise, appropriate conditions for access to data and its subsequent re-use must be guaranteed. In particular, this requirement has important consequences from the point of view of the rules on free competition, in order to avoid, on the one hand, undue situations of prevalence and/or concentration in a given market

[15] In fact, it has been labelled as an 'umbrella term' categorising several closely related concepts. See E Curry, S Scerri and T Tuikka, 'Data Spaces: Design, Deployment and Future Directions' in E Curry, S Scerri and T Tuikka (eds), *Data Spaces* (Cham, Springer 2022) 3.

and, on the other hand, cases of re-use of data that are unlawful or, where appropriate, contrary to the principles and objectives previously established when the corresponding space was created.

It is particularly important to design a governance model that precisely establishes the conditions for the participation of the various actors involved. This includes their rights and obligations, the definition of who will be responsible for adopting the decisions relating to the design of the space and its subsequent practical implementation, and the mechanisms for the resolution of potential conflicts that may arise, notwithstanding the possibility of a judicial process, which in principle would always be available.

In short, sectoral data spaces constitute a model that goes beyond the mere exchange of data between various subjects, and also beyond the re-use of public sector information, although this may be included depending on the case. This is therefore a particularly suitable paradigm for smart cities, where multiple data sources are integrated with significant diversity in terms of the applicable legal regime.

Data spaces are ecosystems in which, in general, the private sector is called upon to play a relevant role – which is fully consistent with smart cities – without preventing the participation of the public sector. The latter acquires a special importance since the local government is the main actor, responsible not only for providing public services but also for the project.

7.6.2. Common European Data Spaces in the Scope of the Public Sector

As mentioned above, the firm commitment to common data spaces at a European level is one of the main axes of the European strategy for data approved in 2020. The document already announced this approach as a basis to support the promotion of public policies and to facilitate the development of innovative products and services based on data intelligence and machine learning.

However, the availability of large sectoral datasets required, as a prerequisite, an appropriate cross-cutting regulatory framework that would make it possible to establish the conditions of viability and security from a legal standpoint. In this respect, after the consolidation of the reform of the Directive on the re-use of public sector information and open data in 2019,[16] the Regulation on data governance was approved in 2022,[17] and the Data Act in 2023.[18]

With these initiatives already adopted and the recent official publication of the Regulation on artificial intelligence,[19] the promotion of data spaces takes on

[16] Directive (EU) 2019/1024 of the European Parliament and of the Council of 20 June 2019.
[17] Regulation (EU) 2022/868 of the European Parliament and of the Council of 30 May 2022.
[18] Regulation (EU) 2023/2854 of the European Parliament and of the Council of 13 December 2023.
[19] Regulation (EU) 2024/1689 of the European Parliament and of the Council of 13 June 2024.

a special importance, especially in the public sector, to ensure the availability of sufficient and high-quality data. However, it is important to remember that, despite the prominent role of public bodies, the main objective of this legal framework is to promote the development and competitiveness of the European data market.[20]

The European strategy for data[21] already envisaged the creation of common European data spaces in several sectors and areas of public interest, although, at the same time, new ones were not ruled out. New spaces have been announced in recent years, such that the current number has increased considerably.

Although a general characterisation of data spaces can be provided based on a series of common notes, there is great diversity from a legal perspective in terms of the purposes they pursue, the conditions under which data are shared and the subjects involved. This heterogeneity is also inherent to those data spaces related to the public sector, ie those in which there is a prominent role of data generated by public administrations and other public bodies in the exercise of their main activities, to which the 2019 Directive on re-use and open data is therefore fully applicable.

At the beginning of 2024, a second version of the 'Commission Staff Working Document on Common European Data Spaces'[22] was published to provide an updated view of the European regulatory framework for data spaces, as well as to identify European initiatives on data spaces in order to assess their level of maturity and the main challenges for the future of each of them.

Specifically, as far as public bodies are concerned, the legal data space, the space related to public procurement, the space related to the 'one-time' technical system in the context of e-government and, finally, the security data space for innovation are being considered. These are very diverse initiatives, some of which have reached a very advanced stage of development and have received quite solid institutional support, while others are only sketched out and require a considerable effort in terms of design and implementation.

7.6.3. Towards a Smart Cities Data Space?

In view of the analysis carried out, would the creation of a specific data space for smart cities be appropriate? The main purpose of data spaces is to promote the sharing and exchange of reliable and secure data in strategic economic sectors and areas of public interest. It is therefore not simply a matter of

[20] See S Sapienza, M Palmirani and S Greco, 'Data Sharing Governance in Digital Twins and Smart Cities: The European Data Strategy' in A Kö, G Kotsis, A Min Tojoa and I Khalil (eds), *Electronic Government and the Information Systems Perspective. 13th International Conference, EGOVIS 2024* (Cham, Springer, 2024) 187–88. See also F Bravo, 'Data Governance Act and re-use of data in the public sector' (2022) 3 *European Review of Digital Administration & Law* 13, 13–14.

[21] See n 14.

[22] SWD(2024) 21 final.

promoting large data sets but, above all, of supporting initiatives that provide access to data according to appropriate governance models, which will ultimately enable data interoperability across the EU on the basis of appropriate technological infrastructures.

Although the EU is not currently considering the creation of a specific data space for smart cities among those already planned for the public sector, there would be no objection to the Member States taking up this idea at their national level or involving municipalities or geographical areas that are not part of the EU. It could even be a great opportunity to promote local ecosystems of data sharing, taking into account the specificities of the municipalities in the Mediterranean area.

In particular, the main advantage of setting up such an initiative would be to facilitate the exchange of data derived from municipal management and, more generally, from the provision of public services, on the basis of minimum interoperability conditions, which would necessarily include respect for the maximum legal guarantees regarding the protection of fundamental rights and freedoms. It could therefore be an initiative formalised by a group of municipalities belonging to different countries – even outside the EU –which, through this space, could establish minimum conditions of legal feasibility to facilitate the exchange not only of projects and initiatives of interest but, above all, of data obtained during the development of their activity according to a set of previously established parameters.

However, for this goal to be achieved with legal certainty, the model of access and re-use of information must be first defined and implemented in each municipality. It would not be enough to simply digitise the activities carried out by each local administration, since information management must be oriented to data rather than documents. To this end, the various legal conditions (limits on access and the purposes of re-use, anonymisation, evidence of the conditions of legal compliance, etc) must be set up by default and by design, so that the interconnection of information systems can be carried out in real time, in an automated manner and taking into account the conditions and guarantees previously established to respond to the rules applicable in each country.

The inherent complexity of smart cities can be considered as a fundamental reason for choosing the data space model. Indeed, as highlighted above, there are multiple and diverse public and private actors involved in this type of environment, either as providers or as recipients of services.

The dynamism of local life and its projection in administrative management requires the immediate availability of updated data on the most diverse circumstances (traffic conditions, drinking water supply problems, mobility incidents, etc), a challenge for which high-value data are certainly useful. Finally, technological innovation requires us to go beyond mere digitisation and aspire to a real transformation from the keys of open government, which implies recognising a prominent role for society in the co-creation of technologically advanced services.

All these circumstances justify the need to promote data spaces that make it possible to face the unique challenges of smart cities as a response to the major problems that municipalities currently face. In short, given that the process of digitisation of public entities is now largely established, the main challenge for data spaces in this area is to provide adequate technical, legal, and organisational conditions to facilitate data availability and interoperability,[23] especially in complex areas with a high economic and social impact, as it is the case with smart cities.

7.7. Final Remarks

In order to achieve a minimum level of consistency, local governments should be committed to establishing an appropriate governance framework for smart cities, which requires the formal approval of projects. This is essential not only for the use and re-use of data to achieve the public interest at the local level, but also to ensure the highest respect for citizens' rights and freedoms and to meet advanced democratic requirements from the perspective of open government.

Apart from the fact that it involves the creation of a specific data space, the formal approval of the smart city ecosystem by the city council is also the most appropriate option to proceed, taking into account the specificities of data spaces. It would allow for the participation of society and all the affected stakeholders, and could reinforce transparency, especially as the legal framework in this field should be applied.

In addition, it would also facilitate compliance with certain formal obligations, such as the Data Protection Impact Assessment required under EU data protection rules. This is an obligation of major importance for the rights and freedoms, despite its limited effectiveness in a technologically disruptive environment. It should therefore be implemented with a more dynamic approach[24] and, above all, with a human-centred perspective beyond the specific technologies used.[25] Finally, it would enable judicial review of this administrative decision approving the smart city ecosystem.

[23] Valero (n 1) 41.

[24] GJ Ritsema van Eck, 'Algorithmic mapmaking in "smart cities": Data Protection Impact Assessments as a means of protection for groups' in A Daly, SK Devitt and M Mann (eds), *Good Data* (Amsterdam, Institute of Network Cultures, 2019) 310–11.

[25] Mantelero (n 8) 13–14, 79.

PART III

The Cultural Component of the Mediterranean Digital Space

8

Mediterranean Cultural Heritage and Data

MIQUEL PEGUERA POCH

8.1. Introduction

Paphos Castle, in Cyprus, and the Cittadella of Gozo, in Malta, are two remarkable examples of Mediterranean cultural heritage. The medieval castle of Paphos, a defensive fortress located in the port of Kato Paphos, has gone through earthquakes, destructions and reconstructions over the centuries, reflecting several historical periods of the island. In 1980, it was included in the UNESCO World Heritage List. The Cittadella of Gozo is a historic fortified town, located on a naturally defensible hill in the centre of the island. Despite centuries of decline, the Cittadella retains significant architectural heritage, showcasing styles from the late medieval period to the Baroque era.

One of the elements both monuments have in common is that they have been digitised in 3D under the recent EU's Twin-it! campaign.[1] Known as 'Twin it! 3D for Europe's culture', this campaign was launched in 2023, inviting the ministries of culture of EU Member States to submit at least one 3D digitised heritage asset from their country to the common European data space for cultural heritage which is currently under deployment.

This is just an example of the ongoing trend of preserving cultural heritage by means of 3D digitisation, allowing non-intrusive access and analysis, particularly of assets in a vulnerable state, and of those, such as the Citadella of Gozo, which face challenges of massive tourism.

The Mediterranean area is immensely rich in a diverse cultural heritage accumulated over centuries of civilisation. The conservation, dissemination, access,

[1] About the Twin it! campaign, see pro.europeana.eu/page/twin-it-3d-for-europe-s-culture. A list of submitted 3D files can be consulted at pro.europeana.eu/post/discover-the-heritage-gems-submitted-to-the-twin-it-3d-for-europe-s-culture-campaign. Other examples of submitted 3D files include the ruins of the Momjan castle, in Croatia, or – outside from the EU – the Zekate House, a historical mansion located in the city of Gjirokastër, Albania.

reuse and enjoyment of such a legacy is being increasingly entangled with digital technology. This, in turn, as in any other sector in our digital society, means abundancy of data, both personal and non-personal. Cultural heritage may indeed benefit from enormous opportunities in a data-driven economy, an expectation it shares with almost any other field of human activity.

This chapter will focus on the relevance of data and digitisation in the preservation and promotion of cultural heritage, using as a case study certain aspects of the EU strategy on data, which has led to the creation of several common European data spaces, including a common data space for cultural heritage. While the initiative is not specifically focused on the Mediterranean region, it does encompass much of its northern part and is open to international collaboration. Moreover, it addresses aspects that are likely common challenges for many Mediterranean countries.

8.2. Some Context: Safeguarding Cultural Heritage

Cultural heritage has been at the centre of national and international instruments and policies. Particularly relevant in this regard is the Convention Concerning the Protection of the World Cultural and Natural Heritage ('World Heritage Convention'), adopted at the General Conference of UNESCO in Paris on 16 November 1972.[2] The World Heritage Convention acknowledges the importance of cultural and natural heritage[3] for all the peoples of the world and establishes a system of collective protection of heritage of exceptional value from the perils of deterioration and destruction – a protection for which individual nations often lack the appropriate resources. The Convention created the World Heritage List[4] to include cultural or natural

[2] See www.whc.unesco.org/en/conventiontext.

[3] Cultural heritage may either consist of *monuments* ('architectural works, works of monumental sculpture and painting, elements or structures of an archaeological nature, inscriptions, cave dwellings and combinations of features, which are of outstanding universal value from the point of view of history, art or science'), *groups of buildings* ('groups of separate or connected buildings which, because of their architecture, their homogeneity or their place in the landscape, are of outstanding universal value from the point of view of history, art or science') or *sites* ('works of man or the combined works of nature and man, and areas including archaeological sites which are of outstanding universal value from the historical, aesthetic, ethnological or anthropological point of view'). See Art 1, World Heritage Convention (emphasis added). Natural heritage may include '*natural features* consisting of physical and biological formations or groups of such formations, which are of outstanding universal value from the aesthetic or scientific point of view; *geological and physiographical formations* and precisely delineated areas which constitute the habitat of threatened species of animals and plants of outstanding universal value from the point of view of science or conservation; *natural sites* or precisely delineated *natural areas* of outstanding universal value from the point of view of science, conservation or natural beauty.' See Art 2, World Heritage Convention (emphasis added).

[4] See www.whc.unesco.org/en/list.

heritage of outstanding universal value, which is administered by the World Heritage Centre.[5]

In October 2003, the General Conference of the UNESCO adopted Convention for the Safeguarding of the Intangible Cultural Heritage, which entered into force in 2006.[6] The intangible cultural heritage refers to the 'practices, representations, expressions, knowledge, skills – as well as the instruments, objects, artefacts and cultural spaces associated therewith – that communities, groups and, in some cases, individuals recognize as part of their cultural heritage'.[7] Such heritage may be represented through different means, including oral traditions and expressions; performing arts; social practices, rituals and festive events; knowledge and practices concerning nature and the universe; traditional craftsmanship.[8] The Intangible Cultural Heritage Convention aims to safeguard the heritage of communities, groups, and individuals; ensure respect for it; raise awareness; and foster mutual appreciation at local, national, and international levels. Additionally, it seeks to facilitate international cooperation and assistance in this field.

For its part, the Council of Europe (CoE) adopted the Convention on the Value of Cultural Heritage for Society in 2005.[9] The Convention was opened for signature by CoE Member States in Faro (Portugal) and is usually referred to as the Faro Convention. It entered into force in June 2011 and has a specific focus on the relationship between heritage, human rights, and democracy, underscoring the importance of the values that heritage places and objects represent, as well as the meanings people attach to them. The Faro Convention proposes a direct implication of citizens, individually or collectively, fostering civil society creativity and community participation.[10] While the implementation of the Convention is left to the discretion of each participating state, the Faro Convention Action Plan provides guidance on activities and methods for applying its principles.[11] Some Mediterranean states not belonging to the EU, such as Bosnia and Herzegovina, and Montenegro, have ratified the Faro Convention.

Furthermore, over the years, the EU has implemented ambitious policies for cultural heritage, particularly leveraging the opportunities provided by digital technology. In this regard, some recommendations from the EU Commission may be mentioned, such as the Recommendations of 2006 and 2011 on the digitisation

[5] See www.whc.unesco.org/en/world-heritage-centre.

[6] See www.ich.unesco.org/en/convention.

[7] Art 1 Intangible Cultural Heritage Convention.

[8] ibid.

[9] See the text at www.coe.int/en/web/culture-and-heritage/faro-convention.

[10] Some of the activities carried out under the Faro Convention are highlighted in The Council of Europe, Culture and Cultural Heritage Division, 'The Faro Convention at work in Europe: selected examples' (2022), https://rm.coe.int/faro-convention-at-work-in-europe-selected-examples/1680a6e3fc.

[11] See www.coe.int/en/web/culture-and-heritage/faro-action-plan.

and online accessibility of cultural material and digital preservation.[12] And, more recently, the Commission Recommendation 2021/1970 on a common European data space for cultural heritage,[13] which will be considered in some detail later on in this chapter.

Among other initiatives, the European Heritage Label was launched in 2013.[14] Unlike the UNESCO World Heritage sites mentioned above, the sites awarded the European Heritage Label are intended to be milestones in the creation of the Europe we know today. They are selected for their ability to represent European values and history. In this context, the selection of sites emphasises the narratives and history behind Europe due to the roles they have played and the symbolic value they carry.[15]

The 2018 European Year of Cultural Heritage helped to reinforce the EU's agenda in this field, with commitments from Member States to preserve and promote its cultural heritage. The 2019 European Framework for Action on Cultural Heritage[16] followed up on the achievements of the said European Year and proposed a comprehensive list of actions focused on facilitating access to cultural heritage, promoting sustainability, safeguarding endangered heritage, mobilising knowledge and research, and fostering international cooperation.

In 2021, the EU took another step forward by issuing the already mentioned Commission Recommendation (EU) 2021/1970 on a common European data space for cultural heritage.[17] It not only focuses on the technological possibilities to enhance and preserve cultural heritage, but acknowledges the potential that data and data governance may provide for these purposes. In this regard, the Recommendation builds on the EU Data Strategy and adds cultural heritage to the list of strategic sectors selected by the EU to set common data spaces. Those

[12] Commission Recommendation of 24 August 2006 on the digitisation and online accessibility of cultural material and digital preservation (2006/585/EC) OJ L 236 (31 August 2006) 28–30; Commission Recommendation of 27 October 2011 on the digitisation and online accessibility of cultural material and digital preservation (2011/711/EU) OJ L 283 (29 October 2011) 39.

[13] Commission Recommendation (EU) 2021/1970 of 10 November 2021 on a common European data space for cultural heritage, OJ L 401 (12 November 2021) 5–16.

[14] See https://culture.ec.europa.eu/cultural-heritage/initiatives-and-success-stories/european-heritage-label.

[15] Some other EU initiatives worth mentioning include the Cultural and Creative Cities Monitor, a tool to evaluate and benchmark European cities in terms of their cultural and creative performance, with a view to help policymakers in identifying strengths and opportunities with qualitative and quantitative data. See composite-indicators.jrc.ec.europa.eu/cultural-creative-cities-monitor. A spin-off of this project is Cultural Gems (cultural-gems.jrc.ec.europa.eu), an application conceived to map cultural and creative places in Europe thanks to information provided by public and private entities. See V Alberti, F Panella, S Consoli, and C Cocco, 'Cultural Gems Turns Four' (Publications Office of the European Union, 2022) doi:10.2760/070797. Relevant resources related to cultural heritage may be found in sites like The Heritage Research Hub, www.heritageresearch-hub.eu.

[16] European Commission, DG for Education, Youth, Sport and Culture, 'European framework for action on cultural heritage' (EU Publications Office, 2019) data.europa.eu/doi/10.2766/949707.

[17] Commission Recommendation (EU) 2021/1970 of 10 November 2021 on a common European data space for cultural heritage, OJ L 401 (12 November 2021) 5–16.

common data spaces had been put forward in the 2020 EU Data Strategy[18] and are currently being developed.[19]

This chapter will next present the notion and purposes of such common data spaces, and will subsequently show the particularities of the common European data space for cultural heritage.

8.3. Common European Data Spaces

The EU Data Strategy highlights the central role of data in the transformation driven by digital technologies across all sectors and aspects of citizens' lives. The vast amounts of both personal and non-personal data continuously generated by individuals and organisations, along with the ability to efficiently process this data, present enormous potential for growth and innovation in a data-driven economy. It is crucial to harness this potential while simultaneously ensuring the highest level of personal data protection and safeguarding fundamental rights in the collection, processing, sharing, use and re-use of data.[20]

Data enables better decision-making in both the public and private sectors, and the EU is committed to establishing a legal framework that captures the benefits of data while protecting fundamental rights, ensuring safety and cybersecurity, creating transparent and appropriate tools for data governance, and facilitating fair access, use, and re-use. This framework is partly embodied in the General Data Protection Regulation (GDPR),[21] the Cybersecurity Act,[22] the Open Data Directive,[23] the Data Governance Act (DGA),[24] and the Data Act.[25]

A key objective of the EU Data Strategy is the building of a single European data space where data could be used irrespective of its physical storage location in the

[18] European Commission, 'Communication from the Commission to the European Parliament, the Council, the European Economic and Social Committee and the Committee of the Regions. A European Strategy for Data', Brussels (19 February 2020) COM(2020) 66 final.

[19] See European Commission, 'Second Commission staff Working Document on Common European Data Spaces' SWD(2024) 21 final.

[20] See European Commission (n 18).

[21] Regulation (EU) 2016/679 of the European Parliament and of the Council of 27 April 2016 on the protection of natural persons with regard to the processing of personal data and on the free movement of such data, and repealing Directive 95/46/EC (General Data Protection Regulation) OJ L 119/1 (4 May 2016).

[22] Regulation (EU) 2019/881 of the European Parliament and of the Council of 17 April 2019 on ENISA and on information and communications technology cybersecurity certification, OJ L 151/15 (7 June 2019).

[23] Directive (EU) 2019/1024 of the European Parliament and of the Council of 20 June 2019 on open data and the re-use of public sector information (recast) OJ L 172/56 (26 June 2019).

[24] Regulation (EU) 2022/868 of the European Parliament and of the Council of 30 May 2022 on European data governance and amending Regulation (EU) 2018/1724 (Data Governance Act), OJ L 152/1 (3 June 2022).

[25] Regulation (EU) 2023/2854 of the European Parliament and of the Council of 13 December 2023 on harmonised rules on fair access to and use of data and amending Regulation (EU) 2017/2394 and Directive (EU) 2020/1828 (Data Act) OJ L 2023/2854 (22 December 2023).

EU, which must secure both personal and non-personal data, including sensitive business information, while providing businesses with easy access to vast amounts of high-quality data. This single data space is expected to drive growth and value creation while minimising environmental impact. The European data space is also meant to enable businesses to leverage the EU market scale, with common rules and enforcement, and to ensure free flow of data within the EU and across sectors, full compliance with EU values and laws – including data protection, consumer rights, and competition – and fair, clear, and practical rules for data access and use, supported by reliable governance mechanisms.

The EU data strategy acknowledges, nonetheless, that while data is crucial across all sectors, each domain may have unique needs, and that not all sectors are progressing at the same pace. Thus it envisioned the creation of a number of specific or sectoral common data spaces, to facilitate trusted and secure data pooling and sharing in several strategic economic sectors and domains of public interest. Such sectoral and domain-specific common European data spaces will gradually be interconnected to support the single market for data, allowing for the development of more data-driven, evidence-based policies throughout the EU.[26] Common European data spaces should follow the FAIR data principles, that is, making data findable, accessible, interoperable and re-usable.

There are currently 14 sectors and domains where EU-wide common, interoperable data spaces are being developed.[27] Most of them were announced in the Data Strategy, in 2020, while some were added later on, including the common European cultural heritage data space.[28] Specifically, the 14 sectors or domains covered are as follows: (a) agriculture; (b) cultural heritage; (c) energy; (d) financial; (e) green deal; (f) health; (g) industrial (manufacturing); (h) language; (i) media; (j) mobility; (k) public administrations; (l) research and innovation; (m) skills; and (n) tourism.

Each data space is structured and organised by participants and stakeholders according to the specific needs of the particular sector or domain. However, they do present some common features, which relate to the data infrastructures and to the data governance frameworks. In particular, key aspects of a common European data space include: (i) a secure, privacy-preserving infrastructure for the pooling, access, sharing, processing, and utilisation of data; (ii) a well-defined and practical framework for data access and usage that ensures fairness, transparency, proportionality, and non-discrimination, alongside reliable data governance mechanisms; (iii) strict adherence to European rules and values, particularly in the areas of personal data protection, consumer rights, and competition law; (iv) the opportunity for data holders within the space to grant access to or share personal and non-personal data under their control; (v) the flexibility for data to be reused

[26] See European Commission (n 19).

[27] ibid.

[28] Commission Recommendation (EU) 2021/1970 of 10 November 2021 on a common European data space for cultural heritage, OJ L 401/5 (12 November 2021).

either with compensation, including payment, or free of charge; and (vi) the inclusion of a broad range of organizations and individuals.[29]

As noted, these data spaces rely on the EU legal framework, and particularly on two instruments announced by the data strategy, namely the DGA,[30] and the Data Act.[31] Both have already been adopted. The DGA has been applicable since 24 September 2023, and the Data Act since 12 September 2025.

The DGA facilitates the building of the data spaces envisioned by the data strategy. On the one hand, it promotes the activity of recognised 'data altruism organisations', which seek to support objectives of general interest by making available relevant data based on data altruism at scale. Such organisations play a crucial role by facilitating the creation of substantial data pools, based on voluntary data sharing, which support data analytics and machine learning across the EU. On the other hand, the DGA regulates data intermediation services providers, who promote both bilateral and multilateral data sharing, as well as the creation of platforms and databases for the collective use of data. These service providers also establish infrastructure that connects data subjects and holders with data users, acting as orchestrators of data-sharing ecosystems within the context of common European data spaces.

In addition, the DGA establishes the European Data Innovation Board (EDIB) that serves as an advisory body to the Commission on all matters concerning the implementation of the DGA and on cross-cutting issues related to the common European data spaces. In particular, the EDIB will assist the European Commission in issues such as the prioritisation of cross-sector standards to be used and developed for data use and cross-sector data sharing between emerging common European data spaces; the enhancement of cross-border, cross-sector interoperability of data as well as data sharing services between different sectors and domains, building on existing European, international or national standards, with the aim of encouraging the creation of common European data spaces; or the establishment of guidelines for common European data spaces, for the purpose of facilitating data sharing in the Union and reaping the potential of existing and future data spaces.[32]

[29] See European Commission (n 19). The Data Spaces Support Centre defines a data space as follows: 'A data space is a distributed system defined by a governance framework. It facilitates secure and trustworthy data transactions between participants, emphasising trust and data sovereignty. A data space supports one or more use cases.' See dssc.eu/space/BVE/357073006.

[30] Regulation (EU) 2022/868 of the European Parliament and of the Council of 30 May 2022 on European data governance and amending Regulation (EU) 2018/1724 (Data Governance Act), OJ L 152/1 (3 June 2022).

[31] Regulation (EU) 2023/2854 of the European Parliament and of the Council of 13 December 2023 on harmonised rules on fair access to and use of data and amending Regulation (EU) 2017/2394 and Directive (EU) 2020/1828 (Data Act) OJ L 2023/2854 (22 December 2023).

[32] See Art 30 DGA.

An important element for the deployment of the common European data spaces is the easiness of re-using public sector data.[33] The general framework for the re-use of this data was initially established in the 2003 Directive on the reuse of public sector information,[34] which after a number of amendments was recast into the 2019 Open Data Directive.[35] The Open Data Directive introduced the notion of high-value data sets, which were defined as

> documents the re-use of which is associated with important benefits for society, the environment and the economy, in particular because of their suitability for the creation of value-added services, applications and new, high-quality and decent jobs, and of the number of potential beneficiaries of the value-added services and applications based on those datasets.[36]

Article 14(1) of the Open Data Directive ordered the EU Commission to lay down a list of specific high-value datasets belonging to the thematic categories listed in the Directive, namely, geospatial, earth observation and environment, meteorological, statistics, companies and company ownership, and mobility.[37] Those specific high-value datasets which should be made available free of charge, in machine-readable formats, via application programming interfaces (APIs) and, where relevant, as bulk downloads.[38] In December 2022, the EU Commission issued the Implementing Regulation (EU) 2023/138, where it established the list of specific high-value datasets within the said thematic categories as well as the arrangements for publishing and reusing them, in particular the applicable conditions for re-use and the minimum requirements for disseminating data via APIs.[39] The DGA complemented the 2019 Open Data Directive by going further in facilitating to identify which public authorities held relevant data for the purposes of

[33] As noted in European Commission (n 19) 8: 'The open data generated or held by government entities plays a pivotal role in enriching data availability within common European data spaces. It enhances data quality and interoperability and facilitates the reuse of data across borders. Availability of this diverse data also allows for cross-domain insights and the ability to address complex, interconnected challenges more effectively.'

[34] Directive 2003/98/EC of the European Parliament and of the Council of 17 November 2003 on the re-use of public sector information, OJ L 345/90 (31 December 2003).

[35] Directive (EU) 2019/1024 of the European Parliament and of the Council of 20 June 2019 on open data and the re-use of public sector information (recast) OJ L 172/56 (26 June 2019). As noted in Rec 65 of the Open Data Directive, 'Libraries, including university libraries, museums and archives hold a significant amount of valuable public sector information resources, in particular since digitisation projects have multiplied the amount of digital public domain material. Those cultural heritage collections and related metadata are a potential base for digital content products and services and have a huge potential for innovative re-use in sectors such as learning and tourism.'

[36] See Art 2(10) Open Data Directive.

[37] See Annex I Open Data Directive.

[38] Art 14 Open Data Directive. Nonetheless, the requirement to make the data available free of charge does not apply to libraries, including university libraries, museums and archives (see Art 14(4)).

[39] See Commission Implementing Regulation (EU) 2023/138 of 21 December 2022 laying down a list of specific high-value datasets and the arrangements for their publication and re-use, OJ L 19/43 (20 January 2023) 43. Within the category of statistics, a dataset of 'Tourism' flows in Europe is included as one of those specific high-value datasets.

data re-use by means of European register for protected data held by the public sector.[40]

For its part, the Data Act establishes some essential requirements to ensure interoperability within and among common European data spaces, which should be complied with by participants who offer data or data services to other participants. Compliance with those requirements is presumed by complying with harmonised standards or common specifications. In this regard, the Commission may request one or more European standardisation organisations to draft harmonised standards and exceptionally adopt common specifications where such harmonised standards are insufficient. In addition, the EDIB – created by the DGA – is entrusted by the Data Act with an advisory role in further specifying the essential requirements for the interoperability of the common European data spaces.

Common European data spaces benefit from the funding of the Digital Europe Programme (DIGITAL), an EU funding programme focused on bringing digital technology to businesses, citizens and public administrations,[41] established by Regulation (EU) 2021/694.[42] In particular, it has already funded a number of activities related to community-building and preparatory work on a blueprint and governance architecture, a roadmap and the identification of priority datasets for a number of common data spaces. In addition, DIGITAL has funded grants and procurements to support the deployment of some common data spaces, including the common European data space for cultural heritage. This has included grants to support activities of small and medium enterprises in the respective sectors, including the cultural heritage sector.[43] In addition, the Horizon Europe Programme also supports the development of common data spaces.

The Data Spaces Support Centre (DSSC) crucially contributes to the deployment of the data spaces.[44] The DSSC was created under the DIGITAL multiannual work programme for 2021–22,[45] with the task of defining the blueprint architecture and data infrastructure requirements for the data spaces.[46] In order to contribute to the deployment of the common data spaces the DSSC explores the needs of data space initiatives, defines common requirements and establishes best practices to speed up the creation of such spaces. The DSSC is crucial to coordinate all relevant actions on the common data spaces, so that they develop in a consistent and coherent way, and fulfil the interoperability requirements. To benefit from economies of scale, the DSSC provides the data spaces with common practices, components and tools.

[40] See data.europa.eu.

[41] See digital-strategy.ec.europa.eu/en/activities/digital-programme.

[42] Regulation (EU) 2021/694 of the European Parliament and of the Council of 29 April 2021 establishing the Digital Europe Programme, OJ L 166/1 (11 May 2021).

[43] See European Commission (n 19) 10 and Annex I.

[44] See dssc.eu.

[45] See Annex to the Commission Implementing Decision on the financing of the Digital Europe Programme and the adoption of the multiannual work programme for 2021–2022, C(2021) 7914 final.

[46] A version 1.0 of the blueprint is available at dssc.eu/space/BVE/357073006.

8.4. A Common Data Space for Cultural Heritage

The Communication on the Data Strategy provided for an initial list of sectors and domains for which to establish common European data spaces, while noting that the Commission could consider launching additional data spaces in other sectors in a sequential way. In this vein, a 'common European data space for cultural heritage' was put forward by the Commission in its Recommendation (EU) 2021/1970 of 10 November 2021 ('the 2021/1970 Recommendation').[47] This Recommendation builds on and replaces the prior Recommendation 2011/711/EU on the digitisation and online accessibility of cultural material and digital preservation.[48]

In the 2021/1970 Recommendation, the Commission highlights the significance of cultural heritage for the European economy, particularly in tourism, research, and in other cultural and creative industries, such as the video game and film sectors, which benefit from the advanced digitisation and re-use of cultural heritage content. The Commission emphasises that advanced digital technologies provide cultural heritage institutions with more effective tools for digitising cultural assets and reaching wider audiences, including with more immersive experiences, comprising places at risk, sites normally inaccessible or those temporary closed. This allows for improved public access to cultural assets, including for persons with visual impairments by means of tactile experiences.[49] The COVID-19 pandemic further showed the urgent need for digital transformation in this sector, revealing both its strengths and vulnerabilities. While many institutions experienced financial difficulties or closures, those that expanded their digital services managed to retain or even increase their audiences, demonstrating their considerable value to society and the European economy.

The 2021 evaluation of the former 2011 Recommendation on the digitisation and online accessibility of cultural material and digital preservation found that many of the challenges facing the cultural heritage sector 10 years earlier, such as the urgent need to protect and preserve European and endangered cultural heritage, remained by 2021. However, it also noted that the cultural heritage landscape had evolved significantly, presenting new needs as well as new opportunities that could enhance the impact of cultural heritage on the European economy. Thus, there was a need for a policy response that addresses these emerging needs and

[47] European Commission, Commission Recommendation (EU) 2021/1970 of 10 November 2021 on a common European data space for cultural heritage, OJ L 401/5 (12 November 2021).

[48] European Commission, Commission Recommendation of 27 October 2011 on the digitisation and online accessibility of cultural material and digital preservation (2011/711/EU). See also the Commission Staff Working Document Evaluation of the Commission Recommendation of 27 October 2011 on the digitisation and online accessibility of cultural material and digital preservation, SWD(2021) 15 final.

[49] Digitisation allows for new opportunities regarding accessibility. In 2020, UNESCO issued a set of guidelines in this regard. See UNESCO, 'Accessible digital documentary heritage: guidelines for the preparation of documentary heritage in accessible formats for persons with disabilities' (2020), unesdoc.unesco.org/ark:/48223/pf0000374995.

expectations of the cultural heritage sector, the cultural and creative industries, and society as a whole.

EU Member States had already signed a declaration on cooperation on advancing digitisation of cultural heritage in 2019, agreeing to intensify their efforts and work collaboratively for the 3D digitisation of cultural heritage artefacts, monuments, and sites, and to develop and promote interoperability standards and frameworks in digitisation initiatives.[50] The 2021/1970 Recommendation encourages them to go further in those endeavours and strategically plan the digital preservation of their heritage assets, adhering to relevant standards and frameworks in order to accelerate the sharing and re-use of data.

A key role in the deployment of the common European data space for cultural heritage has been entrusted to the Europeana Initiative, a platform that already offers access to over 57 million digitised items from cultural heritage institutions across Europe, including books, paintings, maps, manuscripts, and audiovisual materials.[51] Europeana was initially launched in 2008 as The European Digital Library, with the aim to make European cultural heritage more accessible.[52] As the 2021/1970 Recommendation recalls, Europeana has been strengthening standardisation across borders and providing standardised frameworks for sharing digital content and metadata online, which have been taken up widely in the cultural heritage sector in Europe and internationally. This is the case, particularly, of: (i) the Europeana Data Model,[53] which allows a standardised representation of data delivered by cultural heritage institutions using different formats; (ii) the Rights Statements,[54] which provide 12 standardised rights statements for online cultural heritage, which cultural heritage institutions may use to define how the digital objects may be reused; and (iii) the Europeana Publishing Framework,[55] which makes it easy for cultural institutions to see how the quality of the metadata and content they provide affect the way in which the content can be showcased and promoted in Europeana and how others can access it. The common European data space for cultural heritage will not replace the Europeana Initiative. Rather, Europeana – through its three pillars: Europeana Foundation; Europeana Network Association; and Europeana Aggregators' Forum – will steward the common data space, but will not be the owner or the controller of it.

An important aspect of the common data space is that the metadata associated with digitised cultural heritage assets is optimised to its fullest potential. This is especially relevant because these assets encompass a diverse array of documents and objects, come from a wide range of categories, and belong to various fields

[50] See digital-strategy.ec.europa.eu/en/news/eu-member-states-sign-cooperate-digitising-cultural-heritage.

[51] See www.europeana.eu.

[52] See European Commission, 'Report from the Commission to the European Parliament and the Council on the evaluation of Europeana and the way forward'COM(2018) 612 final.

[53] See pro.europeana.eu/page/edm-documentation.

[54] See rightsstatements.org.

[55] See pro.europeana.eu/post/publishing-framework.

of study, including historical, artistic, archaeological, architectural, landscape, gastronomic, and sociological domains, each with its own methods of cataloguing and description. Enhanced metadata aims to capture and integrate all this richness, reflecting the diversity and complexity of the cultural heritage they represent. In this regard, Europeana has been working for years on 'enrichment' – ie, enhancing metadata to improve its quality and accessibility – and will continue to do so regarding the cultural heritage data space.[56] So-called enrichments are enhancements that aim to augment, contextualise, or correct the authoritative data provided by cultural heritage institutions. These can be either metadata enrichments, which add new information or correct existing details about the asset, or content enrichments, which create additional representations of the cultural heritage object itself in different media formats.[57]

In 2021, the Commission set up an Expert Group on the common European Data Space for Cultural Heritage.[58] The Group's tasks include reviewing and discussing digital cultural heritage policies, aiding the Commission in monitoring the progress and impact of its recommendations, facilitating cooperation and information exchange between Member States and the Commission, contributing to the development and sustainability of the European common data space for cultural heritage and Europeana, supporting the Commission in setting objectives for the data space under the Digital Europe Programme, assisting in monitoring the innovative reuse of digital cultural resources to create economic opportunities, and helping the Commission prepare implementing acts.

The deployment of the data space on cultural heritage started in September 2022, building on the Europeana Digital Service Infrastructure (DSI).[59] The current work on the deployment of the common space is divided into four work packages: (a) development and operation of the data space infrastructure, aiming to provide a reliable data space infrastructure and quality of service, as well as foster innovation, interoperability and compliance with other data spaces; (b) integration of high-quality data, aiming to contribute to a significant and sustained increase in high-quality, usable and accessible data in the data space; (c) capacity building and fostering re-use: this work package aims to strengthen

[56] See H Manguinhas, A Matas, and M Škrinjar, 'Enrichments Policy for the common European data space for cultural heritage' (August 2023), pro.europeana.eu/post/enrichments-policy-for-the-common-european-data-space-for-cultural-heritage.

[57] ibid.

[58] See Commission Decision of 29 June 2021 setting up the Commission Expert Group on the common European Data Space for Cultural Heritage and repealing Decision C(2017) 1444, C(2021) 4647 final. This Expert Group replaces the Expert Group on Digital Cultural Heritage and Europeana, created by Decision C(2017) 1444 of 7 March 2017.

[59] As noted in the FAQs, the common European data space for cultural heritage builds on and expands the existing functionalities and services of the Europeana DSI. The service is provided by a consortium coordinated by the Europeana Foundation, and funded under the EU's Digital Europe programme. Moving from the Europeana DSI to the data space will require both continuity (building on what has already been achieved) and transition to an entirely new context. See pro.europeana.eu/page/the-common-european-data-space-for-cultural-heritage-faqs.

the capacity and capabilities of professionals and re-use communities working with digital cultural heritage; and (d) digital services for the public, aiming to engage audiences with digital cultural heritage by expanding pan-European themes and perspectives, and inspiring use, re-use, and participation.[60]

The deployment of the data space is being carried out under the lead of the Europeana Foundation with the support of the Europeana Network Association (ENA) and the Europeana Aggregators' Forum (EAF), in collaboration with a consortium of 19 partners from nine EU countries.

Recent news on the status of the data space may be found at the data space website,[61] which serves as a dedicated gateway to the common European data space for cultural heritage, providing an overview of ongoing activities and developments, showcasing key products, and evolving as the data space expands.

The data space is expected to boost the re-use of cultural heritage data in domains such as education, sustainable tourism and cultural creative sectors. Examples of re-use in education, research, creative industries, and personal projects are presented at the Europeana data space webpage,[62] which provides comprehensive details on the contractual deployment of the common European data space for cultural heritage, outlines its work strands and projects, explains the role of the Europeana Initiative, and includes FAQs for stakeholders and partners.[63]

Complementary to the data space for cultural heritage, the European Collaborative Cloud for Cultural Heritage (ECCCH), funded by Horizon Europe, will build a digital infrastructure that will facilitate the collaboration of cultural heritage institutions and professionals across the EU, by developing specific digital tools for the sector while removing barriers for smaller and remote institutions.[64] While the common European data space for cultural heritage serves as the main access point for discovering and re-using cultural heritage data across sectors, the Cloud will provide a digital workspace for preservation, conservation, and restoration efforts in the cultural heritage sector. Although they have different missions, the data space and the Cloud can complement each other for mutual benefit. The Europeana Initiative believes it is essential to establish these complementarities from the start to ensure that both initiatives provide shared benefits in resource pooling, broad audience reach, and support for heritage professionals, especially those conducting research with high-quality digital cultural heritage objects.[65]

[60] See pro.europeana.eu/page/data-space-deployment.

[61] See www.dataspace-culturalheritage.eu/en.

[62] See pro.europeana.eu/page/common-european-data-space-for-cultural-heritage.

[63] See pro.europeana.eu/page/the-common-european-data-space-for-cultural-heritage-faqs. In addition, and more widely, the Europeana Pro website, at pro.europeana.eu, is a communications platform for professionals working in and around cultural heritage and offers resources and tools for the sector.

[64] See research-and-innovation.ec.europa.eu/research-area/social-sciences-and-humanities/cultural-heritage-and-cultural-and-creative-industries-ccis/cultural-heritage-cloud_en.

[65] See pro.europeana.eu/page/the-common-european-data-space-for-cultural-heritage-faqs.

8.5. Legal Framework

As noted, the DSSC is working on a blueprint for emerging data spaces, which aims to support them throughout the different stages of their development, from the exploratory, preparatory and implementation phases to the operational and scaling stages. The DSSC has already delivered a version 1.0 of the blueprint.[66] It is structured in so-called building blocks, which are divided in two types. First, there are technical building blocks, which concern the technical elements of a data space and the technical agreements that individual participants and trusted intermediaries within the data space must follow. These building blocks include technical specifications regarding the use of specific technologies and processes required to ensure the functionalities of the data space.

The second category is business and organisational building blocks, namely, business model development, use case development, data product development, and data space intermediary. These blocks are intended to guide and help developing a business plan for the data space, focusing on the relationship between available data products and services, their use by stakeholders and customers, and their integration into a financially sustainable model, as well as on the role of data space intermediaries. Another group of building blocks in this category are those related to the governance of the data space. In particular, a building block on the organisational form and governance authority, and a building block on participation management. They aim to ensure effective decision-making processes as well as participant engagement, trust and data quality. Finally, building blocks regarding the legal framework relevant to the data spaces are provided.

The latter encompasses a broad area with many legal instruments at both the EU and national levels.[67] As mentioned above, the EU has recently developed an extensive set of norms in the data economy, with some, like the Digital Governance Act or the Data Act, specifically addressing different aspects of data spaces. Indeed, an appropriate legal framework is crucial for a data space to succeed and fulfil its purposes. And once this legal framework is in place, it requires the data space to be structured in compliance with all its legal requirements, taking into account the opportunities the legal framework provides when establishing contractual relationships with participants and stakeholders.

A data space typically involves the pooling and sharing of both personal and non-personal data, the reuse of public sector information, the organisation of participant and stakeholder activities, the use of various platforms and technical means, the assurance of interoperability, the implementation of appropriate technical and organisational measures to mitigate risks, the provision of services

[66] See the version 1.0 of the blueprint at dssc.eu/space/BVE/357073006.

[67] See M Frigeri, L King, M Musidlowska and B Peeters, 'From Data Silos to Data Ecosystems: The Role of Data Spaces Support Centre in Addressing the Legal Challenges of the Future Single Market for Data' (May 2024), dssc.eu/space/News/blog/479395848.

and access to databases, interaction with consumers, businesses, and public entities, and the storage and dissemination of creative content, among other functions.

All these and other functions require the application of various branches of law, with particular emphasis on the extensive body of data-related regulations. In addition to the already cited GDPR, DGA, Data Act and Open Data Directive, account must be taken of the ePrivacy Directive, the Regulation on the free flow of non-personal data,[68] the Interoperable Europe Act,[69] as well as, when appropriate, the Artificial Intelligence Act,[70] among other norms. Norms dealing with platforms may also be relevant, in particular the Digital Services Act and the Digital Markets Act,[71] as well as cybersecurity regulation. Consumer contract law also provides relevant rules, as it does intellectual property law, especially copyright.

Copyright law is indeed particularly relevant as cultural heritage assets often consist of protected works of authorship and other protected subject matter. Also in this field, the EU legal framework, namely the 2019 Directive on copyright in the Digital Single Market (DSMD),[72] has adopted measures, related to: (a) digitisation and dissemination of out-of-commerce works that cultural heritage institutions have in their collections; (b) exceptions for making preservation copies by cultural heritage institutions; (c) exceptions for text and data mining for scientific research; and (d) the status of works of visual art in the public domain.

Public cultural heritage institutions tend to cooperate with private parties that are willing to provide financial support for the digitisation of cultural assets. As the EU Commission pointed out, many of these cooperation arrangements grant exclusive rights to the private partners. The Open Data Directive provides for some rules regarding exclusive arrangements in its Article 12. However, such rules only apply to cultural heritage institutions falling under the scope of the Directive. While museums, archives and libraries are included, many other cultural

[68] Regulation (EU) 2018/1807 of the European Parliament and of the Council of 14 November 2018 on a framework for the free flow of non-personal data in the European Union OJ L 303/59 (28 November 2018).

[69] Regulation (EU) 2024/903 of the European Parliament and of the Council of 13 March 2024 laying down measures for a high level of public sector interoperability across the Union (Interoperable Europe Act) OJ L 2024/903 (22 March 2024).

[70] Regulation (EU) 2024/1689 of the European Parliament and of the Council of 13 June 2024 laying down harmonised rules on artificial intelligence (Artificial Intelligence Act) OJ L 2024/1689 (12 July 2024).

[71] Regulation (EU) 2022/2065 of the European Parliament and of the Council of 19 October 2022 on a Single Market For Digital Services and amending Directive 2000/31/EC (Digital Services Act) OJ L 277/1 (27 October 2022); Regulation (EU) 2022/1925 of the European Parliament and of the Council of 14 September 2022 on contestable and fair markets in the digital sector and amending Directives (EU) 2019/1937 and (EU) 2020/1828 (Digital Markets Act) OJ L 265/1 (12 October 2022).

[72] Directive (EU) 2019/790 of the European Parliament and of the Council of 17 April 2019 on copyright and related rights in the Digital Single Market and amending Directives 96/9/EC and 2001/29/EC OJ L 130/92 (17 May 2019).

heritage institutions fall outside the Directive's scope.[73] In its Recommendation on a data space for cultural heritage, the Commission put forward that

> in order to facilitate fair and non-discriminatory access for all to cultural heritage assets, cultural heritage institutions partnering with the private sector, including those not falling under the scope of the [Open Data] Directive, should aim to apply the principles laid down in said Article 12.[74]

8.6. A Broad Mediterranean Region Approach

The preceding sections of this chapter have concentrated on EU initiatives concerning the digitisation and preservation of cultural heritage, particularly with the ambitious goal of a sectoral common data space in this field. Related initiatives are also being pursued in several non-EU countries in the Mediterranean region, both at the individual country level and collectively.

An example of the latter is iHERITAGE: ICT Mediterranean platform for UNESCO cultural heritage,[75] a project that seeks to improve access to UNESCO cultural heritage sites in the Mediterranean region by utilising advanced technologies such as augmented reality, virtual reality, and mixed reality. The initiative involves cross-border collaboration, with the participation of Italy, Egypt, Spain, Jordan, Lebanon and Portugal, and focuses on technological transfer, industry–academia partnerships, and the creation of innovative digital products. The project already provides augmented and virtual reality experiences for heritage sites in Italy, Egypt, Spain, Lebanon and Jordan, as well as a number of immersive products.[76] An output of the project is the Register of Intangible Cultural Heritage of Mediterranean Countries (REIM), which, in accordance with the above mentioned UNESCO Convention for the Protection of the Intangible Cultural Heritage, aims to collect and to connect the whole set of practices, representations, expressions, knowledge and techniques – in the form of tools, objects, artefacts and places associated with them – that communities, groups and in some cases individuals recognise as part of their cultural heritage of the Mediterranean project partners. These are classified into oral traditions and expressions, including language as a vehicle of intangible cultural heritage; performing arts; social practices, rituals and festive events; knowledge and practices concerning nature and the universe; and traditional crafts.

Numerous national initiatives have been implemented in Mediterranean countries outside the EU, which have also made significant progress toward the digitisation of their cultural heritage. A few examples are as follows. Tunisia has

[73] See Art 2(j) Open Data Directive.

[74] Rec 14 Commission Recommendation (EU) 2021/1970 of 10 November 2021 on a common European data space for cultural heritage, OJ L 401/5 (12 November 2021) 5–16.

[75] See www.iheritage.eu/; see also www.enicbcmed.eu/projects/iheritage.

[76] See www.iheritage.eu.

actively participated in this effort through initiatives such as employing virtual reality and augmented reality technologies to create digital representations of the collections of the Bardo Museum in Tunis. Another significant Tunisian project, the Tunisia Digital Library, aims to digitise and provide access to an extensive collection of historical documents and manuscripts.[77] Similarly, Egypt has embarked on numerous digitisation projects, including the digitisation of the Egyptian Museum in Cairo and various manuscripts and artefacts.[78] The Bibliotheca Alexandrina plays a crucial role in digitising historical documents and making them available online.[79] Algeria has also been actively engaged in digitising its cultural heritage, focusing on historical archives and manuscripts that are vulnerable to physical deterioration.[80] Similarly, Morocco has initiated several projects aimed at the digitisation of its cultural heritage. The National Library of the Kingdom of Morocco, for instance, has undertaken efforts to digitise manuscripts, rare books, and other historical documents to ensure their preservation and to enhance access to its extensive cultural heritage.[81] Israel is also actively engaged in the digitisation of its cultural heritage. Several institutions, such as the National Library of Israel, have launched major projects to digitise manuscripts, rare books, photographs, and other historical documents, including architectural archives.[82] Similar initiatives are being conducted in neighbouring Mediterranean countries. Furthermore, Europeana has benefited from contributions of digitised cultural heritage from non-EU Mediterranean countries, including Egypt, through the Egypt Centre within Europeana,[83] as well as from Tunisia, Morocco or Algeria.

The European Heritage Hub project, co-funded by the EU and run by a consortium of 20 partners led by Europa Nostra – the largest and most representative heritage network in Europe, founded in 1963 and covering over 40 countries[84] – provides small grants for enhancing the role of cultural heritage in the digital, green and social transformation. A recent initiative was directed to a number of neighbouring EU countries (Albania, Armenia, Azerbaijan, Bosnia and Herzegovina, Georgia, Kosovo, Moldova, Montenegro, North Macedonia, Serbia and Ukraine).

The EU has been also active in funding heritage-related initiatives in non-EU Mediterranean countries.[85] Furthermore, the EU's New Agenda for the

[77] See rea.ec.europa.eu/news/eu-funded-cultural-heritage-projects-2022-05-03_en.

[78] ibid.

[79] See www.bibalex.org/Libraries/Presentation/Static/12600.aspx?d=0.

[80] See N Ghamouh and M Boulahlib, 'Cultural Heritage Digitization Projects in Algeria: Case Study of the National Library' (2015) 41 *IFLA Journal*, 272, doi.org/10.1177/0340035215603994.

[81] See A Boujdad M'kadem and P Nieuwenhuysen, 'Digital Access to Cultural Heritage Material: Case of the Moroccan Manuscripts' (2010) 29 *Collection Building* 137, doi.org/10.1108/01604951011088862.

[82] N Hysler Rubin, 'Digitizing Urban Heritage: The Digitization of Jerusalem Architectural Archives' (2023) 5 *Jerusalem Journal of Archaeology* 101, doi.org/10.52486/01.00005.7; jjar.huji.ac.il.

[83] See www.europeana.eu/en/collections/organisation/1072-egypt-centre.

[84] See www.europanostra.org.

[85] See, eg, rea.ec.europa.eu/news/eu-funded-cultural-heritage-projects-2022-05-03_en.

Mediterranean, which addresses relations with the 'Southern Neighbourhood', emphasises green and digital transformations while encompassing a broad spectrum of issues, including governance, social and economic development, climate action, and security.[86] Among the various aspects addressed, the agenda seeks to harness the potential of digital transformation by promoting innovative initiatives through the deployment of platforms and policies, including, among others, enhancing digital access to culture and cultural heritage, while ensuring a user-centric approach and the ethical use of technologies in accordance with the EU Charter of Fundamental Rights.[87]

8.7. Conclusion

All the endeavours and experiences briefly outlined in this chapter underscore both the transformative potential of digital technologies and the critical importance of data governance, standards, and interoperability in enhancing access and preservation on a broader scale.

The Mediterranean region, with its shared history, is home to a rich and diverse cultural heritage. While social, political, and developmental conditions vary significantly across the countries within the Mediterranean basin,[88] the drive to protect and preserve this multifaceted heritage remains a common goal, supported by numerous initiatives – some of which have been explored in this chapter.

Central to these efforts is the role of data and its proper governance, along with the legal frameworks that support these initiatives, which are certainly not uniform across the different countries involved. Nonetheless, significant progress has already been made in digitising, sharing, and connecting key elements of cultural heritage in the concerned countries, and further advancements are anticipated. These developments will contribute to greater access, deeper understanding, enhanced preservation, and broader enjoyment of the invaluable and diverse cultural heritage housed in the Mediterranean region.

[86] See European Commission, 'Joint Communication to the European Parliament, the Council, the European Economic and Social Committee and the Committee of the Regions. Renewed partnership with the Southern Neighbourhood – A new Agenda for the Mediterranean' JOIN(2021) 2 final.

[87] ibid.

[88] See D Helly, 'Cultural Heritage Protection in the Mediterranean Region: Beyond Resilience' (2018) *IEMed. Mediterranean Yearbook 2018*, 338–41.

9

Anthropology, Archaeology, Architecture and More: Towards a More Nuanced Methodology for Understanding the Past and Present of Privacy in the Mediterranean

JOSEPH A CANNATACI*

9.1. Thinking about Privacy

Who am I? How did I become who I am today? Whether right-wing or left-wing or centre-liberal or green, how did I explore the world of politics and decide who to vote for, if I ever decided to vote at all? Whether heterosexual, homosexual, trans or anywhere else on the LGBTQi spectrum, how did I explore my own sexuality and decide who and when to sleep with, if ever? How do I decide to spend my money when making purchasing decisions? Who and how will I be tomorrow? Why will I be that way? How free am I to decide for myself? Do I truly decide things for myself or am I constantly being manipulated by others into taking decisions which primarily suit them rather than me, irrespective as to whether that decision is which bar of chocolate, or car to buy, or who to vote for? What part does privacy play in all this? Where do we go from here?

These are only *some*[1] of the questions that are linked to the discussion about privacy in a twenty-first century where information and communications technologies are more pervasive than ever. There could be many more. The answers to these questions are extremely important since they may help us decide the way of life we value for our present and our future, and especially which laws to make and which policies to adopt to ensure that we protect that way of life.

* University of Malta and University of Groningen.

[1] Others could include 'Is my country worth fighting and worth dying for and, if yes, why do I think so?', etc.

It should be clear from the outset that there is an underlying theme in all of this discussion, ie the tension between autonomy and privacy, two subjects which may have often been confused in the past. By the end of this discussion, it will be seen that privacy is an essential enabling condition for maximising autonomy by minimising manipulation by others. When we keep our thoughts, preferences and actions as private as possible, we reduce the risk of others seeking to influence us, to manipulate us into taking decisions which they think are to our advantage and/or which are primarily to their own advantage. It follows that, in order to maximise autonomy of thought and freedom of action, we need to maximise the flows of all types of information towards us, while minimising misinformation and disinformation. The more complete and accurate information we receive or have access to, the more options we may have to explore and choose from, whether deciding what product or service to spend our money on, or who to vote for on election day. In order to ensure that we have the maximum number of options to freely choose from, it pays us to maximise our privacy since without it we become more easily manipulated.

But what is privacy? Why, when and how did it evolve and what relevance does its past have to our present and our future? Can we, should we, write new laws about privacy without understanding what privacy looked like in the past? How and why it evolved? This chapter, purely as a matter of convenience, focuses on technology-relevant dimensions of privacy in the Mediterranean region. Anthropology, archaeology, architecture (at times referred to as 'The Triple A approach') are some of the tools which help us answer these questions. Then again, there's much more than Triple A.

9.2. The Future is in the Past

Or should be. This is not a new finding in retro-causality,[2] but rather the result of reflecting at length on the intellectual challenge set by Mantelero, ie to investigate under-explored topics from a Mediterranean, rather than an EU-centric, perspective. In other words, what makes the Mediterranean special, if at all? In an increasingly globalised world, which parts of Mediterranean culture are especially worth preserving in the digital era? To what extent is privacy part of that Mediterranean culture? How did it evolve to be so? Having identified all that is precious about privacy in Mediterranean culture, one can then think more clearly about devising strategies to preserve and enhance it as Mediterranean societies become more and more digital. The EU should have a strong interest in these

[2] Retrocausality, or backwards causation, is a concept of cause and effect in which an effect precedes its cause in time and so a later event affects an earlier one. For a succinct summary about current trends in physics research see B Ferreira, 'A Growing Number of Scientists Are Convinced the Future Influences the Past' Vice (16 March 2023), www.vice.com/en/article/a-growing-number-of-scientists-are-convinced-the-future-influences-the-past.

strategies since, in addition to their being important to EU Member States on the Mediterranean, they may also have universal value.

In reflecting on Mediterranean digital societies there is obviously a strong interest in not letting history repeat itself. For, in 2025, many of us may be ruing the fact that we have ended up in digital societies which were never properly planned. If there was ever a social contract, this has been radically re-written, if not torn up, since (roughly) the World Wide Web was opened to the public in 1991. Except that it has not been re-written by citizens discussing the subject through their elected representatives in national parliaments or global inter-governmental institutions like the UN. Internet governance exists in name only,[3] but all of the Mediterranean countries are intimately linked to the Internet. The real controllers of the Internet include Meta, Google, Apple, Amazon and X (previously known as Twitter), and have been joined by other non-European, non-Mediterranean global giants like Tik-Tok and Ali Baba. Life without WhatsApp, Instagram, Facebook, Threads, SnapChat, Tinder, Reddit, Google, Apple, Amazon, Tik-Tok, Ali Baba, X and so on would be as unthinkable for people in the Mediterranean as it would be for those in Brazil, Asia, Australia or the USA. On the other hand, the business model for most of these companies is fundamentally that of profiling their users and acting as vehicles for advertisers to reach those users. It is not a business model that any Mediterranean prime minister has asked their voters to endorse, but it is certainly one that puts at stake the privacy of everybody in the Mediterranean and outside it. Even more would be at stake if the ruler/government of any Mediterranean states would use infringements of privacy to cut down on other fundamental rights like freedom of expression, freedom of association and freedom of religion.

The Mediterranean is where democracy was born, a key value that this chapter takes as a given. Though true democracy is not yet, in 2025, strongly embedded and functioning well in every Mediterranean country, the effective participation of the citizen in the governance of the state is taken to be a fundamental value which basic human rights like privacy also serve to protect and promote. This is where the wiser residents of the Mediterranean may also choose to learn from events which have taken place beyond their sea. The history of the use of the Internet to manipulate voters in, say, the 2016 presidential elections in the USA or the 2024 presidential elections in Romania is still being written, but strategies for preventing or at least minimising such manipulation need to be worked out for all countries in the Mediterranean too. That being said, the discussion runs deeper, for how are we to devise strategies which would protect particularly Mediterranean characteristics of privacy[4] if we could not identify them today or

[3] The Internet Governance Forum has existed since 2005, but it only discusses the subject and exerts no real governance function.

[4] It should be noted at the outset that the investigation in the research projects underpinning this chapter remains open to a Nil outcome, ie that, when later carrying out comparative analysis with the rest of the world, it may very well transpire that there is nothing particularly special

determine why, how, when and where they may have evolved in the five millennia leading up to 2025? If we wish to protect and promote these values in the future, we therefore need to look back deeply into our past to establish why privacy became and remains so valuable. This is also why it is important to devise and deploy the right methodologies for investigating the past and the present of privacy.

9.3. KAPOSIA[5]

To a considerable extent this chapter is a reflection on methodologies. It attempts to explore which blend of techniques is best to dissect the component elements and contributing disciplines which, when dovetailed together, help us understand what privacy was in days gone by, what it is today and what it should be in the digital age. The Mediterranean provides us the stage, the assortment of places grouped around the Middle Sea where one can demonstrate how the methodology works well. If it can be shown to work satisfactorily for the Mediterranean region, the methodology can hopefully then be extrapolated and refined further to be used in other regions of the world.

Before proceeding to demonstrate the KAPOSIA methodology in greater detail it is worth explaining that it builds on the thinking I previously developed in *The Individual and Privacy*,[6] in which I presented a conceptual framework whereby privacy could be examined *concurrently* through the lenses of *time, place and space* (TPS), with the place here being the Mediterranean.

about privacy in the Mediterranean and that the primary concerns may be universal rather than regional. On the other hand, it is reasonable to assume that focusing on the Mediterranean in the first instance would be, of itself, a valuable exercise in providing benchmarks and pointers on what to look for in other regions.

[5] KAPOSIA is both an acronym and a word in its own right. As an acronym it is made up of the first letters of *K*ipling, *A*ristotle, *P*ersonal *O*bservation *S*ciences, *I*nterviews & *A*nthropology. As a word derived from the (North American Indigenous) Dakotan Kapozha meaning 'light of foot' or 'not encumbered with much baggage', it also serves as a convenient pun – for this author arrived on the scene without much mental baggage and did not set out to prove anything in his four-decade-long exploration of privacy. He had – and he has – no definite hypothesis, no theory to prove or disprove. In that sense, he 'is not encumbered with much baggage'. On the other hand, he undoubtedly carries with him the baggage of conscious, subconscious and unconscious thinking about privacy for over 40 years, coupled with the experience of meeting with and interviewing hundreds of people across five continents, many of whom may have felt their privacy to be violated. Some theories may therefore evolve over time, fashioned from collective experience and observation, but they never become dogma. 'We do not do dogma.' Theories and even legal principles established in international or national law remain work in progress, continuously tested in different times, different places, different spaces, and with variations on a theme being provided by the same working hypothesis or theory being also explored and tested in the same place and possibly the same space but at different times. In early 2025, however relatively proven in practice, KAPOSIA is still a work in progress as a methodology under development and is expected to be refined and expanded further over the coming years.

[6] JA Cannataci (ed), *The Individual and Privacy* (London, Routledge, Taylor & Francis, 2015).

Firstly, it is submitted that, like many other topics, privacy may be conveniently explored using the traditional Kipling-esque approach epitomised in the following poem:

> I keep six honest serving-men
> (They taught me all I knew);
> Their names are What and Why and When
> And How and Where and Who.
>
> I send them over land and sea,
> I send them east and west;
> But after they have worked for me,
> I give them all a rest.[7]

So, for our purposes here, the questions *What?*, *Why?*, *When?*, *How?*, *Where?* and *Who?* will be applied to various dimensions of privacy at various points in *time* in various geographical locations (*place*) around the Mediterranean. When doing so, they will be deployed in different types of physical *space*, including both domestic and public spaces.

9.4. What Really Happens – And Happened – In Public and Private Spaces?

As will become clearer in a later section, Kipling's six honest serving men will also be deployed using a methodology exploring Aristotle's understanding of public and private places. Thus, it will be in the Greek part of the Mediterranean that we shall first seek inspiration for a better understanding of privacy. While always wary of using modern benchmarks to understand the concept of Ancient Greece, using the tools provided by anthropology[8] and especially archaeology within the KAPOSIA framework, we should attempt to draw parallels to the way that human interactions take place in the digital age.

It is here useful to reflect about the relationship between privacy and *space*. For most of the history of humanity, there were no telecommunications.

[7] 'The Elephant's Child' in R Kipling, *Just So Stories* (London, Macmillan, 1902).

[8] See American Anthropological Association, 'What is Anthropology?', https://americananthro.org/learn-teach/what-is-anthropology ('Anthropology takes a broad approach to understanding the many different aspects of the human experience. Some anthropologists consider what makes up our biological bodies and genetics, as well as our bones, diet, and health. Others look to the past to see how human groups lived hundreds or thousands of years ago and what was important to them. Around the world, they observe communities as they exist today, to understand the practices of different groups of people from an insider's perspective. And they study how people use language, make meaning, and organize social action in all social groups and contexts … In the community of anthropologists in the United States, these four fields – human biology, archaeology, cultural anthropology, and linguistics – are understood to be the pillars on which the whole discipline rests').

Communicating at a distance is something very new[9] and is still often considered to be a poor substitute for in-person communication. When examining how people interact with each other, it is therefore important to examine *where*, ie the physical space that they share – and which they choose to share. This physical space may often be divided into two main categories: public space and private space.

Private space as distinct from public space is not homogeneous: it is not one space. While it would be possible to describe private space as all that physical space which is not public, the sub-divisions of private space would also be susceptible to having areas which are private (in the proper sense of the word) and others which are shared with members of the household and/or guests, thus rendering them less private. Indeed, the term 'non-public household space' might be more useful to us since this would help differentiate between those spaces inside a household which are *less* private and those which are *more* private. For example, some members of the public may have access to parts of a private residence designated for receiving visitors (semi-public), but they would not normally have access to those parts of a residence deemed to be more private and reserved exclusively for some members of the household. Again, not *all* members of the household would have unfettered access to *all* areas of the household at all times.

Therefore, research on privacy, by definition must include studies of household spaces across the millennia in an effort to understand why, how, where and when certain similarities – and differences – in attitudes to privacy may have developed in all kinds of people (our 'Who' in this case). This is where privacy meets archaeology, for the latter discipline helps us understand the formation and development of households, especially before we could obtain detailed and reliable written accounts of what actually happened in such a household at a given moment in time.

This interest in privacy and households has led to the creation of a number of research projects, each with a specific focus, but eventually interlinked with other projects. The Mediterranean has been the main focus but not the exclusive zone of interest for these projects, and we shall draw on three of them for some of the reflections in this chapter.

For many years, the PRIVATUS project has studied *P*rivacy in *R*oman *I*nsulae, *V*illas & domus in *A*frican *T*erritories, E*U*rope and related *U*se of *S*pace. While primarily looking at privacy in domestic space in the 700 years from 300 BC to 400 AD, PRIVATUS also occasionally looks *before* that period to houses in the Carthaginian era/zones of control as well as after that period, to developments in the period 650 CE–1450 CE in those lands conquered as part of the Arab expansion around the Mediterranean littoral. Looking to the antecedents of Roman households in the Hellenistic period, necessarily led us to the influence of Greece and certain elements of Greek culture which may be intrinsic to privacy. Thus

[9] Take your pick from telegraph, telephone, video-phone, etc.

the PANAGIAG project was born focusing on *P*rivacy *A*nd *N*udity *A*nd *G*ender *I*n *A*ncient *G*reece. The relevance of nudity to privacy had also become apparent during the study of Roman households, as well as Roman public spaces such as baths and stadia. Those Roman games where athletes competing naked in stadia to which women were not permitted entry[10] harked back to the traditions of nudity in gymnasia in Greece.[11] PANAGIAG[12] took off as a long-term project, with close links to PRIVATUS, examining genderisation of spaces, nudity and privacy in both public and non-public spaces in Ancient Greece as well as the wider areas under Hellenistic influences.

The main tasks of these projects are to seek out, sift, collate and analyse the anthropological, archaeological, epigraphic and literary[13] evidence. Some of their preliminary findings may be found in the conclusions section of this chapter.

Literature meets archaeology in both Greek and Roman times when considering privacy-related concepts such as silence, secrecy and confidentiality. Archaeology provides us with many statues and statuettes of Harpocrates,[14] the God of silence, secrecy[15] and confidentiality, which were to be found in many

[10] *Flagiti principium est nudare inter civis corpora* ('The beginning of the scandal is to expose the bodies of the citizens') (Enn. Sc. 395 Vahlen). This famous quotation of Ennius, which is cited with approval by Cicero (Tusc. 4.33.70) to support his criticism of the Greek gymnasia, seems to represent the typical attitude to public nudity in the Roman Republic, which accounts to a large extent for the Romans' dislike of Greek athletics at the time. However, when nudity became more acceptable to the Romans, at least to the average citizen if not to the intellectual, then Greek athletics also became a more acceptable and attractive part of Roman life. NB Crowther, 'Nudity and Morality: Athletics in Italy' (1980–81) 76 *The Classical Journal* 119.

[11] With eminent Romans such as Cicero initially keen to time a visit to Greece to coincide with the games, this helps illustrate the extent to which Greek culture continued to be attractive to and have an impact on Roman culture.

[12] While PRIVATUS and PANAGIAG remain largely Mediterranean in focus, many of their objectives are now pursued concurrently in projects outside the Mediterranean such as the Baltic (BANYA-PEST is the Estonian component of BANYA-P *B*altic *A*nd *N*ordic *y* *A*ttitudes to *P*rivacy) and North and South America (PEATITA – *P*rivacy: *E*thno-*A*rchaeology, *T*echnology & *I*ndigenous *T*raditions in *T*he *A*mericas).

[13] Literary sources are dominated by Greek, the first *lingua franca* of the Mediterranean from the Myceanean Age and its successor, Latin. Part of the scientific basis for often choosing Greek sources for our evidence base is the fact that the Greek language has the oldest documented history of any indo-European language with the Greek alphabet in use for at least 2,800 years and its precursors in Linear B script dating to approximately 3,400 years ago, ie somewhere between 1350 and 1450 BCE. Phoenician adds itself to Latin and Greek as well as Egyptian hieroglyphics and various form of Cuneiform script when considering epigraphic evidence.

[14] In the Mediterranean, see, for example, A Bonanno, AJ. Frendo, and NC Vella, 'Excavations at Tas-Silg, Malta: a preliminary report on the 1996-1998 campaigns conducted by the Department of Classics and Archaeology of the University of Malta' (2000) 13 *Mediterranean Archeology* 67. For finds from Alexandria in Egypt, see D Meadows, 'Harpocrates in "Devotion and Ritual" Exhibition' (2010) The Rogue Classicist, https://rogueclassicism.com/2010/04/17/harpocrates-in-devotion-and-ritual-exhibition; A Holloway, 'Ancient Greek amulet with strange palindrome inscription discovered in Cyprus' (2015) Ancient origins, www.ancient-origins.net/news-history-archaeology/ancient-greek-amulet-strange-palindrome-inscription-cyprus-020151.

[15] In the earliest works in sociology, privacy-neighbouring concepts were often explored when discussing phenomena such as secrecy. See for example G Simmel, 'The Sociology of Secrecy and of Secret Societies' (1906) 11 *American Journal of Sociology* 441.

Greek and Roman households or private temples.[16] Since the cult of Harpocrates extended from the Hellenistic period well into Roman times, it is no surprise that archaeological evidence of Harpocrates has also been found far beyond the shores of the Mediterranean to various places where Roman rule may have reached in antiquity or where trade with Hellenistic cultures may have occurred.[17] Literature likewise provides us with references to why representations of the rose were painted or sculpted in many rooms where visitors where greeted or hosted to dine. The expression *sub rosa* or 'under the rose' is still defined by dictionaries[18] to mean 'in confidence or under pledge of secrecy'.

Interestingly enough, in classical antiquity, we note the link between places where wine was consumed and the representations of roses that adorned such spaces, suggesting that any secrets spilled under the influence of wine were not to be divulged. Where it can still be observed in sites around the Mediterranean, whether in medieval sites or dating back to antiquity in the times of the Roman empire, the painting or the sculpting of the rose is a reminder of the fact that concerns about information flows and privacy are age-old. The concern for confidentiality of what may have been communicated while drinking wine in a semi-private space such as a dining room are also age-old.

The tradition of painting or carving roses inside or outside meeting rooms, or indeed actually suspending a real rose in a meeting room such as a council chamber

[16] See M Attia, www.flickr.com/photos/130870_040871/51656280007 ('The only private temple discovered (1936) so far in Alexandria was situated in the Ras el-Soda area on the agricultural road leading to El Montazah and Abu Qear and near the eastern company of Linen. In the early 19th and 20th centuries, the temple was transported to Bab Sharq. It was built by the Roman charioteer Ezadoras (Isidore) as a thank-giving for Isis, on the recovery of his foot which was broken when he fell off his chariot. There are also four Ionic marble columns and five marble statues were placed between them; The 2nd statue: It belongs to god Harpocratis who is depicted as a naked child with his thumb in his mouth, he is also shown with a side lock of hair. Harpocrates (Ancient Greek: Ἁρποκράτης) was the god of silence, secrets and confidentiality in the Hellenistic religion developed in Ptolemaic Alexandria (and also an embodiment of hope, according to Plutarch). Harpocrates was adapted by the Greeks from the Egyptian child god Horus, who represented the newborn sun, rising each day at dawn. Harpocrates's name was a Hellenization of the Egyptian Har-pa-khered or Heru-pa-khered, meaning "Horus the Child". Horus is represented as a naked boy with his finger to his mouth, a realisation of the hieroglyph for "child". Misunderstanding this gesture, the later Greeks and Roman poets made Harpocrates the god of silence and secrecy').

[17] Including places as far away from the Mediterranean as Silchester in Britain, M Kennedy, 'Relic of Harpocrates, the god of secrecy and silence, found at Silchester' *The Guardian* (16 July 2010), www.theguardian.com/science/2010/jul/16/egyptian-god-relic-identified-silchester and found in the village of Faw, the capital of the ancient kingdom of Kindah today in Saudi Arabia, M Marie, 'Heracles, Harpocrates statues unveiled in Greece' *Egypt Today* (27 March 20190, www.egypttoday.com/Article/4/67574/Heracles-Harpocrates-statues-unveiled-in-Greece.

[18] *Sub rosa* literally means 'under the rose' in New Latin. Since ancient times, the rose has often been associated with secrecy. In ancient mythology, Cupid gave a rose to Harpocrates, the god of silence, to keep him from telling about the indiscretions of Venus. Ceilings of dining rooms have been decorated with carvings of roses, reportedly to remind guests that what was said at the table should be kept confidential. Roses have also been placed over confessionals as a symbol of the confidentiality of confession. *Sub rosa* entered the English language in the 17th century, and even before then, people were using the English version, 'under the rose'. Earlier still, *unter der Rose* was apparently used in Germany, where the phrase is thought to have originated; www.merriam-webster.com/dictionary/sub-rosa.

or carving a rose into wooden Christian confessional boxes, can be detected across the past two millennia, eventually spreading to lands quite distant from the Mediterranean.

The form and the function of rooms in classical antiquity is just as important as their decoration. Courtyard houses are not an architectural phenomenon exclusive to the Mediterranean, nor were they necessarily first created in this region,[19] but, over the millennia, they have certainly become characteristic of much of the Mediterranean lands. In examining the use of household space in courtyard houses in the Mediterranean, the KAPOSIA methodology is simply a means of bringing to privacy scholars that which Amos Rapoport did for architects and historians in his seminal early study.[20] Rapoport argued that house form is not only a subject of architecture, but is also related to cultural and social sciences such as anthropology, geography, history and city planning, benefiting also from cross-cultural studies. Rapoport's conceptualisation of the subject may also be mapped out onto Aristotle's discussions of *polis* and *oikos*, which will be briefly touched upon later in this chapter:

> Given a certain climate, the availability of certain materials and the constraints and the capabilities of a given level of technology, what finally decides the form of a dwelling, and moulds the spaces and their relationships is the vision that people have of the ideal life. The environment sought reflects many socio-cultural forces, including religious beliefs, family and clan structure, social organization, way of gaining livelihood and social relations between individuals.[21]

The climate in the Mediterranean is conducive to much outdoor activity especially in the relatively more private and sheltered courtyard. Whether decorated with a fountain and statues or just offering easy access to something as functional as a well, the courtyard, sometimes also a home to one or more shady trees, lends itself to several household activities such as cooking, washing clothes, spinning yarn, weaving cloth, pressing olives or grapes, and feeding animals. In some houses, a large oven in a corner of the courtyard can be used for baking bread and some courtyards were undoubtedly used for leisure, taking meals in, meeting members of the family and occasionally even privileged outsiders. Elif Bilge sums it up thus:

> The courtyard accordingly defines … a private area for a household, is a climatically efficient space in hot regions, has an efficient use of space in dense urban settlements, acts a circulation space in the domestic area and thus is an inclusive space performing all these tasks within the confined boundary of the domestic realm.[22]

[19] See for example F Abass, LH Ismail and M Solla, 'A Review of Courtyard House: History Evolution Forms, and Functions' (2016) 11 *ARPN Journal of Engineering and Applied Sciences* 2557.

[20] A Rapoport, *House Form and Culture* (Lebanon, Pearson, 1969) 47.

[21] ibid.

[22] E Bilge, 'The 'Courtyard House': A Spatial Reading of Domestic Architecture in Ancient Anatolia and Greece' (2019), thesis submitted to the Graduate School of Social Science of Middle Est Technical University, 20, https://etd.lib.metu.edu.tr/upload/12623056/index.pdf.

Rapoport claims that different shapes can define the same public–private relations within the same form, or the same shape create different forms in terms of public–private sphere. In his argument, the public and private spheres are connected through a 'lock' which is fundamental in the form of a house in terms of the relation between the private and public domains. The lock is a spatial feature, and can take the form of a semi public/private space, or it can be a bordered/controlled/closed area. It can also refer to physical arrangements or sequence of architectural elements such as walls, windows, doors and passageways. In ancient Greece, for example, the courtyard itself, as an indispensable part of the house, can be evaluated as a 'lock' which regulated the spatial relations between public and private. It also regulated the social interaction between the members of the household and the guests, and also between the members of the household themselves.[23] In a much later work, Rapoport explicitly examines how an important attribute of a courtyard house is its capacity in operating the 'privacy mechanism' often as a 'lock'.[24]

Of note too, when discussing courtyard houses in the Mediterranean as well as beyond, is the dimension of *visual privacy*. What can one see of the inside of the house when in the street outside the house? What can one see of the inside of the house when inside the entrance hall of the house or from the courtyard of the house? This is especially important when considering our previous observation that some parts of a house may be *semi-public* or, when viewed from the opposite perspective, *semi-private*. Sigalos illustrates this quite interestingly in his diagram of a Byzantine period house in the Athenian agora, showing the different visibility fields into the courtyard house from the entrance (more limited) and the centre of the courtyard.[25]

This is also where archaeology meets Aristotle. It is possible to write several chapters, indeed entire books, as to how archaeological remains all around the Mediterranean demonstrate how Greek houses evolved from the Megaron house in the eighth century BCE to the courtyard house in the third and second centuries BCE. Space constraints in this chapter do not permit such a detailed analysis, but, suffice it to say that 'The evolution of Greek houses, from larger, generalized spaces towards much more segmented, and specific rooms, signified a different and new level of organization in the household.'[26]

What actually happened in the Mediterranean and specifically inside the Classical Greek courtyard space has, over the decades, led to a discussion which is

[23] ibid.

[24] A Rapoport, 'The Nature of the Courtyard House: A Conceptual Analysis' (2007) 28 *Traditional Dwellings and Settlements Review* 57.

[25] L Sigalos, 'Housing People in Medieval Greece' (2003) 7 *International Journal of Historical Archaeology* 195.

[26] A Hoffer, 'Organization of space in Houses and Households of Ancient Greece' in A Glazebrook et al (eds), *Houses and Households in Ancient Greece* (2022), https://ecampusontario.pressbooks.pub/housesandhouseholdsancientgreece/chapter/organization-of-space.

of relevance to privacy scholars since it also concerns the possible genderisation of space. Hoffer summarises much discussion thus:

> [T]he courtyard house was able to offer much more specialized spaces and by many accounts did. Women's spaces would include the cooking space and other domestic labouring spaces (such as for weaving, etc.), while men's spaces would include an andron and other recreational spaces. But we can see from visual evidence on vases, as well as written accounts, that female entertainers were invited into the andron space during symposia, meaning that the room's 'men only' policy was geared towards the women who lived in the house, as well any wives or daughters of the guests. In addition, evidence of the activity of women appears throughout the house. Gendered space seems to be much more of a suggestion than a concrete area where a given activity must be done. Overall, one can see that there is some confusion in the evidence around the use of gender to divide the house into various spaces. The increased number of different spaces was not a result of subdividing spaces based on gender. Time of day, for example, would have been an effective way to divide up activities and keep men (especially non-kin males) and women separate.[27]

At this point it is worth pausing to note that, as in many other manifestations of different cultures around the Mediterranean and beyond it, one should always bear in mind the notion of portability of the vast majority of household objects. Cooking utensils, hand looms, musical instruments and even bedding could be easily transported from rooms inside the house to the courtyard (and vice versa) at different times of the days as well as different times of the year. Unlike the situation in many households of developed countries today, the location of most tasks was not fixed since the equipment required could easily be transported to the part of the house which was more climatically suitable. In many cases, for many months of the year in the Mediterranean, the courtyard may have been the place where light was best for some tasks and coolness was best for others. Whereas households in parts of countries outside the Mediterranean moved between a winter kitchen and a summer kitchen, in the Mediterranean the courtyard itself may have often doubled as the summer kitchen. Portability of household objects including bedding is relevant to privacy since it permits a space which is communal to the family or household during some times of the day to become private at other times.

Privacy in the Mediterranean of 3,000, 2,000 and even 1,000 years ago was also affected by cultural and economic phenomena. Chief among these was, perhaps, slavery. Many urban houses in ancient Greece and Rome had a complement of slaves: the economies of Greece and Rome in classical antiquity depended heavily on slaves[28] as a significant part of the means of production, and the

[27] ibid.

[28] See 'Confronting Slavery in the Classical World, September 29 – December 19, 2021', https://carlos.emory.edu/exhibition/confronting-slavery-classical-world ('Estimates suggest that in Athens between 450 and 320 BCE, 80 to 100,000 people may have been enslaved, amounting to one in four inhabitants; and that by the late first century BCE in Italy alone, 1 to 1.5 million people were enslaved, representing 15 to 25 percent of the population.'). See also P Hunt, 'Ancient Greece as a "Slave Society"' in CM Cameron and NL (eds), *What Is a Slave Society?: The Practice of Slavery in Global Perspective* (Cambridge, Cambridge University Press, 2018).

household was no exception. In middle and upper-class households many of the tasks, especially the growing of food, looking after animals and cooking, were carried out by slaves, not by the slave owners. This meant that activities today regarded as private, including bathing and toilet functions, may have been carried out in front of the household slaves. The slave emptied the chamber pots in the bedroom, ran errands around town, including buying the bread,[29] cooked, served food and drink at table, and slept in the household, albeit in quarters sometimes quite separate and distinct from those of their owners. Slaves were everywhere and saw, heard or otherwise witnessed most happenings, if not all, inside the household.

To a significant but incomplete extent, the slave in the Greek or Roman household was the equivalent of the all-seeing, all-hearing screen in Winston Smith's apartment in Orwell's *1984*. Except that, unlike the screen in 1984, the slave did not automatically breach privacy and communicate what was seen or heard inside the household to the holders of power in the country outside the household. And, unlike the screen in *1984*, which could not be switched off, the slave could be ordered out of the room or indeed the house.

The risk of breach of privacy by a slave was further mitigated by dimensions such as personal loyalty, dependence on the masters of the house, etc – but the risk remained. The issue of slaves and the ideal size of a household in order to be able to have slaves was the subject of much reflection and discussion by Aristotle, but that would be too much of a digression beyond the scope of this chapter.

Where Aristotle is a useful springboard for discussion about Mediterranean digital societies is what he may have said about privacy. In Book One of *Politics*, Aristotle carefully distinguishes between the *oikos* – the private family life – and the *polis* – the public realm of political affairs. When reflecting about what Mediterranean digital societies should be like in future and what should be the role of technology law in fashioning such a future, it pays to revisit Mediterranean thinking about private family life and the public realm of political affairs. Much has been written, especially by philosophers and political scientists, about what Aristotle really meant, how best to understand him and whether he was right or not. Some of those writings ventured into privacy, perhaps most famously those of Hannah Arendt:

> The emergence of society – the rise of housekeeping, its activities, problems, and organizational devices – from the shadowy interior of the household into the light of the public sphere, has not only blurred the old borderline between private and political; it has also changed almost beyond recognition the meaning of the two terms and their significance for the life of the individual and the citizen. Not only would we not agree with the Greeks that a life spent in the privacy of 'one's own' (idion), outside the world of the common, is 'idiotic' by definition, or with the Romans to whom privacy offered but a temporary refuge from the business of the res publica; we call private today a sphere of

[29] Unless the bread was actually baked inside the household.

> intimacy whose beginnings we may be able to trace back to late Roman, though hardly to any period of Greek antiquity, but whose peculiar manifoldness and variety were certainly unknown to any period prior to the modern age.[30]

Some scholars like Brendan Nagle have explicitly argued against Hannah Arendt's interpretation of the classical Greek distinction between public and private in *The Human Condition*. Nagle holds that 'it could be said that all polities aim at self-replication through their households. Although this is true to some extent, no other political entity possessed the degree of integration of public and private realms that were to be found in the *polis*, which in turn placed such a heavy burden, educational and otherwise, on the household. The interpenetration of economic, political, social, moral, and religious aspects of life – of public and private realms – was much more intense and complete in a *polis* than in any other form of state ancient or modern'; polities aim at self-replication through their households Nagle then further suggests (intriguingly only in a footnote) that:

> This understanding reverses the public-private dichotomy advocated by Hannah Arendt and her followers. Large implications result from this reversal, especially as it concerns gender relations. I agree strongly, though not always for the same reasons, with the sentiments of Patterson 1998 that '[t]he engagement of the long separated 'private and public spheres' enlarges the historical stage and increases our appreciation of the historical drama …. If … the family – its interests, structures and relationships – can be seen as an important participant in the historical development of Greek society, so also will women enter the historical realm. And they will enter not solely as objects of male gaze but as participants in social institutions …. The family is not the passive relic of political development, but the active fashioner of relationships and identities from which and with which its members engage the larger world.[31]

Nagle is a historian and his principal work on Aristotle examines the demographics of Greek households and cities as Aristotle would have known them with a view to showing that there was a distinctively close relation between them in Aristotle's thought. For Nagle, the household was both the economic foundation of the city and also, 'in some way, its moral basis'.[32] Philosophers and political scientists have spent the best part of 20 years arguing whether Nagle is right in thinking that this has important implications for the understanding of citizen education, slavery and the place of women in Aristotle's political theory.

While remaining neutral on these later debates, it is the accuracy of the demographics and the history that concerns us most in this chapter. It is not Aristotle's political theory but information policy and governance for the twenty-first century that concerns us most. For our purposes here, Nagle's most significant insight into Aristotlean Greek society is 'it was this unusual melding of public and private that gave the polis household its special character and imposed on

[30] H Arendt, *The Human Condition*, 2nd edn (Chicago, University of Chicago Press, 1998).
[31] DB Nagle, *The Ancient World: A Social and Cultural History*, 8th edn (New York, Pearson, 1998) 10.
[32] ibid 155.

it heavy responsibilities'.[33] The key reflection here is that Mediterranean digital societies must very carefully and in great detail consider the melding of public and private as impacted by the Internet, smartphones and other technologies in order to maximise democracy and protection of fundamental human rights. Aristotle's concerns about participation of the individual in the *polis* should also remain with us as we take into consideration the mountain of other evidence that has accumulated since the fourth century BCE when determining how law should regulate technology in the period 2025–2075 CE.

Before moving on from Aristotle, it is useful to recall at this stage the functions of a household and the differences between a modern household and those prevalent in the Mediterranean 2,000 years ago and more. Whereas a modern survey identifies five elements as characteristic of households generally – production, distribution, transmission, reproduction, and co-residence[34] – Nagle identifies the following distinctions between ancient and modern households:

> The differences were profound and manifold. In the eyes of Greeks, most modern households would have been seen as deficient, incomplete economic entities failing in the all-important aspect of being, at least minimally, self-sustaining. In this regard, modern households are the reverse of polis households in that they are, by and large, dependent for their subsistence on income originating from outside the household. Without jobs provided by the disembedded, non-household economy, modern households could not exist. Households of this type are merely consumer and reproductive units. By contrast, the Greek oikos was expected to be a self-sustaining joint enterprise, almost invariably agricultural, undertaken by husband and wife for the specific goal of the perpetuation of the *oikos* and the passing on of its resources to the next generation.[35]

It is submitted that Nagle's assessment of the Greek understanding of the household[36] is a useful way for twenty-first-century society to understand how best to apply some interpretations of Aristotle's world view to its own realities, and especially because most citizens today live both inside *and* astride real space and cyberspace. From a privacy scholar's perspective, the way that an individual's activities in cyberspace are monitored and surveilled may have implications for both politics and security, including national defence. This then becomes another key law and technology insight for Mediterranean digital societies. Aristotle was

[33] ibid 10.

[34] RMcC Netting, EJ Arnould and RR Wilk (eds), *Households: Comparative and Historical Studies of the Domestic Group* (Los Angeles, University of California Press 1984).

[35] DB Nagle, *The household as the foundation of Aristotle's polis* (Cambridge, Cambridge University Press, 2006) ch 1.

[36] Neither Netting's definition nor Gallant's adaptation of it is an adequate basis for fully grasping Greek understanding of the household and, in turn, Aristotle's analysis of it. In their introduction, Netting et al (n 36) 12, note that they do not discuss 'household activities that fall outside [the] five spheres – such as defense or political action – although these can be of overriding importance in some cases'. This brief statement speaks volumes about modern assumptions regarding the household. For Netting and his contributors, politics and defence are not central to 'households' but peripheral, whereas their five other characteristics – production, distribution, transmission, reproduction and co-residence – are definitional.

very keen in his analysis to examine the role of the citizen in society (the *polis*) outside the household (the *oikos*) while carefully maintaining that the *oikos* was the building block of the *polis*.

If Mediterranean digital societies wish to become or remain democracies they must also be very careful to regulate activities in cyberspace, including politics, security and defence. As a number of elections worldwide[37] have shown, thanks to the Internet, the individual citizen can be reached, manipulated and mobilised without ever having to be displaced from the comfort of their own home. In the political world, votes can be bought outright or nudged 'in the right direction' because the Internet user has been carefully and incessantly profiled by website controllers for years on end. This means that hostile foreign powers may insidiously manipulate voters in another state to produce national governments more favourable to that foreign power. Likewise liberty, personal security and the treatment of criminal offenders can be enhanced or threatened by intrusive digital technologies such as electronic ankle bracelets, which can be useful measures when dealing with probation, prison overcrowding, domestic violence and femicide.

This is where we can bring into thinking about Mediterranean digital societies, reflections largely co-ordinated from the northern part of Europe. Recently the inter-disciplinary efforts made by IPG[38] and STeP[39] in developing anthropological approaches to privacy research have been complemented by The Danish National Research Foundation Centre for Privacy Studies (PRIVACY), which was established in September 2017. The PRIVACY research team examines how notions of privacy and the private shape relations between individuals and society across diverse historical contexts. They are particularly interested in indications of privacy as a quality and threat: in the emergence and development of the idea that too little privacy threatens the individual while too much may ruin society. PRIVACY focuses on the period 1500–1800, which saw critical changes in individuals' relationship to society. It brings together the fields of church history, history of architecture, history of ideas, legal history and social history.[40]

One of the important contributions made by our Danish-led colleagues has been the recent articulation[41] of the concept of privacy as heuristic zones.

The PRIVACY scholars deploy a heuristic set of zones, depicted above, 'that represent early modern areas of theoretising, regulation and practice related to privacy and the private. These zones are neither exhaustive nor absolute, but they

[37] Including the USA in 2016 and Romania in 2024.

[38] The Department for Information Policy & Governance in the Faculty of Media & Knowledge Sciences at the University of Malta, Malta.

[39] The Security, Technology & e-Privacy (STeP) Research Group within the Department for Transboundary Legal Studies in the Faculty of Law at the University of Groningen in the Netherlands.

[40] Abstracted from https://teol.ku.dk/privacy/about-privacy.

[41] See the diagram of heuristic zones in M Birkedal Bruun, 'The Centre for Privacy Studies Work Method' (2019), https://teol.ku.dk/privacy/research/work-method. The footnotes in that paper include an indication of some of the previous attempts to articulate privacy in terms of zones or spheres.

do offer a common structure'[42] that enables the Danish-led group to correlate widely different sources and disciplinary approaches. Birkedal Brun describes an approach which is uncannily similar to the one adopted by IPG and STeP teams since the late 1980s:

> The zones serve as a catalyst for historical analysis. They point to spatial registers that are relevant not least but not only, in relation to architecture, and they delineate particular practices and ideal entities as well as their intersections. Each zone thus gives rise to historical debates regarding privacy, and the thresholds between zones potentially involve a negotiation where the contours of an individual or a group of individuals come to the fore. We take special interest in the thresholds: how and where is the boundary between, say, the street and the house, demarcated and described; is the retreat into an alcove perceived as an escalation of privacy; how are the difference of activities and characteristics pertaining to respectively the body and the mind classified – and are such classifications related to privacy or the private?
>
> Just as interesting, however, are the overlaps between zones. When we consider such overlaps, our attention is directed to questions such as: to what extent and by which means do rulers and societies access and regulate the minds of subjects; which societal circumstances provoke a change in this regard; and how do members of, for example, a civic community gain access to private homes; how do the collective norms of a community or a household determine the bodily practices of an individual? Such questions spring from the zone structure and aid our joint focus on, for example, legislative boundaries between household and community, decrees regarding individual bodies or the theoretizing of the household (oeconomia) viv-a-vis the societal order (politia) as well as the regulation of practices that come out of it.[43]

In outlining this conceptual framework for the analysis of privacy, Mette Birkedal Brun also shares the same preoccupations held to the fore by the IPG and STeP teams since 1988:

> The heuristic zones help us to put such questions to the sources and to establish common ground between disciplines. Since the work with the zones takes as its point of departure conceptions of privacy that are to some extent modern, this approach comes with the risk of anachronism. We pay heed to possible projections of our own more or less conscious assumption that certain phenomena are particularly private, be they artefacts (particular pieces of clothes, mementos, containers for personal belongings, activities (sleep, sex, hygiene, contemplation), spaces (home, bed, bedroom, latrine, confessional), forms of communication (letters, one on one conversations, coded communication, sharing of secrets) and so forth.[44]

This explains the particular caution with which the IPG/STeP teams are currently approaching their work in North Africa and the eastern littoral of the Mediterranean, especially when investigating the overlap between those heuristic zones where religion and gender are concerned. It also explains why we take

[42] ibid 3.
[43] ibid 3–4.
[44] ibid 5.

Aristotle's analysis of *oikos* and *polis* and attempt to understand and validate or simply be inspired by his analysis through the lens of interlocking and overlapping spheres.

Nagle has argued that:

> In emphasizing the integration of private and public sectors, of household and *polis*, I do not wish to return to an older view of the *polis* that saw the household's privacy minimised and subordinated to the intrusive authority of the state.[footnote omitted] The private realm of the household was a culturally recognised space distinct from the public, although integrated with it in complex ways. A common designation of enemies was *hoi thurathen*, those outside the courtyard gate of the house.[footnote omitted]

It is precisely *the complexity* of the integration of the private realm with the public space that again demands our attention in the twenty-first-century regulation of Mediterranean digital societies. It is submitted that Nagle's analysis of public/private in the Greek Mediterranean societies of 2,000 years ago could be mostly valid when applied to Mediterranean digital societies of the twenty-first century:

> Yet the terms 'public' and 'private' (*dēmosios/idios*) were flexible concepts subject to a variety of interpretations depending on the particular *polis* and the matters at hand more complementary than binary opposites.[footnote omitted] A recent interpretation, for instance, asserts the concept of 'a protected private sphere as one of the constitutive characteristics of a democratic society.'[footnote omitted] *An individual could play different roles in private and public without having to be a political figure in our sense of the word.*[45] Attending the assembly, serving as a juror or as a member of a chorus could all be viewed as public activities conducted by private individuals. Perceptions of what activities pertained to private and public differed considerably from modern assumptions in this regard. While adultery in developed countries is generally regarded as a private affair between consenting adults, laws prohibiting it notwithstanding, in democratic Athens, adultery was regarded as a dangerous violation of *public* order and a potential threat to the state because it destabilized the relationships between households and initiated intergenerational feuds. Yet, an adulterous wife was not punished directly. Her punishment was that she could not participate in public religious functions, which was a severe punishment in its own way because religion was of such importance to all aspects of life. Penalties for homosexuality were also indirect. They included prohibitions against participation in politics in the public realm and the holding of a wide range of public and administrative offices. Yet, actual homosexual activity between consenting adults was left unregulated in the private realm (it was a different matter if seduction was involved). Laws were directed at protecting boys and young men from seduction because it could affect their capacity at a later date to participate fully in the civic life of the city. Homosexuals were punished directly only if they violated the prohibition against their participation in politics. Although privacy was thus protected from the intrusion of the state, this did not protect practitioners from social and religious censure. Demosthenes reports a litigant as claiming that 'in a democracy a man has a

[45] Emphasis here added for relevance to the role of the individual in digital societies.

> right to do and say whatever he likes as long as he does not care what reputation such conduct will bring him'[46]

One of the ways in which the modern Mediterranean differs from that of classical antiquity is that it offers significantly more scope for complexities thanks to digital technologies. In many instances, for example, adultery can be both detected and condemned using a combination of smartphone cameras, spyware, Internet access, open source intelligence and social media. Homosexuality can be explored in private on the Internet and, indeed, private meetings with others on the LGBTQI spectrum or, indeed, between heterosexuals, can be set up using the Internet in ways which would be much less public than those in classical Greece or Rome. At the same time, men and women can carve out private spaces in cyberspace where their conforming or otherwise with, say, the norms in Catholic or Muslim societies may be neither noticeable nor surveillable. Social and religious censure is still possible in Mediterranean digital societies but, in point of fact, the digital element may actually help mitigate or avoid outright the full extent of such censure. If, on the other hand, however, many or all of our online activities were open to prying eyes, that lack of privacy would render us vulnerable in many more ways than was possible in classical antiquity.

The reflections above, Aristotlean or otherwise, remain useful when using the Triple A approach to investigate developments outside classical Greece and Rome when it comes to the third and fourth spheres in the PRIVACY representation of the heuristic zones of privacy as cited previously, ie 'chamber/alcove/studio' and 'home/household'. While we can detect many similarities, it quickly becomes clear that the Mediterranean is not homogeneous. The courtyard house was already spreading across the Mediterranean before the Roman Empire engulfed all of that sea. If form often follows function in architecture then good ideas like courtyards either spread from one region to another or else develop independently. Whatever the reason, the Mediterranean house with a central courtyard is the most common type of housing to be found in the pre-Roman Carthaginian city of Kerkouane[47] in modern-day Tunisia. The different rooms of many houses in Kerkouane are arranged around the patio or courtyard, which provided ventilation and light. Little is known as to the precise extent to which Carthage had been influenced by Hellenistic civilization, but the courtyard house was something that the Greeks and the Carthaginians and other peoples had in common.

We are here less interested in who came up with the design first, but rather that it seems to have been appreciated and persisted. So when the Romans took over modern-day Morocco, Algeria, Tunisia and Libya, it is no surprise that they built many courtyard houses across most of North Africa. Those houses

[46] Nagle (n 35).
[47] 6th–3rd century BCE: www.patrimoinedetunisie.com.tn/en/sites/kerkouane.

appear to have been taken over in many instances by the later settlers of these lands. It is not known whether the seventh-century CE Arab expansion across North Africa by the Rashidun and Umayyad caliphates brought with them any new ideas about courtyard houses, but what is clear is that this approach to design persisted in the region until blocks of flats began to be erected in the colonial period, which spanned the second half of the nineteenth century and the first half of the twentieth century. As a design permitting private, semi-private and semi-public spaces, the courtyard house proved itself climatically and economically, with a number of variations on a theme, as adopted for use by households embracing all the major religious faiths to be found across the Mediterranean littoral.[48]

9.5. Personal Observation[49]

Choosing the Mediterranean for the case study of the project on digital society underpinning this book was not accidental. It has also permitted the use of classical anthropology tools, including regular full-immersion study in a community, with some special twists. As happened in these pages, such an international research can take advantage of the observations of a scientist who has been embedded in the Mediterranean community[50] for long periods of time, yet on and off for years on end, across the span of six decades. Add to that the value of one who was born in the Mediterranean, one who has worked in various roles across at least 18 of the countries that border the Mediterranean, coupled with the insights and detachment obtained after having lived in various places outside the Mediterranean for several years. The findings are far more than being merely anecdotal. They may occasionally be imperfect and not necessarily as comprehensive as one would wish, but they remain accurate, intimate and detailed.

[48] Space constraints do not allow further detailed analysis about developments relevant to architecture and privacy in North Africa and Anatolia, but see the relevant chapter in J Cannataci, *Privacy imperilled: post-Snowden, post-COVID* (Bristol, Bristol University Press, forthcoming 2026).

[49] The P in KAPOSIA may well have been 'Participant' rather than 'Personal'. Indeed, in classical anthropological categorisation of fieldwork, the term 'participant observation' may well be applied to what the author has been carrying out for decades. The term 'personal' was chosen, however, as a reminder that there was a period of gradual transition (many decades ago) from being a member born into the community to becoming a participant-observer, at which point 'the anthropologist does not have exactly the same quality of experience as these activities evoke in local people. This is so first of all because the anthropologist does not merely participate in routines but is highly conscious and observant, taking nothing for granted and noting the experience in great detail'. See HJ Birx, *An Encyclopedia of Anthropology* (London, Sage, 2006) vol 3, 966.

[50] Admittedly, the embedding was accidental and not part of a carefully thought-out project design. On the other hand, once it happened, and once one can look back on an accident of history and makes allowances for all sorts of bias, then one might as well make use of a number of intimate insights and the maturity that pensionable age hopefully brings with it.

9.5.1. Interviews

Access to interviews, both formal and informal, carried out over the past forty years add to the value of the KAPOSIA methodology. Interview responses not only permit validation and calibration of findings obtained independently, but also occasionally provide novel insights, especially in situations outside the direct personal observation and experience of the scientists involved in the research.

9.5.2. A Personal Journey

The reader will hopefully forgive the personal nature of this writing, especially when they form part of the personal observation sciences[51] component of the methodology. It is sometimes difficult to explain to friends and colleagues from outside the Mediterranean what it means to have been born and lived there. It's not just sun and sea, swimming and sailing.

To give but one example, take the flat roofs of Malta and many parts of Morocco, Algeria, Tunisia, Libya, Egypt, Israel, Lebanon and Greece. Even friends in the more northern part of the Mediterranean itself, let alone those born and living in landlocked cities like Turin in north-eastern Italy, do not know what it means to have flat roofs rather than sloping ones. In many parts of the Mediterranean (though not all), we do not need sharply sloping roofs on our houses because there is no snow to shake off during the winters. A very gentle incline – just enough for what little rainwater there is to find its way to the drainpipe running down to the well – is sufficient, thus creating spacious outdoor terraces. This means that, especially in the heat of the long summer months, the roof becomes a natural extension of the interior living space. In those many, many centuries, millennia even, prior to the advent of air-conditioning, in the hot months we slept close to or actually *on* the roof of our houses when the summer nights rarely dip below 22 or 24 degrees. In 2025, even if they do not often sleep there any more, many families in Malta, Tunisia, Morocco, Algeria and Egypt still use their rooftop terraces to take mint tea or coffee or drink cool lemonades, or regularly cook barbeques, and even entertain guests. The climate permits –indeed encourages –it.

In the past, living at least partially on the roof was even more of a necessity. For my boyhood and throughout my adolescence and well into my twenties, my room on the roof was where I lived, with three windows and two doors but no air-conditioner. When I moved to Norway in my mid-twenties a different reality hit me. The Norwegians could occasionally enjoy the *aurora borealis*, but sleeping on the roof, looking at the stars, enjoying the evening cool or sipping a cold ginger ale in the roof garden was not something any child born and living in Norway

[51] See explanation of 'participant observation' in n 49.

was going to experience. Nor those living in Germany, nor England, nor dozens of countries to the north of the Mediterranean where the lack of a flat roof make a terrace or roof garden impossible, indeed unthinkable in most places. This was a very personal way of finding out that the geographical location determined the climate – and that the climate had given rise to cultural differences in the nature and use of domestic living space. But, while accepting that in many places in Europe the roof is not a living space, to what extent was/is the Mediterranean flat roof terrace a private space or a public space? Especially if it could be overlooked or easily accessed from the neighbour's roof?

As I started travelling and working across North Africa in the early 1990s, I encountered many other rooftop terraces which acted as an extension of the living space of the houses below. I encountered the same Mediterranean rooftop culture indirectly in literature[52] and eventually even cinema[53] where the flat roof terrace, often provided with some form of awning and partial privacy, was also occasionally the chance or preferred place for sexual encounters and even part of sexual awakening.[54] Not to mention that the Bible stories on which we were raised also very much fitted in with narratives of a busy life happening on flat terraced roofs.[55] This very Mediterranean phenomenon was one of the reasons why I started factoring in geography and topographical and climatic differences quite early on into my thinking about privacy. As four decades of research and thinking about privacy went by, I was to find out that I needed to factor in many other aspects in addition to geography in my attempts to better understand the rather complicated and multi-dimensional phenomenon that, in European law, we identify as 'private and family life'.[56]

The very same warm climate that encourages the use of roofs as an intrinsic part of domestic space in the Mediterranean also encourages other practices which ultimately impact the nature of private and family life in one form or another. If you did not go up to the roof when it was too warm to stay inside and you wished to catch the evening breeze, the children sat on the doorsteps while their elders brought out chairs and folding armchairs. Life indoors literally spilled out onto the pavements and the streets and squares of the town or village in a way which is discouraged by the cold weather of cooler climes. This created social interaction that was often inimical to privacy since neighbours sitting together on the pavement tended to observe each other, exchange news and generally gossip. If they

[52] See the Cairo Rooftop in N Mahfouz, *Palace Walk* (New York, Doubleday 1990) 34 ('This roof, with its inhabitants of chickens and pigeons and its arbor garden, was her beautiful, beloved world and her favorite place for relaxation').

[53] *Halfaouine; Boy of the Terraces* (1990).

[54] ibid.

[55] The Old Testament in the Christian Bible provides us with various tales of breaches of privacy and sexual activity, with the roof terrace featuring prominently in some instances: 'One evening David got up from his bed and walked around on the roof of the palace. From the roof he saw a woman bathing. The woman was very beautiful' (2 *Samuel* 11:1–12); 'So they set up a tent on the palace roof where everyone could see it, and Absalom went in and had sex with his father's concubines' (2 *Samuel* 16:22).

[56] See Art 8 European Convention on Human Rights.

ventured from their homes for a late afternoon or evening walk on the seafront promenade, they also tended to meet, chat and gossip – as they did in the open-air cafes and terraces. Life outdoors, where it was cooler in the evenings, especially in coastal areas as the sea breeze came in over the Mediterranean, encouraged people to go out and intermingle. This was typical post-war across much of the Mediterranean until the mid-1950s when economies started to recover from war.

The story remains very personal to this author: although solidly middle class, we had no air-conditioners in our spacious homes so, yes, my parents, sister, cousins and other relatives and friends spilled out onto the roof, into the yards and onto the pavements as well as the seaside promenade. We children played in streets largely devoid of traffic;[57] this was also because, except for reading, there was much less entertainment to be had at home: television sets only started to creep into Mediterranean homes in the late 1950s and 1960s. Even then, the number of channels was small and the TVs were black and white. Colour TV and the multiplicity of channels that emerged with the liberalisation of broadcasting and the arrival of satellite TV were only gradually introduced in the period 1975–1995, so staying indoors was not necessarily such an attractive proposition.

It is therefore important to note what has happened over the past 70 years or so. Some of the social interaction prevalent in the warm Mediterranean as described above has since been impacted and diminished by three key technologies which have accompanied prosperity and which have caused people to mingle less with their neighbours: 1) air-conditioning permits people to remain inside their houses with an even more reliable source of cool air than that provided outside by Mother Nature; 2) television entertains people inside their houses more than neighbours' stories; and 3) the exponential surge of cars on the road means that the streets are no longer full of children playing all sorts of games since relatives anxious for their safety have mostly chased them back inside.

This is not to say that many people in the Mediterranean do not still take walks on the seafront promenade or mingle in open-air cafes. They do, but for many of them, less frequently than in the past, since they remain inside the comfort of their own homes, especially since, post-COVID, more and more people became accustomed to – and ready to pay for – the convenience of being able to order almost any kind of food to be brought home. The Internet not only permits a multitude of home entertainment channels, but also the means to work from home and order food and drink to be brought in. You may still wish to go out and interact with other human beings but, in point of fact, you have less need to do so. The prospect of peace and quiet in the comfort of one's home away from the hustle and bustle of crowds and without needing to brave the traffic, for many Mediterranean dwellers

[57] Where my father was the first person to own a car in the street when he bought his Austin A30 in 1955. Likewise, my father-in-law was the first to own a car in his street, in 1956, albeit in another town in Malta.

has decreased in-person social interaction in a way which has still to be properly measured.

Indeed, as you drive around the Mediterranean littoral today, as a rule, the more inland you go and the more rural and less prosperous a village, the greater the chance that you will observe the older way of life being followed, with children playing outside on the street, and the use of rooftop terraces rising in inverse proportion to the presence of air-conditioning units – likewise in some of the Medinas of the North African states, where road traffic is much less intense or impossible, and where air-conditioning is not yet affordable for everybody. When and where the climate and economic circumstances encourage people to mingle more, individual privacy becomes less prominent. It does not disappear completely – for some things are still kept private and, anyway, some people are more private than others – but, as a rule of thumb, the smaller the community and the greater the social intermingling, the more neighbours know about each other. Indeed, in some communities, it is the extent of collective privacy rather than individual privacy which may need to be properly investigated for, in some Mediterranean communities,[58] what goes on inside the community is often protected from strangers. The transition experienced in the last 50–70 years or so needs to be further examined.

9.5.3. Mare Nostrum

In 2020, one of the insights that Alessandro Mantelero[59] developed into the idea for a Jean Monnet Chair[60] was

> to promote Mediterranean studies in digital technologies and law through an inter-disciplinary contamination. This aimed to amplify the voice and participation of Mediterranean countries in the regulatory and policy debate in the EU and to create a bridge between the cultures of EU and non-EU Mediterranean states.[61]

This idea was and remains intriguing since it provides us with the opportunity to study when, how and why privacy was developed in the past within one of the cradles of civilisation, and thus hopefully help us think better as to when, how and why privacy should be protected in the future both within the EU and outside it. It does so by helping us identify what were the core values that characterised life in the Mediterranean in the past and then explore what dimensions have been added by a digital present and future.

[58] See for example certain small towns and villages in southern Italy, Sicily, Greece, Portugal and Spain.

[59] Professor of Law and Technology at Politecnico di Torino.

[60] An EU scheme which funds the opportunity for higher education institutions to host a teaching post with a specialisation in EU studies for university professors.

[61] Digital Mare Nostrum, Jean Monnet Chair in Mediterranean Digital Societies and Law, DIGIMED, https://digimed.polito.it.

When first discussing this idea with one of my mentors in 1986, I explained to Jon Bing that it was inevitable that developments in information technology would shape the future of societies that then, and possibly still today, we may view as being quite different from each other. The digital technology would however be the same in all of these Mediterranean societies and would possibly create opportunities for increasing similarities and peaceful interchange. It was still too early to foretell how the use of smartphones linked to an ubiquitous Internet would influence the gatherings of Cinque Stelle in Italy or Gilets Jaunes in France or the Arab Spring across North Africa, but it was not too early to understand that computers could be used to both enable and simultaneously monitor behaviour across borders as well as within all of these countries.

As we moved into the early 1990s, which saw the advent of the World Wide Web, it became clear that we had created cyberspace, a place which is both linked to and distinct from the physical space that our bodies inhabit. Cyberspace adds dimensions to where we go, whom we meet, what ideas we can discover and explore, who to share them with, and how and when to do something about ideas in physical space.

Over the past four decades, it had long struck me that there may be interesting similarities in patterns of development in the Mediterranean in the ancient past and the digital present. For more than 3,000 years, peoples, their ideas, their beliefs, their goods and their languages, as well as their skills and their technologies, had moved to the north and south of the Mediterranean using rafts, ships, mules, donkeys, horses, camels and even elephants. These peoples intermingled, their ideas about the human body and medicine were interchanged, and their architectural designs were occasionally intertwined, but the climate and geography of the Mediterranean remained constants which influenced the extent to which things were different or things remained the same, wherever you travelled across the north, south, west and east of this *mare nostrum*.

What would digital technology add to life in the Mediterranean? These were some of the thoughts that went through my mind in July 1993 as I wandered through the narrow streets of the Medina of Tunis, gazed at the blue doorways leading to the courtyards of the whitewashed houses of Sidi Bou Said and navigated the walls and alleyways of Kairouan. But it was as I walked past some of the hammams in the Medina of Tunis and glimpsed times and dates and occasionally entire bath houses where only women were admitted, that another dimension of privacy struck me. For why would women renounce the privacy of their intimate bodies to a public gaze, albeit that of other women? While the socialising dimension was immediately apparent, the economic and technological dimensions immediately added themselves.

It was more common, 30–50 years ago, for Tunisian houses in the Medina (as well as those outside it) not to have running water and certainly not central heating. If you needed water you either raised a bucket out of the well where you collected the rain water that ran off your flat roof or, if that was unavailable and if a solitary tap had not yet been installed in your house off the water mains running beneath the street outside, you took a walk from your home to the nearest communal water fountain and brought a pitcher of water from there. Unless you bothered to heat it, since there was usually no plumbed-in bathroom in many homes, bathing for hygiene purposes was restricted to what could be done using the pitcher and basin in your bedroom or bathroom (a space which, if you were lucky, contained a tin or cast iron bath which had to be filled and emptied manually). For many centuries, for most people except the very rich,[62] the lack of indoor plumbing and modern conveniences meant that it was impractical to have regular hot baths at home since it was difficult to transport and heat water. In most countries across the world, it was only in the latter half of the nineteenth century and the first half of the twentieth century that the technology required to deliver running water to every household made a daily warm bath or shower a reality.

Tunisia was no exception to this global trend. For more than 2,000 years, the solution to what was basically a problem created by developments in water technology and its affordability, was, for most people except the rich,[63] the creation of a central location in the neighbourhood that had the capacity to bring in enough water and heat it for anyone who wanted to go and bathe. The concept of public baths in the Mediterranean dates back at least 2,500 years to the baths which dotted many cities in the Greek world. The Romans learned from and developed the Greek concept of public baths, and these are typically found in the corners of the vast Roman empire which was the very first regime to have transformed *all* of the Mediterranean into a Mare Nostrum.

Two thousand years later, the public baths of the Roman occupation of Tunisia had given way to the hammams which characterised the three centuries of Ottoman rule and survived through French colonial rule until the emergence of Tunisia as an independent state in 1957. As I walked through the Medina of Tunis in July 1993, and during several visits since, even until my very last visit there quite recently, this communal approach to personal hygiene, massage and socialising has still been evident in the various hammams operating across the old city. Quite often, the arrangement was that women could spend hours in the hammam during the days and men could do so in the evenings after work. In Tunisia, they remain quite practical because most homes do not have central heating and, unless you own a modernised bathroom with an electric or gas heater (a much more common phenomenon in 2024 than it was in 1957[64]), the hammam often remains the one

[62] If you were rich enough you could afford to have slaves or servants to warm the water, fill and empty baths, as well as fetch water and dispose of waste water and the contents of chamber pots. If you were not rich enough, then bathing for hygiene purposes was rarely a daily ritual but could be once a week or once a fortnight when members of the household took turns to heat the water and use the bath, often also taking turns and using the same water in the same bath.

[63] If you were rich enough you normally had bathing facilities of varying complexity installed in your own house, obviating the need to leave the house to go to the public baths if hygiene were the only reason for going there.

[64] Some Tunisian friends and acquaintances claim to still go to the hammam once or twice a week even though they own modern bathrooms, since they find the experience of the hammam to be superior to that of bathing alone at home.

place people can go to do their bathing in a hot (or at least moderately warm) room.

Yet, it was the walks across the Tunis Medina, as well as coming across hammams in many other cities in North Africa, which made me recall another childhood memory as well as other family tales. The stone houses in the towns and cities of my native Malta were generally relatively spacious affairs, built with high ceilings and good ventilation to help keep rooms cool in a hot climate but, for most, including those built in the nineteenth and early twentieth centuries, you would be lucky to have a small space that could be used as a toilet. While these small spaces were gradually connected to the public sewers, with some notable exceptions, bathrooms with baths permanently installed tended to be add-ons in Maltese domestic architecture until independence in 1964. Until then, a sizeable bathroom was often an after-thought added at the rear of the building in pre-war terraced houses, or close to some internal yard. The toilet equipped with a (cast-iron) flushing mechanism made its appearance earlier than fully fledged bathrooms. While many houses had bathrooms with cast iron baths and pedestal sinks added mostly after World War II, I clearly remember many other houses belonging to family and friends, including that of one of my grandmothers, where no bathroom at all existed even in the 1980s, where no permanently plumbed-in water heater was installed and where a pitcher and water basin remained the order of the day if you wished to splash some cold water and brush your teeth. If you had the money in pre or post-war Malta, you installed a bathroom. If not, you made do.

These reflections established water technology and the economics of bathroom affordability as two other important dimensions when thinking about privacy. If you were rich enough you had a separate space or room where you could bathe. If you were not rich enough, until fairly recently, you often had to bathe in the same room where you slept, often with other members of the family. In this, the Mediterranean appears to have been no different to most other places around the planet: water technology and its affordability are key dimensions to where and what you do for intimate hygiene.

Water technology also had other impacts on social interaction. For millennia, many people would need to leave their homes to go and fetch water from a stream or a well. The local water supply point such as the well or stream thus became a meeting place where people would socialise and gossip. It was one of the few places, apart from the local church, where teenage boys could eye teenage girls and even occasionally make bolder moves.[65] In some countries, even today, procuring water still occupies one or two hours every day in rural areas, especially in sub-Saharan Africa. In Malta, as in other Mediterranean countries, it was not only potable water that drew people to the pumps, fountains and water troughs to be found in village and town squares.

[65] My father-in-law first spotted my mother-in-law at the water pump in the local square and romance blossomed.

In a number of places, the availability of water and a suitable space led to the creation of communal laundry centres where the womenfolk would gather to wash clothes and sheets, at least three of which were still in use around the island in my childhood. All this changed with progress in technology. The invention of electricity made possible the distribution of water under pressure using pumps to deliver that precious liquid, now often chlorinated, to all corners of a town or village. At first, the communal tap in the local square or street corner simply replaced the well or stream, so people still gathered there and chatted as they sought to bring potable water back to their homes. In time, the same mains pipe which fed the communal fountain or water trough was tapped into at several places along the street and steel pipes were run into homes, thus obviating the need to walk in the streets outside with a heavy pail or pitcher to collect water from a communal point. In some houses, the steel pipe leading to the solitary tap close to the water metre behind the front door remained a fixture for decades. Gradually that same steel pipe was extended from behind the front door to the first toilet inside the house and its flushing mechanism. Later still, that same steel pipe would be extended into the kitchen and then the bathroom. This expansion of pressurised water pipes into the home did not happen overnight. In some Mediterranean houses it took the best part of 50 years at a tempo dictated by the prosperity of the household and the progressiveness of its outlook.

The improvements in and the increasing affordability of water technology thus impacted privacy in a number of ways. Not only was there less opportunity to meet at the local water fountain or pump and gossip, but the need for communal bathing and/or washing of clothes was reduced or downright eliminated. People could more commonly bathe in the comfort of their own homes, increasingly no longer in the presence of other members of the family, but in a private space designated as a bathroom. At first, these were often flimsy affairs – in some places an accretion or an outhouse built of cheaper materials, sometimes hardboard or plywood – but eventually they were replaced by more solid structures with running water and gas or electric devices for heating both the water and the bathroom itself.

The last 50 years have witnessed the next major development: one bathroom in a household is simply not considered to be enough. Two, three and more bathrooms are increasingly becoming the norm with en suite bathrooms gradually becoming the rule rather than the exception. Prosperity, convenience and privacy march hand in hand when it comes to bathrooms wherever you may be in the Mediterranean, as in many places outside it. People are increasingly reluctant to have to wait to use a bathroom, let alone share one. Whoever can afford to, installs more and more bathrooms. Today, in some Mediterranean houses the bathroom has become, after the kitchen, the most expensive room in the house. Factor in the arrival and dominance of automatic washing machines since the 1970s and you will find that, across the Mediterranean, there is much less incentive today to go to communal bathing places such as hammams, or to use a communal laundry. You bathe and wash your clothes in your own good time in the comfort of your own home, often juggling these with other domestic tasks, or even work from home.

The years 1991–1993 were heady ones for people working in technology law. Technology lawyers, especially those participating in BILETA[66] events, were beginning to join the dots between the potential for hypertext and the newly invented World Wide Web. In July 1993, having just returned from the BILETA conference in Liverpool, the domestic architecture of Tunisia as well as its Roman remains at Dougga caused me to reflect on what has remained constant in the Mediterranean as well on what was beginning to hit us in terms of technology. To put things in context, within 12 short years, when the Internet Governance conference was held in Tunisia in 2005, we had witnessed an explosion in information technology far beyond the Mediterranean, across our entire planet. The Internet, the World Wide Web and Web 2.0 spread like wildfire and without any meaningful political discourse or public debate about its design, business model or its future. The pace was dizzying. We had barely begun to adopt Blackberries and other Internet access-enabled mobile phones, like the iPhone (launched in 2007) when, four short years later, smartphones were being hailed as the greatest innovations for journalism in Mediterranean countries like Egypt and Tunisia, during the Arab Spring of 2011.

Yet, throughout these extremely intense decades, a number of seriously niggling thoughts remained, for it was clear that there were some things which are private in Tunisia and Saudi Arabia but which are not private in, say, France, and vice versa. This gave rise to questions like 'It's the same Mediterranean; it's the same Internet and other forms of information and communications technology, so should we have the same approach to privacy?', and 'There may well exist a universal right to privacy, but does that equate to an identical concept of privacy?' Whether it does or does not, should we aim for universality or for uniformity when it comes to making laws protecting privacy? Or should be aim for 'diversity within universality'?[67]

9.6. Conclusions

While the world may very well be our oyster, the Mediterranean is a conveniently fascinating place for the study of the origins and development of privacy. Moreover, taking the Mediterranean region as a starting point for our study makes the research project a more manageable one. Whether one chooses to call it 'Triple A' or KAPOSIA or nothing at all, a methodology which dovetails many disciplines together provides us with the evidence we need to understand the roots and growth of humanity's hunger for privacy. This is where disciplines like anthropology, architectural history and archaeology come together to complement disciplines

[66] See www.bileta.org.uk.

[67] For inroads into some of the answers to these questions, see the relevant chapter in Cannataci (n 48).

like geography, technology and economics, and provide important findings for the privacy scholar, the technology lawyer and the policymaker. In no particular order, the findings of a number of projects that remain work in progress around the Mediterranean suggest that:

Shelter from the elements may have been the primary driving force behind the development of architecture, but archaeology demonstrates that form followed function and that one single, multifunctional space, however sheltered, was not the preferred choice for Mediterranean households over the millennia.

Once they mastered certain building technologies, men and women chose to develop their dwellings from ones which consisted of larger, undivided, more generic spaces to smaller, subdivided spaces which were more suitable for various functions and which thus led to the creation of semi-public, semi-private and private spaces within a household.

The same space did not always retain the same function or the same level of privacy during the day. Its use may have changed and the level of privacy may have changed in line with this. To this very day, non-fixed privacy devices such as portable screens, awnings and curtains continue to be used both inside and outside in the Mediterranean. Even if a modern architect builds a house using an open-plan approach, especially in certain cultures such as some Muslim households, these portable privacy devices are employed within the home to create spaces with various levels of privacy.

It is relatively easy to determine that visual privacy often took priority in the design of household space. Acoustic privacy may possibly also have been valued,[68] but the affordability and availability of technology for achieving acoustic privacy seems to lag behind that for visual privacy.

Economical factors kicked in very early on: when and where the household could afford it, as far back as the Romans of classical antiquity, especially private spaces such as the *cubiculum* were created. From, at the very latest, the times of Ancient Greece, if one could afford to do so, one could choose to bathe in the comfort – and the privacy – of one's own home. In the latter case, convenience and the desire for privacy would occasionally however be tempered by socialising in public bathing facilities.

Climate may have helped determine which places were private or rendered private at different times of the day. Even where the heat prompted residents of a house to seek cooler spaces like courtyards and rooftops, awnings not only provided shade but also a degree of visual privacy.

From the earliest of times, alcohol was consumed in semi-public/semi-private spaces within domestic dwellings. While the discussions therein may have regarded more private matters, some of the other activities during those gatherings were probably considered to be private too, occasionally including sex, whether heterosexual or homosexual. The deleterious effects of alcohol have long

[68] Research on acoustic privacy is still work in progress across many of our projects.

been recognised and thus, from, at the very latest, the Hellenistic period, we find evidence of tremendous respect for the bedfellows of privacy, especially through the deification of secrecy and confidentiality as well as the presence of reminders for the need for secrecy in various spaces within a house.

Whether literary, architectural, archaeological or epigraphic, all the evidence suggests that people enjoyed sex and increasingly preferred to have sex in private (though exceptions could be made). While nudity was not necessarily always linked to sexuality, it often was and this may have led to social attitudes to the genderisation of spaces outside the household as well as within it.

Sanitation and toilets:[69] while technology, affordability and economic means marched hand in hand, it is not certain what came first when it comes to urination and defecation. From the earliest forms of architecture, the more prosperous households had the means to urinate and defecate in relative privacy, but this probably arose because it was more convenient to answer nature's call in the privacy of one's home, and often one's bed chamber, than rush out to some public convenience. When, in addition to a chamber pot, there was also a fixed toilet facility, whether connected to a public sewer or, much more often, depending on a cess pit, Mother Nature also prompted privacy if nothing else because of the general unpleasantness of malodours and all the insects and vermin that continued to live off the faeces. Thus, the privacy of fixed toilet facilities bcame part of the culture in most Mediterranean societies. If you absolutely had to, you did your business in public, but if you could afford to do so, you urinated and defecated in private. In such circumstances, privacy became a habit for good reason.

Sanitation and bathing: personal hygiene was most visibly impacted by the development of water technologies. For thousands of years until the twentieth century, the water pitcher and basin, often in a bed chamber, were essential equipment in a domestic setting. While heating water to bathe with at home was possible, it was a chore more easily afforded by the rich who could order servants or slaves to heat the water for them. Since the time of Ancient Greece, until the end of the nineteenth century, water distibution and heating technologies made it more convenient to have communal baths where one simply went along and made use of facilities open to the public. More than 2,500 years ago men and women appeared to have discovered that communal baths not only enabled personal hygiene in chore-free warmth, but also afforded opportunities for various forms of socialising, meeting friends and neighbours, gossiping, trading, negotiating deals, having a massage and, for some (not necessarily all or many), enjoying sex with varying degrees of openness.

Communal baths like hammams continue to exist around the Mediterranean (as they continue to exist outside it) because they developed into places where personal hygiene is not the primary motivator, especially if, in the twenty-first

[69] For a well-reasoned, evidence-based approach, see AO Koloski-Ostrow, *The Archaeology of Sanitation in Roman Italy* (Chapel Hill, The University of North Carolina Press, 2015).

century one has running water, hot water and a modern bathroom at home. Cultural factors and attitudes to sexuality may have genderised the space in ways generally requiring men and women to enjoy communal bathing at different times and, more rarely, different spaces, but 'enjoy' is the operative term. Humanity continues to enjoy communal bathing spaces because many people (not necessarily all) have fun frequenting them. Had it not been such fun the hammams would have died out completely, rather than living on in various guises both inside the Mediterranean and outside it.[70]

Engagement in politics has long been a reason for individuals to leave a household's private spaces and interact with others in public spaces. The arrival of the Internet has rendered personal interaction more complex especially since cyberspace is relatively ill-regulated and opportunities for manipulation in political activities have significantly increased. The use of smartphones in the Arab Spring around the Mediterranean, and especially its use by women, points to the possibility of digital societies which have as much potential for respecting human rights as for breaching them. It can be argued that the private space of the Mediterranean household has (or should have) now been extended to wherever one carries one's smartphone and/or wherever one accesses the Internet. Mediterranean digital societies need to remain vigilant and exert the required policymaking and regulatory effort to ensure that the values inherent to privacy in households developed over the millennia may continue to be protected and promoted in the Internet Age.

Religion and architecture seem to have influenced each other. The courtyard houses of the Carthaginians, Greeks and Romans of antiquity were taken over and replicated by the Arab-speaking cultures flowing in from the east from the seventh century onwards. The Muslim religion of these invaders evolved in different directions, but the way that privacy and especially segregation of women to varying degrees developed both inside and outside the household demonstrates different levels of privacy in a domestic setting.[71] These developments in some cases even led to separate entrances to dwellings for members of the public and members of the family.

Technology moved hand in hand with affordability. As soon as water technology made it affordable, many Mediterranean societies progressed from wells to taps, to comfortable heated bathrooms in every home, to mulitple bathrooms (many en-suite) where prosperity so permits. Convenience, affordability and privacy have, anthropologically, marched hand in hand when it comes to bathrooms.

[70] Indeed in the BANYA projects we are investigating the history and continued popularity of communal bathing and especially saunas in places like Estonia and Finland.

[71] The religion of the Ottoman Empire may have been predominantly Muslim, but there are discernible differences between, say, the Turkish-speaking and the Arab-speaking parts of that Empire, as there are differences in the architecture of parts of that empire where climate, building materials and geography facilitated/encouraged the development of one form of architecture rather than another. The study of privacy-relevant similarities and differences between different parts of the far-flung Ottoman Empire is still work in progress within PRIVATUS and other projects at present. The economical dimension of privacy was never far away even in Muslim households; see Aleppo.

Thus, all the available evidence indicates that, for more than 3,000 years, possibly far longer, many Mediterranean peoples have increasingly built their houses with privacy in mind, developing their domestic architecture to create distinct flows between the public and the private. While in some instances privacy became an expectation[72] or a necessity, in other instances it became a useful habit.[73]

Digging deeper, the evidence also suggests that privacy is and always was a complex phenomenon, co-existing with the needs and desire of men and women to interact with persons outside the household as well as within it. Security of the community, both internal as well as defence from external aggression, required social organisation at a scale most often occurring in public spaces. The political organisation of society required human interaction in both public and private spaces. While places of worship at home have been commonplace since antiquity, cultural phenomena such as religious beliefs and practices have driven men and women to interact in public places of worship as well as in rituals elsewehere outside the home. The interplay between what happened in public and private in such instances is still being understood as archaeology, epigraphy and literature bring more evidence to bear, increasingly in an interdisciplinary manner.

All this evidence and much more, suggests that privacy in the Mediterranean evolved as a value long before, in many cases *millennia* before, it was recognised by the Universal Declaration of Human Rights of 1948 or the European Convention of Human Rights of 1950. There is no persuasive evidence that, after having developed privacy over at least 3,000 years, probably much more, today Mediterranean societies are suddenly prepared to jettison privacy and throw it overboard just because technology has moved them into the digital era. If laws have codified the protection of values in various ways around the Mediterranean for well over 3,000 years, it follows that the role of law in the twenty-first century therefore must also protect a value as fundamental as privacy.

Digital technologies have already impacted and will continue to radically impact the way commerce is carried out in the Mediterranean. They may even permit meaningful political participation in a way which would have been impossible in the circumstances of Aristotle's Greece. Digital technologies may also enhance leisure pursuits and sexual life. To do so in the right way, however, requires technology law to evolve in the right direction, one where privacy, together with other enabling rights such as freedom of expression, information, religion and association, ensure that the individual's over-arching right to free, unhindered development of personality is facilitated rather than fractured by pervasive digital technologies. Anthropology, archaeology, architecture and history show us what, why, how, when and where we have become whom we have become. If we wish to continue to be whom we have become then we need law to regulate digital technologies accordingly.

[72] As in the cubiculum in Roman houses or bed chambers for millennia.

[73] Such as in toilet functions and facilities.

INDEX

www.ingramcontent.com/pod-product-compliance
Ingram Content Group UK Ltd.
Pitfield, Milton Keynes, MK11 3LW, UK
UKHW020820290926
15470UKWH00003B/1269

9 781509 983674